The Hiking
Trails of
North
Georgia

Third Edition

The Hiking Trails of North Georgia

Tim Homan

Updated trail information
gathered in collaboration with

The Georgia
Conservancy
(Beth Giddens, Editor)

PEACHTREE
ATLANTA

Published by
PEACHTREE PUBLISHERS, LTD.
494 Armour Circle, NE
Atlanta, Georgia 30324

Third Edition
Text © 1981, 1986, 1987, 1997 by Tim Homan
Cover photo © 1992, 1997 Craig M. Tanner

Manufactured in the United States of America

Book and cover design by Loraine M. Balcsik
Cover photo by Craig M. Tanner
Composition by Darren Schillace
Maps by Doug Ponte

10 9 8 7 6 5 4 3

Library of Congress Cataloging in Publication Data

Homan, Tim.
    The hiking trails of north Georgia / Tim Homan. —3rd ed.
        p. cm.
ISBN 1-56145-127-4
        1. Hiking—Georgia—Guidebooks. 2. Trails—Georgia—Guidebooks.
3. Georgia—Guidebooks. I. Title.
GV199.42.G46H65 1997
917.58—DC20   95-52151
                                                                 CIP

Cover photograph: Autumn ferns along the Tennessee Rock Trail
at Black Rock Mountain State Park.

Publisher's Note

This 1997 edition of THE HIKING TRAILS OF NORTH GEORGIA, the third since its original publication in 1981, bears a legacy of excellence borne of the knowledge and attention to detail of its author Tim Homan.

As the trail system in North Georgia expanded, the task of revising this reference loomed large. A thorough revision was needed, and Tim Homan would never be content to produce a revision that was not as excellent as its predecessors. He turned to The Georgia Conservancy to provide the interest and encouragement that would set this revision in motion with the assistance of their volunteers.

With preliminary information gathered, Tim immersed himself in the data, confirming what he knew to be accurate, and questioning and rehiking trails about which he lacked personal knowledge. It is inspiring to work alongside an author who takes such care with his writing. And it is humbling to encounter a man like Tim Homan who will not offer an opinion about a subject unless he knows and understands it thoroughly. This is why THE HIKING TRAILS OF NORTH GEORGIA has become the reference for our state's serious hikers. This is the type of attention to detail that you will find in this new, third edition.

Peachtree Publishers issues this third edition at the start of our twentieth anniversary. The first edition of this book was one of Peachtree's earliest titles, one that has lived happily with us for many years. We are proud of this book and its author. And to honor it, we have done what we believe befits it best—we have taken great care in our editing, fact-checking, proofing, and design. We believe our readers will recognize and appreciate the results.

Table of Contents

Preface to the Third Edition

This is the second major revision of THE HIKING TRAILS OF NORTH GEORGIA. I first hiked all of the trails in 1979 and 1980; the first edition was published in 1981. That first book, a skinny 216 pages, described 80 trails that totaled 349 miles.

In 1986 I hiked all the trails with a measuring wheel for the first major revision—the redball jet edition—which came out in 1987. Nine trails from the first edition were deleted (one changed usage, the rest were no longer considered trails) from the second edition, which had grown to 92 trails totaling 438 miles.

By the mid-1990s, because of the usual responsibilities, I no longer had the time to travel to the mountains for extended hiking trips. In the fall of 1993 The Georgia Conservancy and I agreed upon a plan whereby we, in a cooperative effort, would update the guide and keep it in good running order. Although the project took longer than we had first envisioned and we hit a few unexpected bumps along the way, we persevered, finished the job, and are now proud of the results of our efforts.

In this latest edition, we have added 23 new trails, 8 new sections of the Benton MacKaye Trail, and detailed the numerous substantial changes and additions to old trails. THE HIKING TRAILS OF NORTH GEORGIA now includes 124 trails totaling 532 miles. And as you can see, it has been reformatted for the information age.

Acknowledgments

I wish to extend special thanks to the following people for their help:
Margaret Quinlin of Peachtree Publishers for her support of this project.
Amy Sproull of Peachtree Publishers for her work on the manuscript.
Vicky Holifield of Peachtree Publishers for her editorial work.
Bonnie Jackson of The Georgia Conservancy for her help wheeling trails and checking directions.
The volunteers from The Georgia Conservancy for their assistance in gathering and verifying trail information.
Jud Germon of the Georgia Appalachian Trail Club for providing mileages for the Appalachian Trail.
Rachel Schneider, Jeff Owenby, Larry Thomas, Tom Fearington, Tom Hawks, Edwin Dale, Francis Mason, and David Kuykendall of the US

Forest Service for answering all my questions.
George Owen and Marty Dominy of the Benton MacKaye Trail
Association for their editing and fact-checking.
Bill Tanner, Anthony Lampros, and Alan Padgett of the Georgia
Department of Natural Resources for the tours, help, and information.
My wife Page Luttrell, Gary Crider, and Maggie Nettles for hiking with me.

—*Tim Homan*

Scope of the Book

For a number of good reasons—mountains, clear streams and waterfalls, extraordinary views, spectacular wildflower displays, and designated
wilderness among them—the scope of this book is limited to Georgia's
northernmost counties. All of Georgia's highest mountains, the largest
solid blocks of dry public land, and all but one of the state's longest trails
are found within this northern tier of counties. These trails, especially
those in the Blue Ridge, are the most popular, the most frequently
inquired about, and the most scenic in the state. They offer us beauty,
knowledge and spiritual enrichment, adventure and physical challenge—
and if we need them—solitude and escape.

Definition of a Trail

With few exceptions, the mountains of North Georgia are laced with
dirt roads, old logging roads, old railroad beds, and jeep trails. Footworn
paths lead away from them in all directions and continue unknown distances. Countless other paths created primarily by fishermen meander
along streams and often end in a tangle of rhododendron. Roads that
were barely passable for four-wheel-drive vehicles and open for walkers
quickly grew up in briers and saplings after wilderness designation. The
Southern Nantahala Wilderness, in particular, has had many such roads
quickly reclaimed by forest.

To avoid confusion, the term "trail" as used in this guide must be further defined. With the sole exception of the Old-Growth Forest Trail, the
trails detailed in this guide are designated as such; they are at least mini-
mally maintained, and they have definite starting and ending points.
They are closed, where possible, to vehicular traffic. Their lengths are known,
they are often blazed, and for the most part they are easy to follow.

Because of the trend toward multi-designation trails, hikers have often had to share trails with bikers and horseback riders. Mountain bikes are not permitted in wilderness, so all wilderness trails are either foot travel only or horse and hike only. During the trail selection process for the second revision of this guide—a hiking guide—we decided to include only single- and double-designation trails. Thus all the trails included in this guide are foot travel only, hike and horse only, or hike and bike only.

We may change our philosophy and include a few triple-designation trails in the future. But those trails would have to possess exceptional features, and one of their usages would have to be nearly nonexistent, such as a trail too steep and rocky for bikes. Such trails would be de facto double-designation trails, and therefore have a higher expectation for a less crowded, less hectic, and more enjoyable hike.

The Information Column

Each trail description includes an information column listing ten to thirteen categories. The first of these categories is the physiographic province—Blue Ridge, Cumberland Plateau, Ridge and Valley, or Piedmont—where the trail is located. Because of its great width across northernmost Georgia, the Blue Ridge province has been subdivided into eastern and western sections.

The second category is the subregion—a mountain, a group of mountains, a ridge, a river, a river basin—which serves to further pinpoint a trail's location. (The gray bar across the top of a page also identifies the subregion.) The third listing provides the name of the specific designated area: wilderness, state park, recreation area, scenic area, National Wild and Scenic River, section of long trail, etc. A few national forest trails are located on general forest land that has no specific designation.

Distance follows "features." Mileage figures for linear trails are one-way distances; mileages for loops are the total out and back distances, from trailhead around the loop and back to the trailhead.

This guide employs five difficulty ratings: easy, easy to moderate, moderate, moderate to strenuous, and strenuous. An easy rating means that the trail is flat or nearly flat; a strenuous trail climbs steadily at a sharp grade or makes frequent large (500 feet or more) elevation gains and losses. The intermediate ratings are gradations between the two. These ratings are for mountain trails, where at least mild elevation changes are the norm. These trails are compared to each other and ranked accordingly.

Nearest cities have been included to aid in locating trailheads on road maps and to help in the planning of weekend trips and vacations.

The names of all necessary topographical quadrangles have been provided. These USGS topo sheets are the 7.5 minute series, 1:24,000 scale. These maps can be ordered for a small fee by calling the phone number provided in the back of this guide. Other relevant maps are listed for each trail. The Administrative Map for the Chattahoochee National Forest covers the entire forest, even the disjunct Armuchee District in northwest Georgia. Instead of listing this comprehensive map over and over again for each national forest trail, we have only listed the administrative map here and in the back of the guide.

Water sources are noted only for the longer trails where drinking water might become a concern for day hikers and backpackers. Drinking untreated water in the mountains, even from high, cold springs, is at your own gastrointestinal risk.

Camping is not permitted in state parks except at designated campgrounds or backcountry sites. In the Chattahoochee National Forest, however, camping is permitted throughout the forest (unless posted otherwise) as well as in the recreation area campgrounds and Appalachian Trail shelters. There are many long-established trailside camping areas throughout the Chattahoochee. The Forest Service, however, does not consider these areas to be official campsites; camping at many of these sites is obviously at odds with current environmental guidelines. They also believe that providing information about trailside camping areas would further concentrate use and further degrade the sites. We agree. Thus we have not listed mileages to trailside camping areas. Please practice no-trace camping whenever possible.

The final category—Ranger District—applies only to national forest trails.

When using this guidebook, keep in mind that conditions on hiking trails are constantly changing and trails are occasionally rerouted. To be sure of current conditions, contact the local agency responsible for trail maintenance before planning a hike.

To conserve space, certain abbreviations are used within the text.

AT   Appalachian National Scenic Trail
BMT   Benton MacKaye Trail
BT   Bartram Trail
DNR   Department of Natural Resources
EBR   Eastern Blue Ridge
FS   Forest Service
GA   Georgia primary road
WBR   Western Blue Ridge
WMA   Wildlife Management Area
US   federal highway
USFS   United States Forest Service

Holcomb Creek Trail

EBR
Rabun Bald

From the road, this short trail quickly zigzags past several large tuliptrees, then tunnels through rose-bay rhododendron thickets as it descends toward Holcomb Creek Falls. At 0.3 mile, the trail crosses a footbridge. Even though you hear this isolated waterfall well before you see it, its size and beauty take you by surprise. As you walk out over the bridge across Holcomb Creek, the fall comes suddenly into view. Almost as long as it is high, this 120-foot waterfall is a picturesque combination of wide freefalls, splashing cascades, and quick slides that careen around raised slabs of bedrock.

The trail continues past several giant eastern hemlocks a short distance to another waterfall—Ammons Creek Falls. Like many other North Georgia waterfalls, Ammons Creek is more churning cascade than sheer plunge. The water drops above and below the stilted observation deck. Above, the stream begins its rush down the mountainside directly in front of you as a foaming, pure-white, 40-foot falls. Below, the longer, less vertical portion of the falls makes an S-curve into a narrow, squirming raceway between boulders.

Forty yards before its end at the observation deck, the trail passes a sign that points to another way back to Hale Ridge Road. This alternate route coupled with a segment of Hale Ridge Road completes a loop that returns to the trailhead. The side trail is 0.6 mile in length; the Hale Ridge Road segment, to the left and downhill, is slightly less than 0.6 mile.

The alternate route parallels cascading Holcomb Creek all the way to the road. The trail first comes close to the creek on a hillside above the waterfall's uppermost ledge. It is a tempting but potentially very dangerous 35 yards down for a look. Before you try it, think twice, and then be very careful. Better still, stay on the trail.

The trail continues within earshot or eyesight of

Features
Two waterfalls, outstanding forest

Distance
0.5 mile

Difficulty Rating
Moderate

County
Rabun

Nearest City
Clayton

Map
Rabun Bald
Quadrangle, GA-NC

Blazes
None; none needed

Ranger District
Tallulah

the creek. One-tenth mile from the road, a long cascade slides into its shallow, surprisingly large catch pool.

Highlights
Mile 0.3: 120-foot Holcomb Creek Falls.
Mile 0.5: 40-foot Ammons Creek Falls.

Directions
In Clayton, where US 76 turns west, turn east onto Rickman Street (locally known as Warwoman Road). If you are traveling north on US 441, this turn will be to your right at the Hardee's, which is the second building to the right on Rickman Street. Continue a short distance on Rickman Street, then turn right onto Warwoman Road at its sign.

After traveling 10.0 miles from the turn off US 441, turn left onto FS 7 (Hale Ridge Road). FS 7 is the first public road to the left past Allen's Grocery. Follow FS 7 for 6.5 miles to its intersection with FS 86 (Overflow Road). The trailhead, marked with a rock sign, is located at the intersection.

Notes

Rabun Bald Trail

EBR
Rabun Bald

Starting at its "Hiking Trail" sign, this infrequently blazed but easily followed path works its way up to the summit of Rabun Bald (4,696 feet), Georgia's second highest peak. This remote, challenging footpath rises steadily almost from the beginning, ascending nearly 2,200 feet along its 2.9-mile length. The level stretches and short dips between climbs are just long enough to let you catch your breath. The final grade to Rabun Bald is very steep. While it may not be the steepest pitch along North Georgia's trails, there are none much more demanding.

Beginning at about 2,500 feet, the trail rises steadily through a dense forest where mountain laurel thickets and galax patches are common. Galax, an abundant wildflower in the mountains, is easily identified by its shiny green (copper-red in winter), leathery, heart-shaped leaf. You can often detect galax colonies by the scent—a peculiar, sweet skunky fragrance—even before you see them.

At mile 1.5 the rivulet to the left of the path serves as the only water source on the way to the top, and it probably goes dry during drought. Beyond this rivulet, the treadway leads through an open oak forest before it enters an area of boulders and mountain laurel thickets. At mile 2.1 the footpath crosses a grassy glade where lousewort is common. This fernleafed wildflower received the first part of its name from the old belief that livestock became infested with lice upon contact with the plant.

The trail climbs steeply from the glade for slightly less than 0.2 mile before leveling out on a spur ridge. Often tunneling through rhododendron, the final 0.3 mile ascends very sharply. The path enters the small clearing atop Rabun Bald on the side opposite the observation tower's stairs. Here on top of Rabun Bald's crest, a few American mountain ash grow among the short, twisted oaks that surround

Features
Georgia's second highest mountain, scenic view

Distance
2.9 miles

Difficulty Rating
Strenuous

County
Rabun

Nearest City
Clayton

Map
Rabun Bald
Quadrangle, GA-NC

Blazes
Yellow; infrequent at lower end

Water Sources
Mile 1.5: rivulet on left

Ranger District
Tallulah

the man-made clearing.

The Rabun Bald Trail ends at its junction with the Bartram Trail. On clear, hazeless days the high-perched observation tower offers a superb 360-degree panorama. The long sloping ridges and unbroken forests of the 14,000-acre Warwoman Wildlife Management Area spread away to the south. To the east, South Carolina's Lake Keowee shimmers in the distance. To the northeast, near Cashiers, North Carolina, you can see the sheer rock face of Whiteside Mountain. At most other points on the compass, except where the view reaches the rolling landscape of the Piedmont, overlapping rows of ridges and peaks become indistinct in the blue distance.

If streams are full, and if you have binoculars, see if you can spot the waterfall over toward the cliff faces in North Carolina. One more thing: the large crows that call "crunk" rather than "caw" are common ravens.

Highlights

Mile 2.9: Summit of Rabun Bald, Georgia's second highest mountain at 4,696 feet. Excellent 360-degree views on clear days.

Directions

(See page 2 of Holcomb Creek Trail for directions to the FS 7 turnoff.) Proceed 5.5 miles on FS 7; the trailhead and trailhead sign are on the left side of the road.

Notes

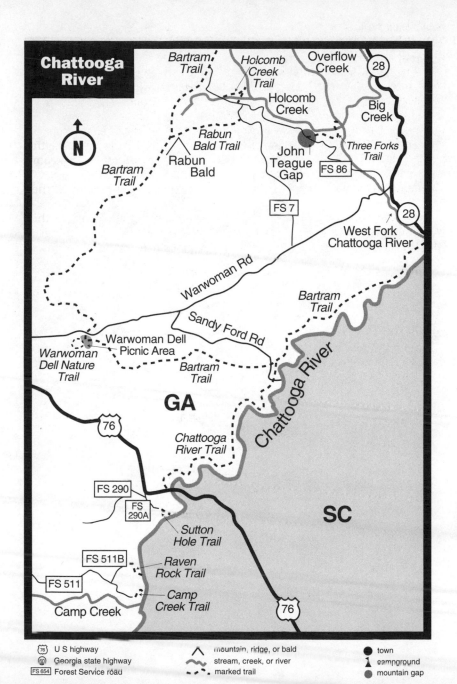

Notes

Three Forks Trail

Three Forks Trail, as it was originally designed, starts at the summit of Rabun Bald and ends beside the West Fork Chattooga River near Three Forks. The trail is named for three creeks—Holcomb, Overflow, and Big—which run together at right angles to create the West Fork. With this design, however, vehicular access can be gained only in the middle sections of the trail, and several miles of the trail are routed onto FS 7 (Hale Ridge Road) and an old road that runs from FS 7 to FS 86 (Overflow Road).

In an effort to provide vehicular access and eliminate confusing, unblazed roads from the middle of the trail, this narrative describes Three Forks Trail from Overflow Road to the end of the designated trail at Holcomb Creek, splitting the Three Forks Trail into two separate ones. Three Forks Trail from Hale Ridge Road to Rabun Bald is described as Rabun Bald Trail. This change takes advantage of trail signs (provided they are maintained), eliminates walking on roads, and helps avoid confusion.

This much shorter version of the Three Forks Trail, starting at John Teague Gap (2,360 feet), leads hikers through forest often dominated by eastern white pine and several species of oak. After traversing 0.7 mile of predominantly level or gently descending terrain, the trail crosses the blue-blazed boundary of the Chattooga National Wild and Scenic River. The immediate Three Forks area and a narrow corridor along both banks of the entire West Fork Chattooga River are protected as part of the Chattooga National Wild and Scenic River.

The trail remains level or slightly downhill until it dips to its three-way intersection with an old jeep road at mile 1.0. Follow the road to the left as it drops sharply for nearly 0.2 mile to a flat, rocky area overlooking a swirlhole-carved cascade on Holcomb Creek. This is the end of the blazed trail; Three Forks

EBR
Chattooga River
Chattooga National Wild and Scenic River

Features
Cascades, streams, bluff at Three Forks

Distance
1.4 miles

Difficulty Rating
Easy to moderate to end of designated trail at Holcomb Creek; final 0.2 mile of unmaintained path beside Holcomb Creek is moderate to strenuous and potentially dangerous when muddy

County
Rabun

Nearest City
Clayton

Maps
Satolah Quadrangle, GA-SC-NC; Chattooga National Wild and Scenic River map

Blazes
Silver diamonds

Ranger District
Tallulah

is to the right, downstream, approximately 0.2 mile from the cascade.

There is an easy, direct way down to the forks—easy compared to bushwhacking, at least. To get there, walk upstream beneath the overhanging bluff until, after 25 to 30 yards, the banks narrow to a jump's width. Cross Holcomb Creek there. Straight ahead from the crossing, a path leads away from the creek. Don't take that one. That one soon forks to the right and left, becomes dimmer and slimmer, deteriorates to a deer run, peters out to a possum track, then snake-wiggles up a tree, and ends in a knot hole. And you are left to bushwhack the slide-on-your-butt, steep lower slopes of High Top.

A few yards to the right of the creek crossing, look for another path entering the woods through a duck-your-head hole in the rhododendron. This trail will lead you downstream, above the long, tilted chutes on Holcomb Creek to Three Forks (1,840 feet). The path becomes progressively steeper toward its bottom end beside Overflow Creek.

Highlights
Mile 1.2: Cascade on Holcomb Creek.
Mile 1.4: The convergence of the three creeks that form the West Fork of the Chattooga River.

Directions
In Clayton, where US 76 turns west, turn east onto Rickman Street (locally known as Warwoman Road). If you are traveling north on US 441, the turn will be to your right near the Hardee's, which is the second building to the right on Rickman Street. Continue a short distance on Rickman Street, then turn right onto Warwoman Road at its sign.

After traveling 14.0 miles from the turn off US 441, turn left onto FS 86 (Overflow Road) immediately after crossing West Fork Chattooga River. Continue 3.9 to 4.0 miles on FS 86 to the cleared pull-off area on the right side of the road at John Teague Gap. Begin looking for the pull-off after cresting a hill. A large rock with "Three Forks Trail" engraved on it marks the trailhead.

Notes

Warwoman Dell Nature Trail

This footpath, which was once an excellent interpretive trail, has fallen on hard times. There is no longer a pamphlet in print, and the numbered posts are gone or are rotting away. The Forest Service is hopeful that they can refurbish the trail in the future.

The trail enters the forest over a wooden walkway beside Warwoman Creek. After it crosses a bridge, its loop begins and ends immediately before the picnic tables. The direction of travel is no longer important. The loop passes beside a small waterfall at its midpoint, then curls back toward its beginning.

From late March through April, the moist area between the pavilion and the waterfall has a good wildflower display. Bloodroots and violets bloom in late March. A month later, in late April, Vasey's trillium, with their large leaves and carmine-colored flowers, bloom along the path.

In addition to having a trail of its own, Warwoman Dell Picnic Area serves as an easily accessible starting and ending point for those walking either of Georgia's two long segments of the Bartram Trail, which crosses Warwoman Road and passes through the picnic area at a point nearly midway along its 37-mile length.

Highlights
Throughout: Good spring wildflower display.
Mile 0.2: Small waterfall at the halfway point.

Directions
In Clayton, where US 76 turns west, turn east onto Rickman Street (locally known as Warwoman Road). If you are traveling north on US 441, the turn will be to your right near the Hardee's, which is the second building to the right on Rickman Street. Continue a short distance on Rickman Street, then turn right onto Warwoman Road at its sign.

EBR
Chattooga River
**Warwoman Dell
Picnic Area**

Features
Small waterfall,
spring wildflowers

Distance
0.4 mile (loop)

Difficulty Rating
Easy

County
Rabun

Nearest City
Clayton

Map
Rabun Bald
Quadrangle, GA-NC

Blazes
None; none needed

Campsites
Camping not permitted in picnic area; this area is day use only and is gated at night

Ranger District
Tallulah

After traveling approximately 3.0 miles on Warwoman Road from the turn off US 441, turn right into the sign-posted recreation area and continue 0.3 mile. The gravel road ends at the picnic pavilion parking lot, where a carsonite sign marks the trailhead.

Notes

Chattooga River Trail

Designated in 1974 as a National Wild and Scenic River, the Chattooga has its origins in the North Carolina mountains and flows southwest into Tugaloo Lake on the border between Georgia and South Carolina. Many scenes in the movie *Deliverance* were filmed from the banks of the Chattooga in the early 1970s.

The Chattooga River Trail may not be what you would expect or want from a trail bearing such a famous name. The trail does not lead you to the wild, colorfully named rapids—Painted Rock, Roller Coaster, Eye of the Needle, The Narrows—along Floating Section III of the river. In fact, it closely parallels the river for only 1.6 miles, from mile 6.3 to mile 7.9.

Starting from US 76, the trail heads northeast along the Georgia side of the Chattooga River. The first half of the trail frequently loops outside of the blue-blazed river corridor, where motorized vehicles are allowed on jeep roads. The last half of the trail, however, remains inside the protected corridor and provides solitude. Alternating from constructed path to old road, the trail winds along the sloping strip of land from the river up to its enclosing ridge. Although the terrain is steep and frequently cut by streams, the trail's numerous grades are all easy or moderate. And most of the moderate grades are short.

At the southern trailhead, the white-blazed Chattooga River Trail begins behind two sets of vehicle-blocking boulders, at an elevation of about 1,200 feet. One of them now serves as the trailhead sign. The path follows an old jeep road through mixed deciduous-evergreen forest to 0.7 mile, where it curls down and left to cross Pole Creek, the first of many streams. From this point, the treadway winds along the lower slopes of Lion Mountain for several miles, often crossing rivulets above their steep-sided coves. Occasionally, you can hear the roar of powerful

EBR
Chattooga River
Chattooga National Wild and Scenic River

Features
Chattooga River

Distance
10.7 miles

Difficulty Rating
Moderate

County
Rabun

Nearest City
Clayton

Maps
Rainy Mountain Quadrangle, GA-SC; Chattooga National Wild and Scenic River map

Blazes
White diamonds

Water Sources
Numerous tributary rivulets and streams

Ranger District
Tallulah

rapids below; the loudest emanates from Bull Sluice, a Class V rapid.

At mile 4.1 and mile 4.4 the trail crosses unnamed Chattooga tributaries that are nonetheless big enough for bridges. Beyond the second, a slow-moving stream with a floodplain, the footpath curves right then passes within 40 yards of the river. After allowing a quick glimpse of the water, the trail climbs to the ridge on an old road. Once on top, it rises and dips with the road along the protected corridor to mile 5.9, where it bears right onto a path and descends to the river.

At mile 6.3 the path swings parallel to the Chattooga, usually green and always beautiful. For the next 1.6 miles, occasionally through dense stands of eastern hemlock, the trail heads upstream above the river's low shoals and long, calm pools. At mile 6.8 it crosses a bridge over Licklog Creek, then continues alongside deep green swimming holes before crossing Buckeye Branch at mile 7.4. Sandy beaches and boulders make great spots to enjoy lunch or watch the rafts float by.

At mile 7.9 the trail bends backward to the left and away from the river onto an old road. It climbs a hill then turns 90 degrees to the right. A moderate grade leads to the ridge, where the path gently undulates on or near the ridge line to mile 9.8. Following a 0.2-mile downgrade, the Chattooga River Trail crosses Rock Creek and Sandy Ford Road in quick succession. Another inscribed boulder marks the trail's crossing of Dicks Creek Road. The remainder of the footpath is easily walked to its Y-shaped junction with the Bartram Trail. This junction (approximately 1,640 feet) is designated with a small rock sign inside the Y.

Officially, the Chattooga River Trail overlaps with the Bartram Trail north of Sandy Ford Road and continues into both South and North Carolina. This narrative describes only the lower portion of the Chattooga River Trail in Georgia.

Highlights
Mile 4.8: The trail meets the river at a spot with many small pools and rushing shoals. Sandy banks provide easy access to the river.
Miles 6.3–7.9: The trail meanders beside the river with many opportunities for boulder scrambles out into the water.

Directions
To the southern trailhead: From Clayton, follow US 76 East from its intersection with US 441. About 9.0 miles from Clayton, US 76 crosses the Chattooga River. Park in a small gravel lot on the left, just before the bridge. The trailhead is located behind the two boulders in the back of the lot.

To the northern trailhead: In Clayton, where US 76 turns west, turn east onto Rickman Street (locally known as Warwoman Road). If you are traveling north on US 441, the turn will be to your right near the Hardee's, which is the second building to the right on Rickman Street. Continue a short distance on Rickman Street, then turn right onto Warwoman Road at its sign.

After turning off US 441, travel approximately 6.0 miles and turn right onto unpaved Sandy Ford Road (also known as Dicks Creek Road to locals) immediately past the house with the A-shaped roof over its door. Inside the entrance to Sandy Ford Road, bear right with the main dirt road, continue approximately 0.7 mile from the pavement, and then turn left across a road-level bridge. After this left turn, proceed approximately 3.7 miles to the Bartram Trail sign—an engraved rock to the right of the road.

The northern end of the Chattooga River Trail ties into the Bartram Trail near Sandy Ford Road. If you end your hike at this junction, turn sharp left onto the Bartram and walk the 100 yards to Sandy Ford Road at the Bartram sign. If you wish to walk the Chattooga River Trail north to south, park at the Bartram Trail sign, walk the Bartram to the left (from the way you came) 100 yards, then turn right onto the Chattooga River Trail.

In addition to being fairly rough and rutted, Sandy Ford Road fords the creek twice before reaching the Bartram Trail sign. The second ford may be too deep for low-to-the-ground conventional cars.

Notes

EBR
Chattooga River
Chattooga National Wild and Scenic River

Features
Chattooga River,
Woodall Shoals

Distance
0.3 mile

Difficulty Rating
Easy

County
Rabun

Nearest City
Clayton

Maps
Rainy Mountain
Quadrangle, GA-SC;
Chattooga National
Wild and Scenic
River map

Blazes
None; none needed

Ranger District
Tallulah

Sutton Hole Trail

The trail quickly descends through an oak-pine forest to Sutton Hole, where the Chattooga River is deep and slow enough for swimming. To the right, downstream, you can see and hear the beginning of the river's only lawfully canoed Class VI rapid—Woodall Shoals, a long pitch of white water famous for its whale-sized rock and its boat-holding hydraulic. Depending upon the time of year and level of the river, you can bushwhack, rock-hop, or wade the 300 yards down to the shoals. Woodall's fast water has scoured a beautiful pool, wide and deep and green, with a white sand beach on its Georgia side.

Highlights
Mile 0.3: Sutton Hole, a deep swimming hole on the Chattooga. Woodall Shoals, a Class VI rapid, is just downstream.

Directions
From Clayton, take US 76 East toward Westminster, South Carolina. If you are traveling northward on US 441, the turn will be to your right. After driving approximately 7.5 miles on US 76 East, turn right onto unpaved FS 290, Woodall Shoals Road, and continue on this road for slightly less than 0.3 mile. In the middle of a sharp curve to the right, you will see a narrow road, unmarked and blocked with a dirt mound, to the left. FS 290-A, which leads to the trailhead, is inside and to the right of this blocked road.

FS 290-A (Woodall Shoals Spur Road) should not be attempted in a conventional vehicle. If you don't have a pickup or a jeep but want to see the Chattooga River at Sutton Hole, you will have to hike this road—only 0.5 mile long and easily walked—to the trailhead. There is a pull-off near the entrance of FS 290-A. The trail begins at the turnaround area where further vehicular travel is blocked by dirt mounds. This is also the boundary of the Chattooga National Wild and Scenic River, and travel is by foot only.

Raven Rock Trail

R aven Rock Trail follows an old roadbed, now closed but still used occasionally, that continues from the back right corner of the turnaround area for FS 511-B. After 0.4 mile, where the old road is blocked with felled logs, the trail angles down and to the left on wooden steps and descends, sometimes steeply, 400 feet to the river. A careful eye can pick out ferns, trillium, Indian pipe, redbud, flowering dogwood, wild hydrangea, partridgeberry, and trailing arbutus. Along the way the trail approaches Daniel Creek, then turns left and leads to a level campsite with a fire pit. Here the trail turns 90 degrees to the right, dropping downhill to the Georgia bank of the Chattooga National Wild and Scenic River.

The path ends beneath an eastern hemlock rooted at the top of a tiny white sand beach. Upstream and down, the banks are jumbled with boulders; between them are more pockets of sand. This is a perfect vantage point to watch rafters, canoeists, and kayakers as they come out of Raven Rock Chute and enjoy a breather before tackling the Class IV and V rapids downstream called Five Falls. Directly across a deep, eddying pool, just downstream from a shoal, Raven Rock arches upward from either side, coming to a point perhaps as high as 150 feet, perhaps higher; it is difficult to judge. The cliff face is striated gneiss, vertically streaked with black mineral stains. Stunted eastern red cedars are growing on ledges and out of cracks in the cliff.

During periods of low water in summer and early autumn, it is possible to bushwhack, rock-hop, and wade up and downstream from the sandy beach. The 2.5-mile segment of the Chattooga—from 0.5 mile upstream of Raven Rock all the way downstream to Tugaloo Lake—more than lives up to its designated "wild and scenic" status. Raven Rock Chute and Deliverance Rock Rapids (both Class IV), giant boulders, and a beautiful Long Creek waterfall on the

EBR
Chattooga River

Chattooga National Wild and Scenic River

Features
Chattooga River, Raven Rock, rapids and waterfall nearby

Distance
0.8 mile

Difficulty Rating
Moderate

County
Rabun

Nearest City
Tallulah Falls

Maps
Rainy Mountain Quadrangle, GA-SC; Chattooga National Wild and Scenic River map

Blazes
White

Ranger District
Tallulah

South Carolina side are close by upstream. Downstream, there are pools, rocks, and rapids that build in size and strength as you head toward the lake. Camp Creek Trail, also in this section, provides much closer access to the Class V rapids along the lowermost Chattooga.

The beauty of the river is easily marred by inconsiderate sightseers. Please do not build fires along the shoreline, and remember to leave this small, special place cleaner, if possible, than you found it.

Highlights
Mile 0.8: Small sandy beaches, shading hemlocks, green pools, river boulders, and rapids along the banks of the Chattooga River. Striking view across the river of Raven Rock, a gneiss cliff with dark mineral stains.

Directions
From the Riley C. Thurmond Memorial Bridge in Tallulah Falls, travel on US 441 North for approximately 3.0 miles, then turn right onto paved Camp Creek Road. After driving approximately 1.5 miles on Camp Creek Road, turn left onto FS 511 (Water Gauge Road) just up the hill from a small concrete culvert bridge and immediately beyond a large house on the left. Continue on FS 511 for approximately 2.4 miles, then begin looking for FS 511-B (Daniel Creek Road), a narrow, unmarked road with two entrances, the first dropping down and turning to the left at less than a 90-degree angle. Seventy-five yards farther on FS 511, you will find the second entrance, seldom used, angling toward the first. Beyond the second entrance there is a pull-off place to the left of the road. You should find this road after approximately 2.4 to 2.6 miles on FS 511.

Proceed on FS 511-B only in a four-wheel-drive vehicle. Each dirt road is narrower and rougher than the one before. If you don't have a pickup or a jeep, but still want to see Raven Rock, you will have to hike this road, only a mile long and easily walked, to the trailhead. On FS 511-B, stay on the main road at all forks; it ends at a turnaround area after approximately 1.0 mile. The trail begins at the lower right corner of the turnaround area, where the road once continued.

Camp Creek Trail

EBR
Chattooga River
Chattooga National
Wild and Scenic
River

Features
Chattooga River,
rapids

Distance
0.5 mile

Difficulty Rating
Easy to moderate

County
Rabun

Nearest City
Tallulah Falls

Maps
Rainy Mountain
Quadrangle, GA-SC;
Chattooga National
Wild and Scenic
River map

Blazes
None; none needed

Ranger District
Tallulah

Beginning to the right of the Forest Service bulletin board, the trail heads downhill on the easy, switchbacking grades of an old road. On the way down, the path winds through maturing hardwoods near the edge of Camp Creek's steep-sided ravine. The route reaches a fork, where you can walk upstream or down, beside the Chattooga River at 0.3 mile. Here the main trail curls to the right and closely parallels the wide green river downstream, past sandy beaches and gentle shoals.

The trail ends at another fork just across Camp Creek, a small stream barely big enough to be called a branch. The old roadbed continues upslope and to the right. To the left a prominent path quickly leads to a level, heavily used campsite with the remains of a small stone structure.

If you want, you can follow a bushwhack path a few tenths of a mile farther downstream to the beginning of the Class V rapids—Corkscrew, Crack-in-the-Rock, Jaw Bone, and Sockem Dog. During periods of low water in summer and early autumn, it is possible to bushwhack, rock hop, and wade even farther downstream from Camp Creek. Below the four Class V rapids, there is a very large pool just upstream from Tugaloo Lake. On the South Carolina side of the pool, you will find a beach where rafters often haul out and a small entering stream, Opossum Creek. You can follow the path up this creek to a surprisingly beautiful waterfall, labeled only as "Falls" on the Chattooga National Wild and Scenic River map.

Note: Especially in the last few years, this trail is always eroded and frequently trashy. People in a hurry carrying heavy objects such as kayaks or beer coolers have cut down across the switchbacks, creating small eroding gullies. The parking area often has trash thrown down the banks. The rock-foundation campsite at trail's end is obviously a party spot. A few years ago the campsite was disgusting; in late fall of 1997, it was beyond disgusting. Hundreds and hundreds of beer bottles and beer cans, milk jugs and beenie weenie cans, were piled atop the rock foundation. The pile was so high that it had a slip face like a small sand dune, and its slumping angle of repose caused a trash slide down the bank toward the river.

Highlights
Throughout: Late spring rosebay rhododendron displays along the trail and water's edge.
Mile 0.5: Chattooga River—a series of Class V rapids, including Jaw Bone and Sockem Dog, is approximately 0.3 mile downstream.

Directions
(See page 16 of Raven Rock Trail for directions to the FS 511 turnoff.) Continue on FS 511, a one-lane gravel road, for approximately 4.0 miles to its end at a gravel parking lot. The trailhead is to the right of the bulletin board.

Notes

BLACK ROCK MOUNTAIN STATE PARK

Black Rock received its name from the dark biotite gneiss cliff faces, boulders, and outcroppings scattered throughout the park. On the park's narrow ridges these rock outcrops make splendid natural overlooks that provide panoramic vistas of the nearby valleys and mountains. Black Rock covers a large area—1,803 acres—and its greatest elevation, by far the highest in the Georgia state park system, is 3,640 feet atop Black Rock Mountain.

With nearly 80 inches of rainfall per year, the park's luxuriant vegetation supports a varied wildlife population. Thick patches of evergreen rhododendron provide concealment for turkey, deer, bobcat, and an occasional bear.

Ada-Hi Falls Nature Trail

If only all trails, even those down the worst of dirt roads, were as well marked as Ada-Hi Falls. It begins with a formal trailhead—a wooden doorway frame that heightens the perception of entering and intensifies the difference between the oppressiveness of the pavement and the cool richness of the forest, especially during the glaring drought days of summer. Ada-Hi, the Cherokee word for forest, makes perfect sense for a trail beginning in a hardwood forest dominated by northern red, chestnut, and white oak, and ending in a tuliptree cove.

This short path immediately descends into a moist cove where ferns and wildflowers grow in lush abundance. Vasey's trillium, bloodroot, and jack-in-the-pulpit bloom here in spring; touch-me-not (spotted jewelweed), mountain mint, rattlesnake plantain, and black cohosh in summer. Continuing downhill through a diverse hardwood forest, the trail ducks into a dense arbor-like thatching of rhododendron before dropping to its end at the observation deck

EBR
Black Rock Mountain
Black Rock Mountain State Park

Features
Diverse flora, small, low-volume waterfall

Distance
0.2 mile

Difficulty Rating
Moderate

County
Rabun

Nearest City
Mountain City

Maps
Dillard Quadrangle, GA-NC; park map available at visitor center

Blazes
None; none needed

Campsites
Available with
reservation in park
campground

beside Ada-Hi Falls.

The end of the trail is as botanically rich as the beginning. The umbrella-leaf, an aptly named plant infrequently found on rocky seepage slopes, grows below the left side of the deck. (See Sosebee Cove Trail, page 100, for a description of this unusual plant.)

Calling Ada-Hi a falls, especially in Rabun County, is charitable, to say the least. Depending upon the season and recent rainfall, Ada-Hi varies from glistening rock face to thin veneer of sliding water. Most often, this 35-foot-high Taylor Creek headwater fall is a dripping trickle.

Highlights
Throughout: Botanically diverse area with good spring wildflower display.
Mile 0.2: Ada-Hi Falls at trail's end.

Directions
From Clayton, take US 441 North to Mountain City. In Mountain City, turn left onto Black Rock Mountain Road. A prominent sign marks the turn.

Once inside Black Rock Mountain State Park, turn left at the signs for the Tent and Trailer Camping Area. Across the road from the Information Cabin, next to the Concession Area, a sign denotes the trail's location, and a wooden doorway frames its entrance.

Notes

Tennessee Rock Trail

Tennessee Rock is one of the most varied and scenic state park trails. Anthony Lampros and Dustin Warner have recently developed twenty-five interpretive stations throughout its length; an excellent guide to the numbered posts is available at the visitor center for a small fee. Easily walked in an hour or two, its loop traverses the botanically rich slopes and ridge crest of Black Rock Mountain. Flame azalea, mountain laurel, and numerous species of wildflowers bloom beside the path from mid-April through May.

The wide, yellow-blazed walkway begins with a short, moderate climb up wooden steps. After less than 100 yards, the trail reaches the point where its loop begins and ends. A sign states that the loop is easier to walk to the right, counterclockwise. This description follows that direction.

After turning right, the trail continues on an easy upgrade through a hardwood forest dominated by oaks. Beyond 0.2 mile the path becomes level or slightly descending as it winds along a slope that is alternately moist, then dry. Here the herb layer of the forest displays ferns and wildflowers including Virginia spiderwort, Canada violet, and mayapple. A sign marks the entrance of a 100-yard spur that leads to the base of a small boulder field at post 7.

The loop turns left onto an old road at 0.7 mile. This road soon enters an extensive planting of white pine where pinesaps—saprophytic wildflowers—are abundant. These unusual plants do not produce chlorophyll and obtain their nourishment, with the aid of fungi, from organic matter. Most of the pinesaps in this colony were pale yellowish-orange rather than their more common coloration of reddish-orange. They bloom during the second half of July and early August.

A short distance after the road leaves the pine forest, the treadway turns left and becomes path

EBR
Black Rock Mountain
Black Rock Mountain State Park

Features
View, diverse flora, excellent interpretive trail, Eastern Continental Divide

Distance
2.2 miles (loop)

Difficulty Rating
Moderate

County
Rabun

Nearest City
Mountain City

Maps
Dillard Quadrangle, GA-NC; park map available at visitor center

Blazes
Yellow

Campsites
Available with reservation in park campground

again at mile 1.2. Here the trail makes a moderate-to-strenuous climb to the ridge of Black Rock Mountain. Once on the ridge, the footpath continues slightly uphill through an open deciduous forest. Several patches of starry campions—wildflowers identified by their five fringed, white petals and four whorled leaves—bloom along this section of the loop in late July and early August.

At mile 1.7 the trail climbs wooden steps over the first mound of the gneiss outcrop known as Tennessee Rock, which is part of the Eastern Continental Divide: a series of ridges that separate watersheds and their river systems. Water bouncing off the north side of the rock flows to the Gulf of Mexico, by way of the Tennessee, Ohio, and Mississippi Rivers. Raindrops splattering to the south of the rock contribute to the watersheds that flow to the Atlantic Ocean, by way of the Savannah River.

This narrow backbone crest of the mountain affords surprisingly scenic views of the Wolffork and Germany Valleys, and towns and mountains to either side. Beyond the look-off areas, the path drops to a road, then curls downhill and to the left away from the pavement. The trail's ending segment passes above a colony of Vasey's trillium. They usually flower from late April to late May.

Highlights

Throughout: Interpretive signs describing the features of the Southern Appalachian forest. Also, a wide diversity of wildflowers.
Mile 1.7: Tennessee Rock Overlook (3,625 feet) and the Eastern Continental Divide.

Directions

From Clayton, take US 441 North to Mountain City. In Mountain City, turn left onto Black Rock Mountain Road. A prominent sign marks the turn.

The Tennessee Rock Trail begins along the road that leads to the cottages. Two-tenths mile beyond the fork in the main park road (camping to the left, cottages to the right), turn right into the large day-use play area parking lot. There are signs for Tennessee Rock Trail and James E. Edmonds Backcountry Trail at the back of the gravel lot.

James E. Edmonds Backcountry Trail

The beginning of this path makes an easy, then moderate, descent through a hardwood forest along the lower slopes of Black Rock Mountain. At 0.7 mile the treadway reaches the junction—marked by a double blaze—where its loop begins and ends. This description takes the advice of the sign and follows the loop to the right, counterclockwise. The trail continues easily uphill on an old road. At mile 1.1, where the road turns to the right, the loop turns left onto a path. After this change in direction, it drops sharply until it crosses a paved park road at mile 1.4. Orange paint on the road and a "Trail" sign on its other side clarify the route.

Across the pavement, the trail proceeds steadily downhill, passing through a hardwood cove before swinging parallel to Taylor Creek at mile 2.1. The loop ascends beside this lively, sliding stream before crossing it and a gravel road near Taylor Gap at mile 2.4. Here the path rises moderately by switchback for 0.5 mile to the top of Scruggs Knob. It then rides the ridge down the knob's other side to mile 3.2, where it turns left onto an old road at Scruggs Gap. After following this nearly level walkway for 0.2 mile, the trail comes to an important junction. A sign marks the loop's turn downhill and to the left onto another old road.

The road you were on before the junction continues straight ahead to an excellent view. Its moderate, upridge climb leads to a rock slab outcropping atop Lookoff Mountain, elevation 3,162 feet. The Little Tennessee River Valley is below; Smokehouse Knob is across the valley. Dillard and the US 441 corridor are to the right. The first backcountry campsite is located here at the overlook. (This blazed side trail to the overlook, 0.7 mile round-trip, is included in the 7.2 mileage given for this trail.)

After its left turn at the junction, the loop descends sharply, turns right onto another old road,

EBR
Black Rock Mountain
Black Rock Mountain State Park

Features
View, diverse flora, primitive camping

Distance
7.2 miles (loop)

Difficulty Rating
Moderate to strenuous

County
Rabun

Nearest City
Mountain City

Maps
Dillard Quadrangle, GA-NC; park map available at visitor center

Blazes
Orange circles

Water Sources
Miles 2.4 and 5.2: Taylor Creek; mile 6.1: Greasy Creek

Campsites
Designated campsites at mile 3.7 and mile 6.2; available with reservations only

then continues its descent along the lower slopes of Lookoff Mountain. At mile 5.2 the path crosses the gravel road again; 100 yards farther it crosses Taylor Creek again. Here the trail begins the ascent to the end of its loop at mile 6.5. The upgrade becomes progressively steeper after the Greasy Creek crossing at mile 6.1. (The second designated campsite is just beyond the Greasy Creek crossing.) The final 0.7 mile back up to the parking lot is the trail's toughest climb.

Spring-blooming wildflowers are abundant along the backcountry trail. One of the wildflowers people most want to see—the pink lady's slipper, or pink moccasin flower—is fairly common in Black Rock Mountain State Park. Look for colonies of these native, perennial orchids where the trailside forest is predominantly pine. These colonies should have individual plants in bloom from May 10 through May 25.

The pink lady's slipper, which occurs occasionally on public land throughout the state's mountain region, has been designated as "threatened" in Georgia. The plant received this listing because of exploitation—people picking them or digging them up. Please do not harm them; to do so is extremely selfish and against the law. These plants have a symbiotic relationship with mycorrhizal fungi. If you dig them up and take them away from their natural habitat, they will die. Fungi-independent varieties are commercially available. End of lecture. Enjoy their beauty.

Note: Camping on the Edmonds Backcountry Trail is allowed only at the two designated sites and only by reservation. This is strictly enforced. Once you have reserved a site, that site belongs to your party alone. There is a small fee per person per night. Before beginning your hike, check in at the visitor center to obtain a backcountry permit and a map, and to settle all other details.

Highlights

Mile 3.7: Lookoff Mountain overlook with a view of the Little Tennessee Valley.
Mile 6.1: Small cascade shortly after Greasy Creek crossing.

Directions

(See page 22 of Tennessee Rock Trail for directions to the James E. Edmonds Backcountry trailhead.) The trail starts behind its sign at the back of the gravel lot.

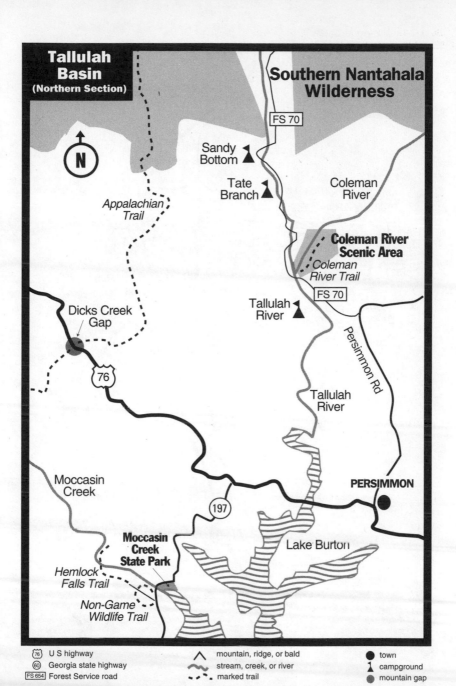

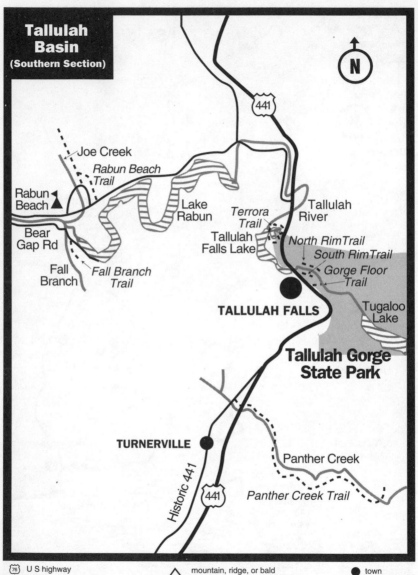

Tallulah Basin
(Southern Section)

N

441

Joe Creek

Rabun Beach Trail

Rabun Beach

Lake Rabun

Terrora Trail

Tallulah River

Bear Gap Rd

Tallulah Falls Lake

North RimTrail

South RimTrail

Fall Branch

Fall Branch Trail

Gorge Floor Trail

TALLULAH FALLS

Tugaloo Lake

Tallulah Gorge State Park

TURNERVILLE

Panther Creek

Historic 441

441

Panther Creek Trail

76	U S highway	mountain, ridge, or bald	town
60	Georgia state highway	stream, creek, or river	campground
FS 654	Forest Service road	marked trail	mountain gap

Coleman River Trail

This enjoyable, highly scenic trail originates just before the bridge by the "Artificial Lures Only" sign and closely follows Coleman River upstream into the 330-acre Coleman River Scenic Area. Shortly after entering the forest, the path comes to a commemorative plaque embedded in a huge boulder. Near the plaque, rockcap ferns grow from the moss on the rock.

By nature, mountain streams are beautiful—the Coleman, bordered by room-sized boulders and wide enough to let the sun in, is especially so. Near the end of the trail the river's fast, shimmering water rushes from cascade to cascade.

Impressive eastern white pine and eastern hemlock flank the Coleman. At 0.2 mile, one of the largest white pines along the trails of North Georgia stands just to the left of the path. Its circumference at 4 feet 6 inches up from the ground is 10 feet 4 inches; the height of its arching tip may be as much as 160 feet, perhaps even higher. Not far beyond the towering pine there is a magnificent old lunker eastern hemlock—13 feet 5 inches in circumference—downslope to the left of the trail.

Eastern white pines are the tallest trees in eastern North America. Judged by the original standard that no longer exists—but is slowly returning in protected areas—the Coleman River pine would hardly be worth mentioning. In America's virgin forests eastern white pines commonly exceeded 160 feet in height; some spired to over 200 feet. On the present site of Dartmouth College, a specimen 240 feet in height was measured.

Two-tenths of a mile farther up river from the pine, look up and to the right of the path. Tucked away in moist pockets between and below trailside boulders are northern maidenhair fern, Indian cucumber-root, Vasey's trillium, and showy orchis.

EBR
Tallulah Basin
Coleman River Scenic Area

Features
Cascades, outstanding forest, huge boulders

Distance
0.9 mile

Difficulty Rating
Easy to moderate

County
Rabun

Nearest City
Clayton

Map
Hightower Bald Quadrangle, GA-NC

Blazes
None; none needed

Campsites
None along the trail; three campgrounds are located along Tallulah River Road: Tallulah River, Tate Branch, and Sandy Bottoms Campgrounds; only Tate Branch is open year-round; the others are seasonal

Ranger District
Tallulah

The trillium and orchis usually begin blooming during late April and early May.

Above the log steps the path narrows, then ends in a jumble of rhododendron and deadfalls.

Highlights

Mile 0.2: Large, impressive white pine and other old-growth trees.
Mile 0.8: Cascades.

Directions

From Clayton, travel slightly more than 8.0 miles west on US 76. Turn right onto paved Persimmon Valley Road at the volunteer fire department and the sign for Tallulah River Recreation Area. Continue for about 4.2 miles on Persimmon Valley Road, then turn left onto FS 70. There is a large sign for Coleman River WMA and another sign for Tallulah River Recreation Area at the entrance of FS 70. Travel FS 70 for 1.6 miles. A few hundred yards past the camping area, a bridge crosses over the Coleman River. The trailhead, marked with its sign and an "Artificial Lures Only" sign, is to the right of the road immediately before the bridge.

Coming from the west, traveling east on US 76, look for the turn onto Persimmon Valley Road approximately 3.0 miles beyond the US 76–GA 197 junction.

Be sure to park only in one of the designated areas. Rangers do ticket cars left outside of these parking spaces. One area is located just past the Tallulah River Campground as you approach the bridge over the Coleman River. You can also park on the trail side of the bridge. If these areas are full, there is more roadside parking around the next bend of the road.

Notes

Non-Game Wildlife Trail

Although this trail is located on national forest land, it was constructed and is maintained primarily by state DNR employees. Questions about the trail should be addressed to Moccasin Creek State Park.

This trail is aptly named. Along its short, easy loop, you will pass by a bat box, a wood duck box, bluebird boxes and several wildlife openings with food plots. The money to construct this trail came from Georgia's nongame wildlife fund—a state tax check-off program designed to benefit nongame species. This trail is easy and educational, an introductory walk especially suited for young children who want to observe wild animals and birds and learn about their habitats.

The trail, now much improved over its original route, follows the first of the many directional arrows that lead walkers beside Moccasin Creek in a counterclockwise direction. American holly is abundant in the understory of the streamside forest. Interpretive signs, wildlife openings, old field succession, a small pond, and an eastern hemlock and eastern white pine grove follow in quick order. At 0.4 mile, just before the loop crosses a road, there is a large patch of running ground pine to the right.

Highlights
Throughout: A variety of bird boxes and forest clearings for wildlife.

Directions
To reach Moccasin Creek State Park from Clayton, travel west on US 76 to the intersection with GA 197. Turn left (south) on GA 197 and travel 3.5 miles to the park entrance.

From the Clarkesville junction of Historic 441–GA 197, travel 21.0 miles on GA 197 North to the park entrance. The corralled trailhead parking area for the Non-Game Wildlife Trail is located on the west side (left if you are heading north) of GA 197 directly across the highway from the entrance of Moccasin Creek State Park. The Non-Game Wildlife Trail begins at the parking area.

EBR
Tallulah Basin
Lake Burton
Wildlife
Management Area

Features
Wildlife openings and food plots, interpretive signs, streams, views

Distance
1.0 mile (loop)

Difficulty Rating
Easy

County
Rabun

Nearest Cities
Clarkesville (S), Hiawassee (NW), Clayton (E)

Map
Lake Burton Quadrangle, GA

Blazes
Frequent directional arrows throughout trail

Campsites
Available with reservation in nearby Moccasin Creek State Park

EBR
Tallulah Basin
Lake Burton
Wildlife
Management Area

Features
Cascades on
Moccasin Creek,
waterfall, bluffs

Distance
1.0 mile

Difficulty Rating
Easy with occasional
rocky, slippery footing

County
Rabun

Nearest Cities
Clarkesville (S),
Hiawassee (NW),
Clayton (E)

Map
Lake Burton
Quadrangle, GA

Blazes
None; none needed

Campsites
No camping permit-
ted next to Hemlock
Falls; primitive camp-
sites available at
trailhead; campsites
also available with
reservation in nearby
Moccasin Creek
State Park

Ranger District
Tallulah

Hemlock Falls Trail

This short, scenic trail leaves no doubt about its exact starting point: it's carved in stone. Behind the trail rock the treadway parallels Moccasin Creek on an often rocky old road. The streamside forest is dominated by eastern hemlock, eastern white pine, sweet birch, basswood, and rosebay rhododendron.

At 0.4 mile a narrow rivulet tributary pours 8 feet onto a rock slab across the creek. The footpath continues beside a long, cascading run—powerful, swift, and foaming white when the water is high.

With 0.3 mile remaining, the path crosses the creek on a sturdy wooden bridge. Beyond the bridge the trail continues to parallel the still-cascading stream to the waterfall. If you walk this trail after leaf-fall and recent rain, along the way you can spot another small-volume, 45- to 50-foot waterfall sliding down the bluff across the creek. Wide and 15 feet high, Hemlock Falls drops into a large, round, mountain-green catch pool. Hemlock Falls is the end of the official, maintained trail.

Note: A patchwork trail once connected path with management area road all the way to Addis Gap on the Appalachian Trail. This unblazed path, which fords Moccasin Creek three times, is now blocked with numerous deadfalls from a blizzard and a hurricane. Moccasin Creek Falls, 30 to 35 feet high and 40 feet wide, is 0.6 mile upstream and one normally easy ford beyond Hemlock Falls.

Highlights
Throughout: Cascading Moccasin Creek and bluffs.
Mile 1.0: Hemlock Falls, 15 feet high and surprisingly powerful during winter and early spring.

Directions
(See Non-Game Wildlife Trail, page 29, for directions to its corralled parking area.) Travel the gravel road that begins next to the corralled parking area 0.5 mile to the Hemlock Falls trailhead and parking area.

Rabun Beach Trail

This wide, rhododendron-shaded trail closely follows Joe Creek upstream. Almost immediately, the brook exhibits a small-scale preview of what's ahead. Just above the first bridge, a gentle, stair-step cascade pours over the same smooth, level ledges that characterize the much higher falls to come.

The easily followed path reaches Panther Falls after slightly less than 0.6 mile. The falls—wide and 35 to 40 feet high—are surprisingly large for such a small and usually peaceful stream. A bedrock ledge serves as a convenient seat at the base of this isolated waterfall.

After the switchbacks beside the upper portion of Panther Falls, the trail continues to a rock crossing over the creek. Here the path becomes a loop, briefly leading away from Joe Creek into a mixed forest of eastern hemlocks, eastern white pines, oaks, American holly, flowering dogwood, hickory, and basswood. But it is only a short distance to the wooden observation bridge in front of Angel Falls—higher (65 feet) and narrower than Panther. At normal water levels Angel is a peaceful series of small falls and slides, framed by rosebay rhododendron and other moisture-loving plants. On cloudless days the late-morning sun bathes the upper falls, fusing with the white water to produce a stunning brilliance.

The Forest Service has constructed a 0.4-mile connector that ties into the regular trail 35 yards from its beginning in Campground 2. Look for the start of this connector at the national forest "tent" sign to the right of the road slightly less than 0.2 mile before you come to the entrance of Rabun Beach Campground 2. Wooden steps and a small carsonite sign mark the trailhead. The connector crosses a small branch that may not be a dry-shod crossing after heavy rains.

EBR
Tallulah Basin
Rabun Beach
Recreation Area

Features
Stream, waterfalls

Distance
0.9 mile: trail beginning inside recreation area; 1.3 miles: trail starting at the road outside of the recreation area

Difficulty Rating
Easy to moderate

County
Rabun

Nearest City
Tallulah Falls

Map
Tiger Quadrangle, GA

Blazes
None; none needed

Campsites
Available seasonally in the recreation area campground

Ranger District
Tallulah

Note: Joe Creek is small, and its waterfalls are usually at their best in winter and spring. During late summer and early fall, especially during drought, you may want to choose a waterfall trail that follows a large stream.

Highlights

Throughout: Abundance of spring wildflowers.
Mile 0.6: Panther Falls, a 35- to 40-foot waterfall.
Mile 0.7: During late April and early May, look for flame azalea in bloom.
Mile 0.9: Angel Falls, a cascading 65-foot series of falls and slides.

Directions

From the Riley C. Thurmond Memorial Bridge in Tallulah Falls, travel on US 441 North for approximately 1.7 miles, then turn left at the Rabun Beach sign immediately before the third bridge. Continue on this paved road for approximately 2.5 miles before turning left at the three-way intersection.

Proceed approximately 4.7 miles, then turn right into Rabun Beach Campground 2.

Once inside the campground gate, turn right and follow the paved road past the rest rooms. Beyond the rest rooms, proceed a short distance (past two roads to the left) to a three-way intersection. The signed trailhead is directly across the junction.

Notes

Fall Branch Trail

EBR
Tallulah Basin
Rabun Beach
Recreation Ara

This trail does not begin or end at Rabun Beach Recreation Area, but because of its close proximity, many people like to walk to beautiful Minnehaha Falls while they are in the area. Tall eastern white pines, thickets of mountain laurel and, closer to the falls, rosebay rhododendron border the short, smooth, easily walked trail.

Like the two waterfalls at Rabun Beach, Minnehaha cascades down numerous rock ledges, but with more exuberance, force, and noise. A bench-like boulder near the base of the wide 50- to 55-foot high upper falls makes a handy seat. If you have some time, spend a few minutes watching the kaleidoscopic water patterns and listening to the "laughing water"—the Minnehaha. Below the sitting rock, the stream careens down the mountain again, this time more slide than falls.

Features
Minnehaha Falls

Distance
0.2 mile

Difficulty Rating
Easy

County
Rabun

Nearest City
Tallulah Falls

Map
Tiger and Tallulah Falls Quadrangles, GA

Highlights
Mile 0.2: A 115-foot long waterslide under a rhododendron grove just before the falls.
Mile 0.2: Minnehaha Falls, a 50-foot waterfall over rock ledges.

Blazes
Red rings mark trailhead

Directions
From the Riley C. Thurmond Memorial Bridge in Tallulah Falls, travel on US 441 North for approximately 1.7 miles, then turn left at the Rabun Beach sign immediately before the third bridge. Continue on this paved road for approximately 2.5 miles before turning left at the three-way intersection.

Proceed approximately 6.3 miles, then turn left and down onto the paved road at the Flat Creek community sign.

Continue on the paved road across the bridge over Seed Lake, and after 0.2 mile, where the paved road curves to the right, follow gravel Bear Gap Road straight ahead. After traveling 1.5 miles on Bear Gap Road, begin looking to the right for stairs cut into the roadbank. There is a small pull-off area on the left just before the steps.

Campsites
Available seasonally at the nearby recreation area campground

Ranger District
Tallulah

TALLULAH GORGE
STATE PARK

> The finest workers in stone are not copper or steel tools, but
> the gentle touches of air and water working at their leisure
> with a liberal allowance of time.
>
> —*Henry David Thoreau*

Opened in the fall of 1992, the 3,050-acre Tallulah Gorge State Park
was created through a partnership between the Georgia Department
of Natural Resources and the Georgia Power Company. The Preservation
2000 program provided the funds for land acquisition. Split by US 441,
the park is located in Habersham and Rabun counties. This large park
encompasses not only the entire gorge, but also 63-acre Tallulah Falls
Lake and the plateau-like forest that stretches southeast along the gorge
all the way to the shores of Tugaloo Lake.

One of the most spectacular gorges in the eastern United States, the
chasm is slightly less than 2.0 miles long and approximately 700 feet
deep at its greatest depth below the rim. While the gorge is impressive, its
quiet walls are no longer alive with sound and reflected river light, its
floor is no longer alive with the power and beauty of a wild river, the
Tallulah. The river was dammed and diverted in 1913. Yesterday's famous
waterfalls—Tempesta, Hurricane, Oceana, and Bridal Veil—have been
slowed to silent trickles most of the time. Our state's most beautiful con-
cert hall is still standing; it has just lost its music and dancers.

A permit is required to hike the rugged Gorge Floor Trail. The park
closes this trail during inclement winter weather and rain, even in summer.

Additional trails and an extensive backcountry system are planned
for the near future.

Because this new park is changing so fast, and because of the inher-
ent risks associated with hiking into the gorge, park officials have asked
that all people visit the Jane Hurt Yarn Interpretive Education Center
before starting their hike.

North Rim Trail

EBR
Tallulah Basin
Tallulah Gorge
State Park

This wide promenade connects the string of five overlooks on the north rim of the gorge. The walkway leading from the back doors of the Jane Hurt Yarn Interpretive Center ties into the trail between overlooks four and five. To the left, the route leads 0.2 mile to overlook five, which features lookouts in three directions. Here the view is of Oceana Falls and down the gorge to the pools below Sliding Rock. North Wallenda Tower lies on its side nearby.

To the right from the Interpretive Center the walkway winds 0.4 mile along the rim to the other four overlooks. Overlook four provides an upstream view of pools, swirlholes, waterfalls (when there is water), and the huge Hawthorne Pool directly below. Overlook three offers much the same view, with perhaps a better look at Hawthorne Pool, but from a different angle. Overlook two is of the dam, which for three generations has shackled the life, beauty, and power of the gorge. Overlook one presents a final look at cliff face and pool. The trail ends here, 0.1 mile from the highway.

The Virginia pine, a tree adapted to dry, poor, rocky soil, is clearly dominant along much of the north rim.

Features
Overlooks of
Tallulah Gorge

Distance
0.6 mile

Difficulty Rating
Easy

County
Rabun

Nearest City
Tallulah Falls

Maps
Tallulah Falls
Quadrangle, GA;
park map available
at visitor center

Blazes
White arrows

Campsites
Available with
reservation in park
campground

Highlights
Scattered throughout: Five overlooks affording views of the uppermost mile of the gorge, from the dam to Sliding Rock.

Directions
From the Riley C. Thurmond Memorial Bridge (Tallulah Lake on left, Tallulah Gorge on right) in Tallulah Falls, continue north on US 441 for 0.4 mile, then turn right onto Jane Hurt Yarn Drive at the state park signs. Proceed 0.8 mile to the Jane Hurt Yarn Interpretive Education Center. The trail begins behind the center.

Tallulah Gorge
State Park

Features
Overlooks of
Tallulah Gorge

Distance
0.3 mile

Difficulty Rating
Easy

Counties
Rabun and
Habersham

Nearest City
Tallulah Falls

Maps
Tallulah Falls
Quadrangle, GA;
park map available
at visitor center

Blazes
None; none needed

Campsites
Available with
reservation in park
campground

South Rim Trail

The South Rim Trail was all but obliterated by a tornado in the spring of 1994. After being closed for extensive cleanup and reconstruction, the trail reopened in the summer of 1996.

A wide walkway with steps, railing, and benches, this trail heads to the east along the chasm rim, connecting a string of five overlooks. The treadway begins at the overlook pavilion, where the view is of Hawthorne Pool, Tempesta Falls, and the sheer cliffs of the gorge wall. The second view is essentially the same as the first, but from a different angle. The third overlook affords a view of Hurricane Falls and its pool—Devils Footbath.

The fourth and fifth overlooks are close together at the end of the trail. The next-to-last overlook provides a good view of Caledonia Cascade (a trickle during summer drought) on the north wall and the gorge floor upstream to Hurricane Falls. The final view is of Oceana Falls and its pools. On warm-weather weekends you can often see rock climbers scaling the north wall.

The chestnut oak is common in the dry, rocky habitat along the gorge rim. This oak is easily identified by the numerous wavy, rounded lobes on its leaf margin. The Piedmont rhododendron, a small-leaved evergreen shrub, is also common in the sunny areas along the rim. This small rhododendron's pink or pinkish-purple flowers usually peak between May 10 and 25.

Highlights
Throughout: Five overlooks affording excellent views of Tallulah Gorge, its waterfalls, pools, boulders, and cliffs, as well as the strangled flow of its creator, the Tallulah River.

Directions
See North Rim Trail, page 35, for directions to the Jane Hurt Yarn Interpretive Center.

Gorge Floor Trail

EBR
Tallulah Basin
Tallulah Gorge
State Park

This old trail has numerous names, none of them official. These names usually include the words "cable," "tower," and "Wallenda," in varying combinations. But since this trail descends to the bottom of the gorge, which has very little to do with the cables and towers of Wallenda's walk, it now has a new unofficial name: Gorge Floor Trail.

No matter what it is called, this route is by far the most strenuous short trail, or short section of trail, in Georgia. One hundred feet of elevation change per 0.1 mile is considered strenuous hiking. This trail loses approximately 560 feet (0.1 mile) in 0.3 mile. The steepest pitches—alternating tilted slabs of rock with high steps from rock to rock—are 40 to 45 degrees. Often a 10- to 30-foot-wide worn swath over rock, the trail winds down the remains of a ridge through a forest of hardy trees and shrubs that have adapted to the harsh habitat.

The trail ends at Sliding Rock: a thin veneer of water sliding down a long, curving, slick pitch of rock to the deep, green catch pool below. From Sliding Rock you can explore the gorge floor upstream to the base of Hurricane Falls and downstream to the Amphitheater.

Features
Gorge views, rugged trail, Sliding Rock, gorge floor

Distance
0.3 mile

Difficulty Rating
Strenuous

County
Habersham

Nearest City
Tallulah Falls

Maps
Tallulah Falls Quadrangle, GA; park map available at visitor center

Blazes
White arrows

Campsites
Available with reservation in park campground

Highlights

Throughout: Georgia's most rugged short section of trail. Numerous partial and open gorge views from or near the trail. The route ends at Sliding Rock and its large green catch pool. There is an excellent view of the mineral-stained gorge wall across the pool.
From trail's end: Exploration of Tallulah Gorge—its pools, slides, boulders, cliffs, and waterfalls—is possible upstream and downstream.

Directions

See North Rim Trail, page 35, for directions to the Jane Hurt Yarn Interpretive Center.

EBR
Tallulah Basin
Tallulah Gorge
State Park

Features
Interpretive signs,
Tallulah Falls Lake

Distance
0.5 mile (loop)

Difficulty Rating
Easy to moderate

County
Rabun

Nearest City
Tallulah Falls

Maps
Tallulah Falls
Quadrangle, GA;
park map available
at visitor center

Blazes
Directional signs

Campsites
Available with
reservation in park
campground

Terrora Trail

Terrora Trail circles (with the help of a bridge) a small cove of Tallulah Falls Lake. Starting at the lake view behind the old jail, the footpath follows the trail sign and heads to the right in a counter-clockwise direction. The route quickly descends through a dry oak-pine forest and crosses a bridge over Slaughter Pen Branch. After rising from the branch, the treadway dips to lake level and an open lake view at slightly less than 0.3 mile.

The trail closely follows the lakeshore another 100 yards to a fork at the benches. Here the route takes the right fork up and away from the lake to the old railroad bed, railroad overlook, and parking lot. The remainder of the loop turns left onto the paved road and crosses the bridge back to the jail.

The trailside forest is often dominated, for now, by the pines—white, Virginia, and shortleaf. Mountain laurel is abundant along the rocky, open shoreline. Colonies of evergreen trailing arbutus and galax grow near the beginning of the loop.

A little-known tree species, one endemic to the Southern Appalachians, lives in the dry, rocky habitats along this trail. Smaller than the eastern hemlock, and having a different needle arrangement, the Carolina hemlock ranges in scattered pockets from southwestern Virginia to extreme northeast Georgia. This hemlock is adapted to dry, rocky areas—slopes, cliffs, bluffs, and ridges. The Carolina hemlock wasn't named until 1881.

Highlights
Throughout: Frequent views of the green-water cove.

Directions
See North Rim Trail, page 35, for directions to the Jane Hurt Yarn Interpretive Center.

Panther Creek Trail

The trail, which follows Panther Creek downstream toward its confluence with the Tugaloo River, begins across the highway from the Panther Creek Recreation Area on Historic 441. A sign marks the trailhead. After slightly less than 0.1 mile, the treadway passes beneath the two bridges of US 441. Until it crosses the wooden bridge at mile 1.4, the path usually remains on the steep slopes above the stream, within earshot of the fast-flowing shoals and low cascades. At 0.9 mile a side trail drops down to a noisy cascade that finishes its run with a long, sliding chute.

You will reach the third set of trail-crowding outcrops slightly less than 0.1 mile beyond the cascade. This time, instead of continuing straight ahead beneath the rock that juts overhead, the trail curls up and to the left, between the narrow gap in the outcrop. At mile 1.4 the path crosses a bridge over the creek at the first of the small signs that guide hikers to the falls. Beyond the bridge, the stream becomes calm and the trail becomes sidewalk flat, at least for a while. Do not mistake the high shoals at mile 2.3 for the waterfall. Panther Creek Falls, still slightly more than a mile away, past a path-narrowing bluff, is much more impressive.

Not knowing what to expect, most people are surprised by the beauty, size and power of the waterfall—really a series of falls, with a splashing slide in the middle. The trail skirts along the upper falls on the outer edge of a bluff, then descends to the small, swirling pool that catches the waterfall's first drop. From here the path becomes somewhat steep, sloping down to the bottom of the falls and the unusually large, enticing pool at its base.

The trail continues for 2.4 more miles. Below the falls, Panther Creek becomes even more scenic: the forest becomes taller and more diverse; shoals are

Piedmont
Tallulah Basin
Panther Creek Recreation Area

Features
Cascades, waterfall, Panther Creek Botanical Area

Distance
5.9 miles

Difficulty Rating
Easy to moderate to falls; moderate beyond

County
Habersham

Nearest Cities
Clarkesville (SW), Tallulah Falls (N)

Maps
Tallulah Falls Quadrangle, GA, Tugaloo Lake Quadrangle, SC-GA

Blazes
Blue

Water Sources
Panther Creek and tributaries

Campsites
Not allowed in recreation area; this area is day use only

Ranger District
Chattooga

more frequent; boulders, occasionally table-top flat, are larger and more numerous; pools are longer, deeper, and greener. Unfortunately, as it is now designed, the trail takes hikers away from the creek for almost half of the remaining distance.

After remaining alongside the creek for 0.6 mile, the trail comes to a low waterfall and its miniature gorge. Forty-five yards beyond this falls, the path turns to the right and climbs away from the creek beside a tributary rivulet. The path crosses the rivulet at mile 4.3, then sharply ascends a hillside for slightly more than 0.1 mile before it reaches the level top of a dry, piney ridge. (Watch for the double blue blazes which signify sudden changes in trail directions.) Descending from the ridge through a forest dominated by mature oak, tuliptree, basswood, and American beech, the trail returns to Panther Creek with a 0.7-mile walk to the bridge, which marks its end.

The US Forest Service has designated two parcels of land along the Panther Creek corridor as the Panther Creek Botanical Area. These tracts, which total 598 acres, preserve and protect unique vegetative communities. The first area, which is the larger of the two, begins below Panther Creek Falls and continues downstream to near where the trail ends. The second area is further downstream, across the section of privately owned land that separates the two tracts.

Spring wildflowers, including three species of trillium, are abundant on the moist, open slopes downstream from the falls. One of North Georgia's rarest wildflowers—gaywings, sometimes called fringed polygala or bird-on-the-wing—blooms by the thousands along the first few miles of the trail. This perennial herb often grows with partridgeberry, forming dense mats of dark green and orchid pink. Gaywings usually bloom in mid-April.

Highlights
Throughout: Spring wildflower display.
Mile 2.3: Impressive high shoals.
Mile 3.5: Panther Creek Falls—scenic, large, and memorable.

Directions
To the Panther Creek Recreation Area trailhead: From Cornelia travel US 441 North for less than 18.0 miles to the sign for Panther Creek Picnic Area and Trail Parking. Turn left off US 441, then quickly turn right onto Historic 441. Continue a short distance on Historic 441 to the recreation area parking lot on the left.

The trail, which follows Panther Creek downstream, begins on the right side of Historic 441 (facing north), beyond the recreation area entrance and across Panther Creek. The trail's entrance is behind its sign, to the right of the dirt road.

To the Yonah Dam trailhead: Travel GA 106 North into the city of Toccoa. Where GA 106 ends, just before a bridge inscribed "Southern," turn right onto GA 17 toward Westminster. Drive 1.0 mile to the third traffic light on Highway 17, then turn left onto GA 17 Conn. After traveling 0.5 mile, turn left at the stop sign, then turn onto the first road to the right, Prather Bridge Road.

Continue straight on Prather Bridge Road for 9.7 miles before you bear left immediately after the bridge near Yonah Park and Dam. After traveling 0.7 mile beyond the bridge, turn left onto a dirt road. Continue straight on this rutted road for 1.5 miles to near where it fords Panther Creek. Park at the pull-off area to the right of the road. If the road is muddy, it is better to park near the power cut on the hill above the ford.

Notes

42

Features
Stream, forest

Distance
4.1 miles

Difficulty Rating
Easy to moderate

County
Stephens

Nearest City
Cornelia

Map
Ayersville
Quadrangle, GA

Blazes
Blue

Water Sources
River and creek
water available
throughout

Ranger District
Chattooga

Broad River Trail

Originally built by the Civilian Conservation Corps in 1939, the Broad River Trail was reopened by the Youth Conservation Corps in 1980. It is located in the middle of the Lake Russell Wildlife Management Area and exemplifies the rolling topography of the upper Piedmont.

This trail has either-end access on Guard Camp Road. Once the trail begins to follow the Middle Fork of the Broad River downstream, its general direction of travel is north to south. Although it is not difficult to walk in either direction, the trail is noticeably easier from north to south, downstream and downhill.

The first mile of the path parallels Dicks Creek— quick and clear, and cascading like a mountain stream—before it meanders through the coves and hillsides along the Middle Fork of the Broad River. The canopy of mixed, mature hardwoods near the river thins out on the hillsides, giving way just out of sight to stands of eastern white pine. The trail, river corridor, and coves remain a ribbon of wildness in the midst of managed forest.

Fairly level throughout, the trail's elevation ranges between 920 and 1,200 feet. Covered in mountain laurel, the river bank is beautiful in May when the clusters of tiny cup-shaped pink and white blooms open. After the first 1.4 miles, the treadway climbs away from the river, traversing hardwood coves dominated by oaks—chestnut, white, black, southern and northern red—as well as tuliptree, blackgum, red maple, sweetgum, and pignut hickory. Along the trail you'll also see sassafras. You can identify this tree by its four distinct leaf shapes (the left-handed mitten, the right-handed mitten, the turkey foot, and the unlobed blade); the leaves turn bright red, yellow, or orange in the fall. Mature American beeches occupy the crotches of seeps, which are easy to walk across or are spanned by foot logs and bridges.

In early fall black-eyed Susans and other members of the aster family, purple lobelia, and strawberry bush add color to the hike. Also called hearts-a-bustin', strawberry bush is a shrub whose inconspicuous greenish-purple flowers bloom in April and May. But the species is known for its rough-surfaced, crimson, half-inch fruit that opens in late September and October to display shiny orange-red seeds pendant between each of the three to five lobes. Partridgeberry and spotted wintergreen are also common on the forest floor along the trail, as is little brown jug, or heart-leaf, whose small, jug-like calyxes appear under thick, arrow-shaped leaves in April and May.

Highlights

Mile 0.6: Waterfall on Dicks Creek. The creek drops 10 feet through a narrow crevice then spreads over sandstone shelves forming a cascade.
Mile 1.0: Flat rock shoals spanning the 30-foot Broad River just below its confluence with Dicks Creek.

Directions

Travel US 441–GA 365 North from Cornelia. Approximately 4.5 miles beyond where GA 365 ties into US 441, turn right at the Clarkesville exit (GA 197). At the stop sign turn right onto Old Highway 197. Continue approximately 2.5 miles on Old Highway 197, then turn left onto Dicks Hill Parkway toward Toccoa. Proceed slightly more than 8.5 miles (pass the first Ayersville Road and Fern Springs Picnic Area) before turning right onto Ayersville Road at the Milliken and Patterson industrial signs.

After turning onto Ayersville Road, continue 0.8 mile, then turn left onto FS 87, Guard Camp Road. If you want to hike north to south (upstream to downstream), travel 2.2 miles from the turnoff at Ayersville Road. The trailhead is on your right. Look for a big brown trail sign about 50 feet down the road bank. You will know you're getting close to the trailhead at mile 2.1 when you pass over a culvert marked with reflectors. Drive 0.1 mile beyond the culvert then look for the northern trailhead on foot.

To reach the southern trailhead, continue on FS 87 another 3.0 miles. It is located 0.1 mile past a single-lane bridge and just before FS 92 forks off FS 87. This trailhead is also marked with a big sign, located about 80 feet off the right side of the road. The trail begins at a sturdy wooden bridge spanning Kimbell Creek.

Guard Camp Road is the only Lake Russell Wildlife Management Area access that remains open throughout the year. However, this dirt and gravel road is subject to closure during and after bad winter weather.

Piedmont
Lake Russell
Wildlife
Management Area
Lake Russell
Recreation Area

Features
Lake Russell, scenic
views

Distance
5.1 miles: 3.3 miles
of trail plus 1.8 miles
of road to complete
loop

Difficulty Rating
Easy to moderate

Counties
Habersham and
Banks

Nearest City
Cornelia

Map
Lake Russell and
Baldwin
Quadrangles, GA

Blazes
Blue

Campsites
Available seasonally
in recreation area
campground

Ranger District
Chattooga

Lake Russell Trail

L ake Russell and the surrounding wildlife management area are named for the late US Senator Richard B. Russell, who served his Georgia constituency
from 1933–71, over half his life.

Lake Russell Trail is a loop that begins and ends at
the Nancy Town Lake parking area. The loop is
designed and blazed to be walked in a clockwise direction, crossing the spillway first. The final 1.8 miles of
the trail, however, follow recreation area roads, all of
which are open to vehicular traffic when the recreation area is open. During the off-season, the main
recreation area road is gated beyond the Lake Russell
boat ramp.

The beginning of this trail crosses the spillway
immediately below the dam at Nancy Town Lake.
Concrete steps, a stride apart except for one gap, make
the crossing relatively easy for most people during low
water levels. When the spillway is releasing a high volume of water, however, the gap can be slippery and
difficult to negotiate. After heavy rains in winter, the
spillway could be particularly difficult without a bridg-
ing board (4 or 5 feet will work fine).

After it climbs the bank, the trail turns to the
right and parallels scenic Nancy Town Creek downstream. The wide, easily walked path reaches the
upper end of 100-acre Lake Russell at 0.3 mile. For
the next 1.3 miles, the trail closely follows the lake's
forested southeastern shoreline, occasionally winding
around deep, inviting coves. This section of the loop
gently undulates to match the shoreline terrain.
Where the lakeside is flat, the footpath remains at
bank level, but where hills drop into the green water,
the treadway rises onto slope, usually only 10 to 30
feet above the lake. Here the shoreline forest alternates between stands of pine—shortleaf, loblolly and
Virginia, their trunks sometimes fire blackened—and
smaller groves of hardwood. Many of the pines are
dead or dying, victims of a beetle infestation.

After crossing a bridge halfway around a large cove, the route rises up and away from the lake for the first time. The loop dips to the Lake Russell Dam at mile 2.3. The walk over the dam affords a good view of the long, narrow lake and its surrounding ridges. Once the trail reenters the forest, it turns left and descends to the floodplain below the dam. Here the path crosses a bridge over Nancy Town Creek, follows the outside arc of the spillway, and then makes a short climb back to lake level.

The remainder of the foot-travel-only trail follows a gravel road closed to vehicular traffic. After traversing a hillside above a cove, the road bends away from the lake at mile 2.9 and ends at a paved road at mile 3.3. Here you have a choice: you can either turn left and complete the loop by road, or you can turn around and backtrack the way you came.

Highlights
Miles 0.3-2.4: Green water views of 100-acre Lake Russell.

Directions
Travel US 441–GA 365 North from Cornelia and follow signs for Lake Russell Recreation Area. Approximately 4.5 miles beyond where GA 365 ties into US 441, turn right at the Clarkesville exit (GA 197). At the stop sign turn right onto Old Highway 197. Continue approximately 2.5 miles on Old Highway 197, turn right onto Dicks Hill Parkway, then proceed less than 1.0 mile before turning left onto Lake Russell Road.

Continue approximately 2.0 miles on Lake Russell Road, then turn left onto FS 591 at the sign for Nancy Town Lake. After 0.1 mile turn right into the trailhead parking area next to the dam at Nancy Town Lake.

Lake Russell Trail begins at its trailhead sign next to the dam.

Notes

Piedmont
*Lake Russell
Wildlife
Management Area*
Lake Russell
Recreation Area

Features
Nancy Town Falls

Distance
2.7 miles (loop)

Difficulty Rating
Easy to moderate

County
Habersham

Nearest City
Cornelia

Map
Ayersville
Quadrangle, GA

Blazes
Blue diamonds

Campsites
Available seasonally
at recreation area
campground

Ranger District
Chattooga

Sourwood Trail

A sign marks the beginning of this loop, which is designed and blazed to be hiked in a clockwise direction, footpath at the beginning and gravel road at the end. The forest along the first segment of the trail, a flat woods road, is dominated by tall, well-spaced loblolly pines. This stand will probably be cut in the near future.

After crossing the iron bridge over an unnamed Nancy Town Creek tributary, the route gradually rises through a regenerating cut (around 1986), where fast-growing pine saplings, including the short-needled Virginia pine, have quickly filled the void. At 0.9 mile the treadway crosses a management area road. Here the loop becomes footpath as it drops into an open hardwood hollow, where chestnut oaks are common.

At mile 1.4 the trail dips to Nancy Town Creek for the first time. A low sign to the left marks the entrance of a side path that heads slightly less than 0.1 mile upstream to Nancy Town Falls. This small-water falls, wide and 20 to 25 feet high, gently pours over large crumpled rocks—tranquil and suprisingly scenic for the Piedmont.

Back on the main loop, the trail often closely parallels the occasionally shoaling creek for 0.6 mile to the next iron bridge. Doghobble and Christmas fern, both evergreen, are common beneath the hardwood forest of the floodplain. Doghobble is the low, arching, thicket-forming shrub that has alternate leaves tapering to a long point.

Beyond the bridge, the treadway passes through a small, recent cut (mid-1990s) before paralleling shoaling Nancy Town Creek again for a short distance. The loop turns right onto a wide gravel road at mile 2.2 and continues, following the metal diamonds, straight ahead on the road back to the trail sign.

Sourwood Trail traverses an area that is actively managed for timber and wildlife. If you would rather not walk through recent cuts, you may want to pick another trail.

Highlights
Mile 1.4: A 0.1-mile path to the left leads to the 25-foot-high Nancy Town Falls.

Directions
(See page 45 of Lake Russell Trail for directions to its trailhead and to the dam at Nancy Town Lake.) Park at the Lake Russell trailhead next to the dam at Nancy Town Lake. Walk paved FS 591 a little more than 0.3 mile beyond its gate—past Nancy Town Lake and a group camping area—to the Sourwood trailhead and sign to the left of the road just before it crosses a bridge. The gate at FS 591 remains closed throughout the year.

Notes

EBR
Tray Mountain
High Shoals
Scenic Area

Features
Two waterfalls

Distance
1.2 miles

Difficulty Rating
Moderate

County
Towns

Nearest Cities
Helen (S),
Hiawassee (N)

Map
Tray Mountain
Quadrangle, GA

Blazes
Blue

Ranger District
Brasstown

High Shoals Trail

The trail, starting at about 2,880 feet, enters the forest on wooden steps to the right of the parking lot. About 100 yards from the steps the trail turns to the right and loops its way down into the 170-acre scenic area. At the bottom of the mountain at 2,560 feet, the path turns left onto an old road and follows High Shoals Creek downstream to a wooden bridge. Across the creek, the trail curls to the left, then parallels the cascading stream as it drops more than 300 feet in a series of five waterfalls. The two largest falls are viewed easily. Two prominent side trails, veering back to the left through mountain laurel and rosebay rhododendron thickets, angle down to the two observation decks.

A few yards past a large vehicle-blocking boulder at 0.9 mile, the first side path takes you down to the deck overlooking Blue Hole—a picturesque pool more than 20 feet deep, scoured over the centuries by the falling rock and water from its accompanying 25- to 30-foot waterfall.

Less than 0.1 mile farther, the next slanting spur trail drops back down to the much larger High Shoals Falls—a jagged, twisting falls over 100 feet high. The falls are more exciting, more powerful, during periods of high water. I once visited High Shoals in late February, after heavy rain and snow had increased the water volume three to four times that of late summer. The falls were in magnificent form, ricocheting off rocks and splashing into the air, sending showers of spray downstream and onto the decks. Though it was sunny and over 50 degrees, the observation decks and vegetation along the fringes of the waterfalls were still coated in ice from the mist and chill of the night before.

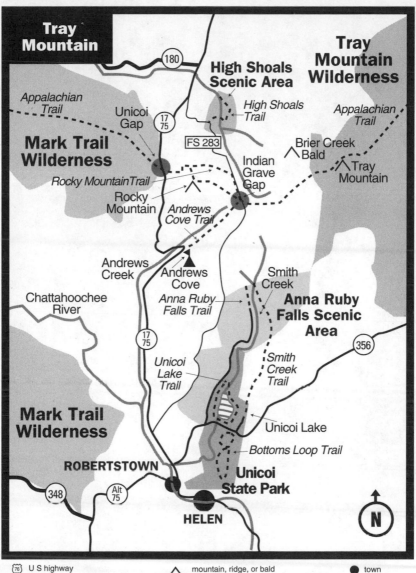

Tray Mountain

Tray Mountain Wilderness

180

High Shoals Scenic Area

Appalachian Trail

Unicoi Gap

17 75

High Shoals Trail

Appalachian Trail

FS 283

Brier Creek Bald

Mark Trail Wilderness

Indian Grave Gap

Tray Mountain

Rocky MountainTrail

Rocky Mountain

Andrews Cove Trail

Andrews Creek

Andrews Cove

Smith Creek

Chattahoochee River

Anna Ruby Falls Trail

Anna Ruby Falls Scenic Area

17 75

356

Unicoi Lake Trail

Smith Creek Trail

Unicoi Lake

Mark Trail Wilderness

Bottoms Loop Trail

ROBERTSTOWN

348

Alt 75

Unicoi State Park

HELEN

N

76 U S highway	∧ mountain, ridge, or bald
60 Georgia state highway	∿ stream, creek, or river
FS 654 Forest Service road	▴▴▪ marked trail

● town
⌇ campground
● mountain gap

Notes

Highlights

Mile 1.0: Blue Hole Falls, a deep pool of clear, cold water.

Mile 1.2: At High Shoals Falls, water shoots through a narrow rock opening and winds down a jagged, rocky ledge.

Directions

From the Chattahoochee River Bridge in Helen, travel GA 75 North approximately 11.3 miles, then turn right onto Indian Grave Gap Road, FS 283. This road is about 2.0 miles north of the large parking area to the right of the highway at Unicoi Gap, where the Appalachian Trail crosses GA 75. It is also the first road to the right after Unicoi Gap.

Once on FS 283, ford the usually shallow stream and keep going straight up the hill. About 1.4 miles from the turn off GA 75, FS 283 reaches a level area and curves right. Look for the trailhead sign and parking area to the left.

The dirt and gravel road is somewhat rough; during winter, frozen ruts make it all but impassable except for four-wheel-drive vehicles. During the rest of the year, regular cars may have trouble with the stream and muddied road after a heavy rain.

Notes

EBR
Tray Mountain
Section 5—AT

Features
AT approach, winter views, Rocky Mountain

Distance
1.8 miles

Difficulty Rating
Moderate

County
Towns

Nearest Cities
Helen (S),
Hiawassee (N)

Maps
Tray Mountain Quadrangle, GA; Appalachian Trail map

Blazes
Blue

Water Sources
Trail crosses head-water rivulets at miles 1.0 and 1.5

Ranger District
Brasstown

Rocky Mountain Trail

The Rocky Mountain Trail was designed as the first leg of a loop beginning and ending at Indian Grave Gap. The loop's total distance—from the gap (3,100 feet) up to and over Rocky Mountain (4,020 feet), then back down to the gap—is 3.5 miles.

From Indian Grave Gap follow the blue blazes on FS 283 back the way you came, to the northwest toward the High Shoals trailhead. After 0.6 mile on the road, which is included in the trail mileage, the route turns left into the forest at the double blue blaze and signs. Here the treadway follows the winding, easy grades of an old woods road through a young, predominantly hardwood forest.

At 0.9 mile the trail leaves the old roadbed, then descends on constructed path to its crossing of a rocky, headwater rivulet. Marginal wood ferns and Christmas ferns add winter green to the slope above the crossing.

Beyond the rivulet, the footpath ascends on easy-to-moderate grades to mile 1.5, where it crosses Rogers Branch. Continuing to gain elevation through a forest dominated by oaks, the treadway curls onto a ridge top, then quickly ends at its junction with the AT.

Turn left onto the AT to complete the loop. The AT finishes the climb over aptly named Rocky Mountain before beginning its occasionally steep and rocky, 900-foot descent to Indian Grave Gap. Along the way there are numerous good winter views. Outcrops on Rocky Mountain's open southern shoulder afford two year-round views reaching to the Piedmont. Yonah Mountain's unmistakable profile is due south.

Highlights

Nearly throughout: Winter views. The large mountain to the northeast is Brier Creek Bald, 4,163 feet. Near the end of the trail, where the path curls onto a ridge top, there is a winter view of Brasstown Bald to the right (northwest). *Miles 1.0, 1.5:* Good spring wildflower displays in the two high, moist, north-facing hollows.

Directions

(See page 51 of High Shoals Trail for directions from Helen to FS 283.) Once on FS 283, ford the usually shallow stream and keep going straight up the hill. Proceed slightly more than 3.5 miles on FS 283 (pass High Shoals Trailhead at mile 1.4) to Indian Grave Gap. Indian Grave Gap is easy to find: the AT crosses the road, the road widens to pull-off parking to the right, and the blue-blazed Andrews Cove Trail ties into the AT at the gap.

From the GA 75–US 76 junction, travel GA 75 South for approximately 6.7 miles, then turn left onto FS 283.

Notes

EBR
Tray Mountain
Andrews Cove
Recreation Area

Features
Cove forest, AT
approach

Distance
1.8 miles

Difficulty Rating
Moderate to
strenuous

County
White

Nearest City
Helen

Maps
Tray Mountain
Quadrangle, GA;
Appalachian Trail
map

Blazes
Blue

Campsites
Available seasonally
in the recreation
area campground

Ranger District
Chattooga

Andrews Cove Trail

Andrews Cove—short, scenic, and somewhat challenging—is an ideal warm-up hike for the springtime. It climbs its cove along an old logging road to Indian Grave Gap, where the AT crosses FS 283. Along the way, it passes through a maturing second-growth forest, dominated by an open, park-like stand of hardwoods. Because Andrews is drier than coves that are higher or north facing, many of its larger trees are either oak or hickory.

The trail begins on a hill above Andrews Creek at an elevation of 2,080 feet. You can see this creek for about 0.2 mile and hear it after that. At 1.2 miles it reappears. You start off on an easy, smooth trail almost devoid of rocks. After three small rivulets, the trail crosses a small feeder branch and then makes a sharp left turn at 0.5 mile. At mile 0.9 you pass a large boulder with a spring under it.

Enjoy the level and downhill walking before you reach the steep ascent to Indian Grave Gap (elevation 3,100 feet). Looking up and to the left, you can identify the steep side of Rocky Mountain to the north. At mile 1.4, the trail becomes very rocky; it is then very steep for the last 0.3 mile to its junction with the AT. The final 0.3 mile averages about 100 feet of elevation gain per 0.1 mile. When a trail does this—climbs at a 20 percent grade—it really goes up. There are few trails in the Southern Appalachians that maintain that gradient for more than 2.0 miles.

On the way down, you'll notice a nice view of the valley back toward Helen, and during the steep section, you'll enjoy a vista of the mountains to the south.

Highlights
Throughout: In fall, enjoy the leaf color and variety—90 percent of trees in the cove are hardwoods.

Hickory, oak, tuliptree, and flowering dogwood abound; a few pines, eastern hemlocks and American holly add year-round greenery. *Throughout:* Good spring wildflower display from late March through April.

Directions

From the Chattahoochee River Bridge in Helen, drive 6.6 miles on GA 75 North. Watch for the Andrews Cove Recreation Area sign on the right as you make a sharp left turn. Turn right into the campground and follow the loop right. Park between campsites 6 and 7.

Notes

EBR
Tray Mountain
Anna Ruby Falls
Scenic Area

Features
Two waterfalls,
streams, rock out-
crops, interpretive
nature trail

Distance
0.4 mile

Difficulty Rating
Easy to moderate

County
White

Nearest City
Helen

Maps
Tray Mountain
Quadrangle, GA;
scenic area informa-
tion available at visi-
tor center

Blazes
None; none needed

Campsites
Available with reser-
vation in nearby
Unicoi State Park

Ranger District
Chattooga

Anna Ruby Falls National Recreation Trail

Combined with adjoining Unicoi State Park and situated near Helen, Anna Ruby Falls Scenic Area is by far the most frequently visited area in the Chattahoochee National Forest. This steeply sloped scenic area lives up to its designated status through-out the year, for it is always "scenic." In addition to the uninterrupted splendor of the falls, each season brings its own beauty to the 1,600-acre tract. The spring blossoms, the shady lushness of summer, the autumn foliage, and the sparkling snow and unob-structed views of winter make Anna Ruby Falls a great place to visit in all seasons.

The asphalt path—which has numbered posts and a corresponding pamphlet that identifies com-mon plants—begins at the upper end of the parking lot next to the information booth and bulletin board. The trail follows Smith Creek upstream through a predominantly hardwood forest to the base of the two waterfalls. Along the way, the turbu-lent brook swirls below the path, picking its way downhill through a maze of boulders. On sunny days the creek is a dazzling mixture of glinting white and green, alternately light with fast-flowing chutes and dark with short pools. Above the path, large rock outcrops and their improbably rooted trees further enhance the short walk.

The trail ends at the base of two waterfalls. To the left, Curtis Creek drops 153 feet in two stages, and to the right, York Creek plunges in a 50-foot col-umn. Both streams originate from springs high upon the slopes of Tray Mountain; below their falls they mingle to become Smith Creek, a tributary of the Chattahoochee River. Collectively known as Anna Ruby Falls, the paired cascades were named for the only daughter of Colonel John H. Nichols, who pur-chased the land surrounding and including the falls shortly after the Civil War.

The area was logged by Byrd-Matthews Lumber Company from 1900 to 1915, and has not been logged since. The falls were used as part of a flume to transport logs. In 1925, the federal government purchased the land to be included in the national forest; the scenic area was established in 1964.

There are two observation decks—one on either side of Smith Creek. The lower deck is nestled close to the bottom of the 153-foot falls. Standing at the forward railing, you see tree trunks, boulders, and surging white water bisecting a framing forest; you feel the water-powered wind and mist.

Across the creek a gravel path leads to the upper deck for a closer look at the smaller falls. On clear days, especially when the sun is overhead, rainbows quiver on the edges of plummeting York Creek.

Please stay on the paved trail. "Take only pictures—leave only footprints" is a good motto for long trails that receive little use. But here, along this short, heavily used trail through a preserved "scenic area," leaving your footprints off the trail not only spoils the beauty of the wildflowers but also eventually destroys their habitat and leaves only mud.

Highlights
Throughout: Cascading Smith Creek, boulders, and rock outcrops.
Mile 0.4: Paired waterfalls with drops from two different creeks. Curtis Creek falls 153 feet and York Creek drops 50 feet.

Directions
From Helen take GA 75 North. At Robertstown, turn right onto GA 356 toward Unicoi State Park. After traveling 1.3 miles on GA 356, turn left onto Smith Creek Road (FS 242) at the sign for Anna Ruby Falls. Follow the signs to the parking lot.

Note: The Forest Service charges a small fee to enter the scenic area. The road leading to the parking area and trailhead is gated at the scenic area boundary. The gate opens at 9:00 A.M. and closes at or near dusk year-round. Visitors have permission to walk the 1.6 mile segment of road before the gate opens in the morning, but entry after the gate closes at night is forbidden.

58

**Anna Ruby Falls
Scenic Area–
Unicoi State Park**

Features
Forest, streams

Distance
4.5 miles

Difficulty Rating
Anna Ruby Falls to
Unicoi State Park:
easy to moderate;
Unicoi State Park to
Anna Ruby Falls:
moderate

County
White

Nearest City
Helen

Maps
Tray Mountain and
Helen Quadrangles,
GA; park map avail-
able at visitor center;
scenic area informa-
tion available at
National Forest
Visitor Center

Blazes
Blue

Water Sources
Follows small
stream from miles
2.5–3.8

Smith Creek Trail

For an obvious reason, you might expect this trail to follow Smith Creek downstream to the lake in Unicoi State Park. Beyond the first 0.1 mile, however, you can no longer see the creek; beyond the first 0.5 mile, you can no longer hear it. And that's it. The trail does not come close to Smith Creek again. Hickorynut Ridge would be a more descriptive name for this trail.

Smith Creek can be walked from either end. This description starts at Anna Ruby Falls at approximately 2,180 feet and ends at Unicoi State Park at approximately 1,760 feet.

From the falls, the trail gently ascends the lower slopes of Smith Mountain through a diverse decidu-ous forest with many large, maturing oaks and hicko-ries. Approximately 1.8 miles of Smith Creek Trail are within the boundaries of the Anna Ruby Falls Scenic Area. Most of what is now the scenic area was logged early in the century, from 1900 to 1915, and has not been logged since. Thus it is likely that most of the larger trees beside the beginning half mile of the trail were either too small to bother with when the tract was logged or have grown from seed since that time.

The trail soon swings eastward along the lower flank of Smith Mountain, continuing above an unnamed branch until it reaches an easy place to cross the branch at the head of its ravine. After cross-ing this small stream at 0.7 mile, the trail gradually climbs to Hickorynut Ridge at mile 1.3. Much of the mountainside from the stream to the ridge top is a wildflower garden during late May and early June. Here the trail tunnels through dense thickets of Catawba rhododendron, also known as mountain rosebay—a heath shrub that has many large deep-pink or pink-purple blossoms.

Both trail and ridge run more or less north and south. For most of the next 0.8 mile the trail heads southward either on top of Hickorynut Ridge or along its western slopes slightly below the ridge line. At mile 2.1, after half-circling a rocky knob, the trail crosses a gap in the ridge, then angles down its eastern side. The path approaches and then turns to the right away from a dirt road at mile 2.5 before it loops down to a seepage area where a rivulet begins. For the next 1.4 miles the trail, descending moderately at first, follows and then closely parallels this rapidly growing stream.

Campsites
Primitive camping is permitted along Smith Creek Trail except within state park boundaries; campsites available with reservation at Unicoi State Park

Ranger District
Chattooga

Between mile 3.2 and 3.9 several small stream crossings take place. Three wooden bridges have been erected to aid crossing.

Two easily identified ferns—the beech and the New York—are common beside the stream. The lower frond segments are diagnostic for both: the beech fern's bottommost frond segments are much wider than those at the top and they fold sharply forward; the New York fern's lower segments become progressively smaller.

The trail crosses the stream and Hickorynut Ridge Road, a four-wheel-drive dirt road, at mile 3.9, then remains nearly level to its southern end within Unicoi State Park. The trail emerges on the Unicoi Park Road, 0.5 mile from the dam.

Highlights
Mile 1.0: Tunnels through thickets of Catawba rhododendron and mountain laurel.
Mile 2.1: Large granite outcrop atop Hickorynut Ridge.

Directions
To the northern trailhead: Smith Creek Trail is reached from the Anna Ruby Falls Trail. (See page 57 of the Anna Ruby Falls Trail for directions to its trailhead and for information concerning the parking fee, gate hours, and regulations concerning entry when the gate is closed.) Walk the Anna Ruby Falls Trail 0.4 mile to its end at the falls. Smith Creek Trail starts behind its sign along the path to the upper observation deck.

To the southern, Unicoi State Park trailhead: Travel GA 75 North through Helen to Robertstown, then turn right onto GA 356 toward Unicoi State Park. Note the turnoff to Anna Ruby Falls after 1.3 miles, but stay on GA 356 across the Unicoi Lake Dam. Just past the dam, take a left. Smith Creek Trail is clearly marked 0.5 mile up on the right, directly opposite the Little Brook Camping Area.

UNICOI STATE PARK

Sandwiched between the city of Helen and the Chattahoochee National Forest's Anna Ruby Falls Scenic Area, Unicoi State Park, formerly an outdoor recreation experiment station, embraces 1,081 acres of forest, field, and lake. Perhaps better known to many for its restaurant, conference lodge, and barrel-shaped cottages, Unicoi also has hiking trails that allow visitors to savor the park's wildlife and wildflowers apart from the crowds. Smith Creek Trail (page 58) stretches from the scenic area to the state park.

The name "Unicoi" comes from the Cherokee word meaning "where the white man lives."

EBR
Tray Mountain
Unicoi State Park

Features
Unicoi Lake, forest

Distance
2.4 miles (loop)

Difficulty Rating
Easy

County
White

Nearest City
Helen

Maps
Helen Quadrangle, GA; park map available at visitor center

Blazes
Yellow

Campsites
Available with reservation in park campground

Unicoi Lake Trail

This loop trail's official beginning and ending is at the back end of the restaurant parking lot, near the park conference center and lodge. This description, however, begins and ends at the picnic area parking lot to the left of GA 356 just before it crosses the Unicoi Lake Dam. The 2.4 mile figure represents the total distance of a complete loop—around the lake, across the dam, and back to the picnic area.

The wide pathway closely follows the western shoreline of Unicoi Lake through a mixed deciduous-evergreen forest. On this side of the 53-acre lake, the treadway is often at or near water level. The loop meanders near or through many of the park's activity areas. At the first such area the path crosses the beach, climbs onto the wooden deck, then continues to skirt the lakeshore.

The trail crosses successive bridges over an unnamed Smith Creek tributary and over Smith Creek itself, the lake's source, at 0.8 mile. Across the second bridge, the path turns right and follows Smith Creek downstream through a picnic area shaded by tall eastern white pines. Look for trout where the stream begins to slacken.

The loop turns away from the lake for the first time at mile 1.3. Near the trading post, where it approaches a paved road, the trail turns right onto a graveled treadway. After it passes in front of the trading post and crosses another bridge, the path turns 90 degrees to the right onto an old road. The remainder of the loop follows this wide walkway beneath a row of cottages set back from the lake. The Unicoi Lake Trail reaches the junction of two paved roads—GA 356 and the road that leads to the park's campgrounds—at mile 2.0. The official ending segment of the trail crosses the camping approach road, crosses GA 356, and then continues a short distance to the restaurant parking lot.

Highlights
Much of the trail: Unicoi Lake.

Directions
From Helen travel GA 75 North. At Robertstown turn right onto GA 356 East and continue a short distance, following signs to Unicoi State Park.

Once inside the park (traveling from Helen) turn left into the picnic area parking lot just before GA 356 crosses the Unicoi Lake Dam. You can begin the loop through the back of the grassy picnic area. This is one of several access points for the Unicoi Lake Trail.

Notes

EBR
Tray Mountain
Unicoi State Park

Features
Streams, view

Distance
2.4 miles (loop)

Difficulty Rating
Easy to moderate

County
White

Nearest City
Helen

Maps
Helen Quadrangle, GA; park map available at visitor center

Blazes
Yellow

Campsites
Available with reservation in park campground

Bottoms Loop Trail

From its stair-step trailhead, the hiking path drops 90 yards to a second set of trail signs before turning to the right. (The green blazes guide the Unicoi-Helen Trail, which is not included in this book.)

The Bottoms Loop descends through a second-growth oak-pine forest dominated by tall shortleaf and eastern white pines. The growth rate of these eastern white pines has been rapid. You can age these trees by counting the whorls of branches, one whorl per year.

At the bottom of the first hill, the trail passes tennis courts and crosses a branch and park road in quick succession. The wide, well-signed walkway arrives at its loop at 0.5 mile. This description follows the loop to the left, or clockwise. One-tenth mile farther, the green- and yellow-blazed trails split apart. The signed "early exit" route begins 100 yards from this junction.

For the next 0.8 mile the treadway winds through an area of small streams, rosebay rhododendron thickets, and low ridges. At mile 1.4 the path dips to the level floodplain—the bottoms—of Smith Creek, a clear, cold mountain stream. Here the trail crosses three bridges before entering a narrow, grassy field that affords open views of nearby low mountains.

From the field, the treadway turns to the right and reenters forest with the wide walkway. The remainder of the loop rises easily near a Smith Creek tributary lined with rosebay rhododendron.

Highlights
Mile 1.4: Trail parallels Smith Creek for a short distance.
Mile 1.6: Small field affords open view of low mountains to the north.

Directions

(See page 61 of Unicoi Lake Trail for directions to the Unicoi State Park entrance.) Once inside the park (traveling east from the Helen area), continue on GA 356 East across the Unicoi Lake Dam, then turn right onto the paved road that leads to the park's conference lodge and restaurant. Immediately after the turn, you will see a set of trail signs to the left. These signs direct day hikers who are walking from elsewhere in the park.

Proceed up the hill, pass through the gap in the buildings, turn left, and park in the back of the lot behind the restaurant.

Notes

64

Features
Wilderness,
Georgia's highest
mountain, excellent
late spring wildflower
display, views

Distance
5.6 miles

Difficulty Rating
Brasstown Bald to
Track Rock Gap:
moderate; Track
Rock Gap to
Brasstown Bald:
strenuous

County
Union

Nearest Cities
Blairsville (W),
Hiawassee (N),
Helen (S)

Maps
Blairsville and
Hiawassee
Quadrangles,
GA-NC, Jacks Gap
Quadrangle, GA

Blazes
Blue, mostly near
Track Rock Gap

Water Sources
None; drinking foun-
tain available sea-
sonally at upper ele-
vation end

Ranger District
Brasstown

Arkaquah Trail

This steep mountain trail through the Brasstown
Wilderness features a point of interest at each
end—Brasstown Bald at the eastern trailhead and
Track Rock Gap Archeological Area at the western
one. Since the trail is accessible by road at either end,
you can choose to walk the trail uphill or downhill
according to your physical condition. Walk down
from Brasstown Bald for a moderate day hike, or
climb from the Track Rock Gap trailhead for a work-
out. If you take the uphill route, you'll gain 2,504
feet in elevation from the gap to the summit of
Brasstown Bald, which requires an extra 0.5 mile hike
from the Brasstown Bald parking lot. The elevation
change from gap to bald is greater than that of any
other trail or combination of trails of equal or shorter
length in North Georgia. Either way, during cool
weather, you'll want to be prepared for strong winds
on the trail's unprotected ridges.

The lower elevation end of this trail has been
rerouted in the past and, according to the Forest
Service, will likely be rerouted again soon. Starting
from Track Rock Gap (2,280 feet), the trail ascends
easily on an old roadbed through a largely deciduous
forest. The grades become increasingly sharp as the
treadway makes switchbacks up the mountainside
until it curls onto Buzzard Roost Ridge at mile 1.7.
Often open, narrow, and dotted with boulders, the
ridge is especially beautiful in late spring when
Catawba rhododendron, flame azalea, and mountain
laurel bloom, frequently at least two of them flowering side by side.

The path remains atop the ridge for the next 1.6
miles. This segment of the ridge crest is a series of
waves and troughs. After the first uphill stretch, the
path is level or descending for nearly 0.2 mile. At
mile 2.3, you ascend Locust Log Ridge, alternating
switchbacks with level passages. The pattern repeats

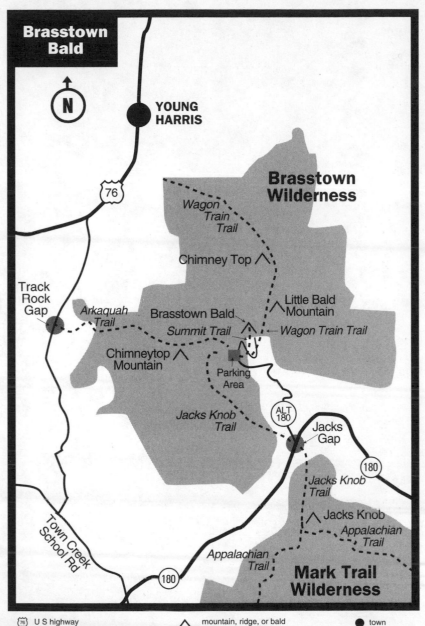

Brasstown Bald

N

YOUNG HARRIS

76

Brasstown Wilderness

Wagon Train Trail

Chimney Top ⋀

Track Rock Gap

Arkaquah Trail

Brasstown Bald

Summit Trail ⋀

Little Bald Mountain ⋀

← *Wagon Train Trail*

Chimneytop Mountain ⋀

Parking Area

Jacks Knob Trail

ALT 180

Jacks Gap

180

Jacks Knob Trail

Jacks Knob ⋀

Appalachian Trail

Town Creek School Rd

Appalachian Trail

Mark Trail Wilderness

180

76 U S highway	⋀ mountain, ridge, or bald
60 Georgia state highway	∿ stream, creek, or river
FS 654 Forest Service road	⋯ marked trail
● town	
⋀ campground	
● mountain gap	

Notes

itself until mile 3.0, where you climb steadily along easy-to-moderate grades to Blue Bluff Overlook.

At mile 3.3 the trail slants off the ridge top and winds below its crest through an area of rock outcrops and moist, fern-draped slopes. Look for splotches of yellow lichen that decorate the eaves of the tallest outcrop.

The hard hiking is over once the path regains the ridge top at mile 3.5. For most of the next mile the trail rises to the crest of Chimneytop Mountain—actually just a named high point on the ridge. The remainder of the trail, following the short descent from Chimneytop, is predominantly easy uphill or level to its end at the Brasstown Bald parking area (4,360 feet). The footpath's uppermost elevations are dominated by heath thickets and almost pure stands of short, low-branching oaks.

Brasstown Bald's uppermost elevations provide habitat for at least two tree species—yellow birch and American mountain ash—that are much more abundant in states further north. These two trees are at the southern limit of their range on the highest peaks in northernmost Georgia.

Arkaquah is an excellent trail for springtime botanizing. Fertile soil and abundant rainfall support a rich variety of wildflowers and shrubs. In May, wildflowers, including four trillium and two orchid species, are numerous.

With the exception of approximately 0.1 mile at either end, the Arkaquah Trail traverses the 12,975-acre Brasstown Wilderness.

Highlights
Near the lower elevation trailhead: One-tenth mile from the Arkaquah trailhead (but not on the trail) is the Track Rock Gap Archaeological Area. This area consists of three large micaceous soapstone boulders inscribed with ancient drawings—petroglyphs—suggesting bird and animal tracks. Though obscured by weathering and protected by a metal cage, they have given this gap its name and can still be discerned. The Cherokee also recognized their import, calling the gap *degayelunha*— "printed (or branded) place."

Mile 3.1: Blue Bluff Overlook

Mile 4.1: Chimneytop Mountain, elevation 4,296 feet, provides winter views. To the north, you can see Peppercorn Cove, the location of the Jacksonville and Young Harris communities; the southwest vista encompasses Rocky Knob.

Mile 5.6: Brasstown Bald—Georgia's highest point at 4,784 feet offers a 360-degree view from the observation platform. You'll have to walk an extra 0.5 mile from the trail's end to reach the summit.

Directions

To the upper elevation, Brasstown Bald trailhead: The Brasstown Bald approach road, GA 180 Spur, heads north from GA 180. This spur is located on the segment of GA 180 between its junction with GA 75 to the east and its junction with US 19–129 to the west.

From its US 19–129 junction, travel GA 180 East 7.5 miles to GA 180 Spur (or from its GA 75 junction, travel GA 180 West 5.0 miles to the approach road). Follow the signs to the Brasstown Bald parking lot.

The Brasstown Bald Visitor Information Center is open seasonally; a small parking fee is charged at the large Brasstown Bald lot. The steep GA 180 Spur is closed during bad winter weather.

The sign-posted path enters the forest to the left of the paved walkway leading to the rest rooms, which are near the concession building.

To the lower elevation, Track Rock Gap trailhead: Take US 19–129 North slightly more than 2.5 miles past Vogel State Park, then turn right onto GA 180 East toward Brasstown Bald. Continue on GA 180 for approximately 2.5 miles before turning left onto Town Creek School Road at the sign for Track Rock Gap Archeological Area. Proceed approximately 5.3 miles on this paved road to a church and cemetery on the left, then turn right onto Track Rock Gap Road.

Travel approximately 3.8 miles to the parking area on the left side of the road. The trailhead is 35 yards beyond and across the road from the parking area. The "track rocks" are just beyond the parking area, farther up the hill.

Notes

Jacks Knob Trail

EBR
Brasstown Bald
**Brasstown
Wilderness and
Mark Trail
Wilderness**

L ike the Arkaquah Trail, the path immediately takes you through dense rhododendron arcades, but the vegetation on this trail soon becomes quite different from that along the Arkaquah Trail. Such a divergence may seem surprising, considering that the two trails begin only a few hundred yards apart; the reason for the difference, however, is easy to explain. Different sides of the same mountain receive different amounts of sunlight each day. South-facing slopes, for instance, get the most sunlight, causing their soils to become dry. Conversely, north-facing slopes receive the least sunlight, allowing their soils to remain damp. Over eons the sun, in partnership with the forest communities it helped create, has significantly altered the soil. North-facing slopes, in general, have better, thicker soils with good moisture-holding qualities. South-facing slopes tend to have poorer, thinner soils with marginal moisture-holding qualities. Pines, which have adapted to poor soils, are a significant component of the trailside forest from Brasstown Bald to GA 180.

This easily followed trail begins at an elevation of about 4,360 feet. After remaining nearly level for its first 0.5 mile, the path starts a switchbacking descent, becoming progressively steeper as it runs down Wolfpen Ridge. There is no water along this first, high section of Jacks Knob Trail. The steep descent takes you past granite boulders, some with a dark, leathery lichen called rock tripe growing on their sides. The wildflower display starts in early spring—trailing arbutus, bloodroot, anemones, bluets, and violets—before the mayapples and pink lady's slippers emerge in May.

At mile 2.3 the trail reaches its second access point—the intersection of highways GA 180 and the 180 spur at Jacks Gap (2,960 feet). This access point, situated in the middle of the trail, provides you with the option of hiking half the trail in either direction.

Features
Wilderness,
Georgia's highest
mountain,
AT approach

Distance
4.5 miles

Difficulty Rating
Downhill section
from Brasstown Bald
to GA 180: moderate; complete trail
and both sections
starting from GA
180: strenuous

Counties
Towns and Union

Nearest Cities
Blairsville (W),
Hiawassee (N),
Helen (S)

Map
Jacks Gap
Quadrangle, GA

Blazes
Blue

Water Sources
Mile 2.8: rivulet;
mile 4.5: spring at
Chattahoochee Gap

Ranger District
Brasstown

At Jacks Gap, the trail bends to the left, crosses both highways, then reenters the forest above a grassy area surrounding a concrete drainage pipe. A sign across GA 180 usually marks the exact location.

The second half of the trail, like the Appalachian Trail it meets, is an undulating series of ups and downs as it follows Hiawassee Ridge toward Chattahoochee Gap. And like the AT, Jacks Knob Trail does not ride the ridge crest up and over every high point. Instead, it often drops off the crest and makes a half circle around a peak well below its crown, then rejoins the ridge where it slopes down to the next gap.

Beyond the highway, the path climbs moderate grades through a hardwood forest to mile 2.7. The next section of Jacks Knob crosses a spring and remains level to mile 3.0, where it ascends into a rich cove. After it loops through the cove, the trail ascends sharply to the end of a ridge at mile 3.3, then drops to a gap at mile 3.6. From the gap, the path climbs a moderate-to-strenuous grade along the western flank of Jacks Knob for 0.3 mile.

The trail gently undulates to mile 4.2, where it passes beside a line of large gray outcrops. The final 100 yards dip to the sign at Chattahoochee Gap (3,500 feet), where the trail ends at the white-blazed AT. The spring-source of the Chattahoochee River is down the slope on the other side of the gap.

Much of the Brasstown Bald to GA 180 segment of the trail is within the 12,975-acre Brasstown Wilderness, and the GA 180 to AT segment, with the exception of its first 0.2 mile, is totally within the 16,400-acre Mark Trail Wilderness.

Highlights

Mile 0: Brasstown Bald, Georgia's highest mountain. Catawba rhododendron blooms here in May and early June.

Nearly throughout: Brasstown and Mark Trail Wildernesses.

Mile 4.5: Appalachian Trail at Chattahoochee Gap. Spring-source of the Chattahoochee River nearby.

Directions

(See page 68 of Arkaquah Trail for directions to the Brasstown Bald parking lot and for information concerning the parking fee.) The Jacks Knob trailhead is located at the end of the Brasstown Bald parking lot opposite from the concession buildings. An opening in the fence and a small sign prohibiting motorized vehicles indicate the start.

Summit Trail

**Brasstown Bald
Visitor Information
Center**

Paved and usually sign-posted, this trail originates between the concession building and the Chattahoochee-Oconee Heritage Association's gift shop cabin. The walkway climbs the final 424 feet to the top of Georgia's highest mountain. Perched on the crown at 4,784 feet is the Brasstown Bald Visitor Information Center with an observation tower affording an outstanding 360-degree view of nearby mountains such as Blood, Slaughter, and Yonah.

The name Brasstown Bald comes from the confusion of the Cherokee word *itse-yi* meaning "new green place" with the word *untsaiyi* meaning "brass." A bald is a mountaintop that uncharacteristically lacks the trees of most of our Southern Appalachian mountains. In some instances balds were created when mountaintops were cleared and used as pasture; sometimes the balds occur naturally. Brasstown is not a natural bald.

Mountain laurel, Catawba and rosebay rhododendron, eastern hemlock, and stunted, wind-swept oaks make up the bulk of trees and shrubs along the trail. The Chattahoochee-Oconee Heritage Association has placed interpretive signs along the trail. In late May and early June, the Catawba rhododendron blooms on the upper slopes of Brasstown Bald, primarily above 4,000 feet.

Bird-watching is usually good in the area around and above the parking lot at the bald. There are two main reasons. The first is simple: the birds are easy to see. As the elevation climbs above 4,000 feet on the high mountaintops across North Georgia, the trees, mostly oaks, are increasingly shorter and lower-branched. So even if a bird is singing from the uppermost canopy, it is still often only 10 to 15 feet above your binoculars.

The second reason is more complex. The summer ranges of many songbirds finger down the cool

Features
Georgia's highest mountain, scenic views, visitor center, interpretive signs

Distance
0.5 mile

Difficulty Rating
Moderate

Counties
Towns and Union

Nearest Cities
Blairsville (W),
Hiawassee (N),
Helen (S)

Map
Jacks Gap
Quadrangle, GA

Blazes
None; none needed

Ranger District
Brasstown

Southern Appalachians only as far south as the mountains of northern-most Georgia. And even within the mountain region there are birds (such as the Canada warbler, the veery, the dark-eyed junco, and the common raven) that require habitats at the very highest elevations. These disjunct habitats are found only on the upper slopes and tops of North Georgia's highest mountains. Two of our most brightly colored high-country birds—the chestnut-sided warbler and the rose-breasted grosbeak—are often seen on Brasstown Bald in June.

Highlights
Mile 0.5: From the top of the observation tower there is a 360-degree view. On clear days you can see into four states and as far south as Atlanta. The bald, at 4,784 feet above sea level, is Georgia's highest peak.

Directions
(See page 68 of Arkaquah Trail for directions to the Brasstown Bald parking lot and for information concerning the parking fee.) The trail-head is located between the concession building and the Chattahoochee-Oconee Heritage Association's gift shop cabin.

Notes

Wagon Train Trail

Winding generally north and south, this trail follows the abandoned bed of an old road constructed to become Highway 66. This highway—routed from Highway 180 over the top of Brasstown Bald, then down to US 76 at Young Harris—was built using convict labor starting in the late 1930s. Now the old roadbed is a wide, easily walked trail through the Brasstown Wilderness. The grades, for the most part easy, are never more difficult than moderate, and remain so only for a short distance.

Ridge-crest and upper-slope trails usually offer good winter views. Bare-tree views last for half the year, even longer at the highest elevations, along North Georgia's major ridge systems. Wagon Train, because of its location (Brasstown Bald), the width of its treadway, and the steepness of its slopes, affords excellent winter views. As you begin your hike uphill from Young Harris, you can soon see your destination, the end of the trail on Brasstown Bald, looming high and far above you.

Starting where the road is gated at the wilderness boundary (2,700 feet), the trail rises easily on a ridge crest through a somewhat scrubby oak-pine forest. After a short distance the treadway angles off the ridge top, slabs south around the highpoint of Granny Knob, then passes through the lower south side of Carrol Gap. The path gradually ascends as it winds around the steep upper slopes of Yewell Cove.

Here in this west-facing cove the trees are much larger than on the beginning ridge and are predominantly hardwood. Near the trail you will occasionally see large old chestnut oaks, passed by during the logging days.

At mile 1.3 the route crosses over Double Knob Ridge at 3,200 feet. Beyond the ridge the trail follows the 3,200-foot contour for nearly 1.0 mile before climbing to cross Buck Ridge at mile 3.2 and 3,840

EBR
Brasstown Bald
Brasstown Wilderness

Features
Georgia's highest mountain, scenic views, wilderness

Distance
5.6 miles

Difficulty Rating
Moderate

Counties
Towns and Union

Nearest Cities
Blairsville (W),
Hiawassee (N),
Helen (S),
Young Harris (N)

Maps
Hiawassee
Quadrangle, GA-NC;
Jacks Gap
Quadrangle, GA

Blazes
None; none needed

Water Sources
Miles 0.9, 1.8, 1.9,
2.4, 2.6, and 3.1:
seasonal seeps and
springs; little or no
water available late
in a hot, dry summer

Ranger District
Brasstown

feet. North and south of Buck Ridge, a western-running spur off Chimney Top, the treadway skirts the upper slopes of a large, bowl-shaped valley open to the west. The uppermost feeder streams of Brasstown Creek flow out of Peabottom, Big Bald, and Little Bald Coves.

Beyond Buck Ridge the trail straightens and heads almost due south. At mile 4.1 the route crosses a gap (4,100 feet), then leaves the ridge top as it slabs around the high point of Little Bald Mountain on the western slope. The remainder of the route crosses back over the ridge at mile 4.9 and gains elevation on the upper eastern slope. Beyond the gate continue straight ahead at the pet grave.

The forest changes as the trail gains elevation on or near Brasstown Bald's north-facing ridge. Pines become scarce, then disappear altogether. Sweet birch, Carolina silverbell, and Fraser magnolia become increasingly common above 3,000 feet. At the trail's upper elevation end there is an orchard-like forest dominated by oaks, yellow birch, and American beech. Rock outcrops and rock-face cuts are fairly common along much of the trail.

The trail's upper elevation end (4,420 feet) is its junction with the short, paved Summit Trail. To the left and down it is 135 yards on the Summit Trail to the Brasstown Bald parking area.

Except for a short distance at its upper elevation end, the Wagon Train Trail is within the 12,975-acre Brasstown Wilderness.

Highlights

Mile 1.0: Overlook into Yewell Cove and the town of Young Harris from the north side of Double Knob Ridge.

Mile 1.3: Winter view of Brasstown Bald and the high ridge leading west toward Chimney Top and Blue Bluff.

Mile 3.4: Winter views to the right of Brasstown Bald and the rhododendron slick on its northern slope.

Mile 4.4: Rock outcrop view open to the west affording views into the forested cove below, the fields near the community of Jacksonville, and Gumlog Mountain to the northwest. To the west is Locust Log Ridge rising to Chimneytop Mountain (southwest). This is the ridge-top route of the Arkaquah Trail leading to Brasstown Bald.

Directions

To the lower elevation trailhead at Young Harris: (The trailhead is reached by a rutted, littered, mile-long dirt road that should not be attempted by regular two-wheel-drive vehicles.) From the US 76–GA 75 junction, travel US 76 West approximately 11.0 miles to the traffic light in Young Harris (where GA 66 heads north). Continue on US 76 0.2 mile past the light, then turn left onto Bald Mountain Road immediately beyond Sharp Memorial United Methodist Church. Proceed 0.2 mile on Bald Mountain Road to the fork behind Appleby Center. The gated fork to the right, which immediately becomes a rough and rutted dirt-gravel road, is the 1.0-mile route to the trailhead. Young Harris College has recently installed this gate; it is sometimes closed.

From the US 76–US 129 junction in Blairsville, travel US 76 East approximately 8.5 miles to the right turn onto Bald Mountain Road just before Sharp Memorial United Methodist Church in Young Harris.

To the upper elevation end at Brasstown Bald: Traveling on US 19–129, turn on GA 180 East. Continue 7.5 miles and turn onto the approach road (GA 180 Spur) to Brasstown Bald. Follow the signs to the parking lot (small parking fee) and look for the beginning of Summit Trail between the concession building and the gift shop cabin. Walk the short, paved Summit Trail for 135 yards, then turn right onto the intersecting road. This road is the trail.

Notes

EBR
*Upper
Chattahoochee
Basin*

**Upper
Chattahoochee
River Recreation
Area**

Features
Chattahoochee
River, waterfall

Distance
0.1 mile

Difficulty Rating
Easy

Counties
White and Union

Nearest Cities
Helen (S),
Hiawassee (N)

Map
Jacks Gap
Quadrangle, GA

Blazes
Blue

Campsites
Available seasonally
in recreation area
campground

Ranger District
Chattooga

Horse Trough Falls Trail

The wide gravel walkway quickly crosses a bridge over Georgia's longest river—the Cherokee's Chattahoochee, "River of the Painted Rocks." Here the creek-sized river is only a short distance from its source spring high in the mountains of Union County. All of the Chattahoochee's headwater branches arise south of the Appalachian Trail, only a few miles north of these falls.

The trail passes beside several large eastern white pines. Toothwort, a perennial in the mustard family also known as pepper-root, is abundant on the forest floor. The toothwort's three, deeply notched basal leaves make it easy to identify.

After slightly less than 0.1 mile, the path ends at an observation deck in front of Horse Trough Falls.

Spilling down numerous small ledges, the falls are wide and over 50 feet high. Horse Trough is a small volume falls from an unnamed Chattahoochee tributary. During a late summer drought there would be little water spilling down the rock face.

Highlights
Mile 0.1: View of the 50- to 55-foot-high Horse Trough Falls.

Directions
From the Chattahoochee River Bridge in Helen, travel GA 75 North approximately 9.5 miles to the left turn onto FS 44. This turn, which is marked by signs for the Mark Trail Wilderness and Upper Chatta-hoochee River Campground, is less than 0.1 mile before the large Unicoi Gap parking area on the right.

Follow FS 44 approximately 4.7 miles before turn-ing right into the Upper Chattahoochee River Campground. Proceed on the main campground road to the second day-use parking area at the signed trail-head for Horse Trough Falls.

From the US 76–GA 75 junction, travel GA 75 South for approximately 9.0 miles and turn right onto FS 44.

SMITHGALL WOODS, DUKES CREEK CONSERVATION AREA

The 5,604-acre Smithgall Woods, Dukes Creek Conservation Area was acquired as a gift-purchase through the Preservation 2000 program. Noted conservationist and businessman Charles A. Smithgall Jr. sold this wild tract, which he had protected and restored, to the state for half of its appraised value. This is one of the most generous gifts that an individual has ever made to the state of Georgia.

Located in White County just southwest of Helen, the conservation area is managed by the Georgia Department of Natural Resources. In addition to its conservation area status, Smithgall Woods, Dukes Creek has also been designated as a Heritage Preserve under the Georgia Heritage Trust Act of 1975. This designation mandates the highest level of protection possible under this act. Only environmental education and low-impact recreational activities such as hiking, hunting, fishing, and picnicking will be allowed. Four and one-half miles of Dukes Creek flow through the area, which first opened in March, 1995.

A system of four trails is scheduled for completion in the next few years. These trails will be routed in the safety zone, which is not open to hunting. The entire 14.0-mile road system is open to walking.

Smithgall Woods, Dukes Creek is open to the public on Wednesday, Saturday, and Sunday, sunrise to sunset. Park Passes must be purchased. The area does not have a campground.

EBR
Raven Cliffs
**Smithgall Woods,
Dukes Creek
Conservation Area**

Features
Interpretive signs,
small streams,
winter views

Distance
1.5 miles (loop)

Difficulty Rating
Easy to moderate

County
White

Nearest Cities
Helen (NE),
Cleveland (S)

Maps
Cowrock
Quadrangle, GA;
park map available
at visitor center

Blazes
None; none needed

Campsites
No campgrounds in
the conservation
area

Laurel Ridge Interpretive Trail

This aptly named, short loop often winds through dark, evergreen mountain laurel and rosebay rhododendron thickets, especially at either end of the trail. Because it passes through a variety of habitats—streamside, moist hollow, and low, dry ridge—and because it is a loop offering maximum change of exposure, this trail features a surprisingly diverse flora for its short length and relatively slight elevation change.

This trail was not yet officially open when hiked for this guide. Interpretive signs were on the way.

This loop is easier to walk to the left, in a clockwise direction. The ends of the loop come together at different locations in the trailhead field. To walk the loop in a clockwise direction, the way it is described, cross the bridge (look for New York ferns below) over the small branch at the near end of the field.

After only 50 yards there is a junction in a field of New York ferns. The loop continues to the left; the walkway to the right heads back to the field. The wide treadway quickly rises up to and over a low oak-pine ridge before dropping to the head of a hollow. For the next few tenths of a mile, the route gently undulates through several hollows, frequently dipping to bridges. The final segment between bridges parallels a rivulet beneath a hardwood forest dominated by tall tuliptrees. Here a long swath of light-green New York fern flanks the stream.

This fern is one of the easiest to identify. Its pinnae (leafy foliage) taper sharply to nearly nothing at either end. New York ferns are common throughout the mountains of North Georgia. They frequently occur in dense monocultural beds that resemble well-tended gardens growing beneath widely spaced trees. The reason for this "cultivated" appearance is simple: the ferns use their own herbicide to poison and eliminate other plants.

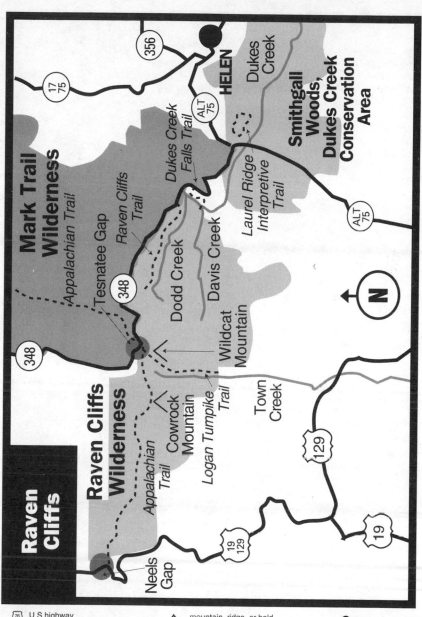

Raven Cliffs

Mark Trail Wilderness

Raven Cliffs Wilderness

Smithgall Woods, Dukes Creek Conservation Area

HELEN

Dukes Creek

Appalachian Trail

Raven Cliffs Trail

Tesnatee Gap

Dukes Creek Falls Trail

Laurel Ridge Interpretive Trail

Dodd Creek

Davis Creek

Wildcat Mountain

Logan Tumpike Trail

Cowrock Mountain

Appalachian Trail

Town Creek

Neels Gap

N

76	U S highway
60	Georgia state highway
FS 654	Forest Service road

∧ mountain, ridge, or bald

〜 stream, creek, or river

-·-· marked trail

● town

⚑ campground

● mountain gap

Notes

At 0.5 mile the path crosses a rivulet, then ascends to and follows the crest of a low ridge. The oak-pine forest is typical of many second- and third-growth, low-elevation, ridge-top woods. Virginia (short needles) and eastern white pine are common. Red maple, sourwood, blackgum, and the oaks—chestnut, white, black, northern red, post, and blackjack—numerically dominate the hardwood component of the woods.

The trail rises steadily with the ridge to mile 1.0, where it begins to descend. The remainder of the loop curls off the ridge and continues to descend, sometimes moderately, back to the field.

Highlights

Miles 0.9–1.1: Good winter views and partial summer views to the left (southeast) from the ridge top. Yonah Mountain's distinctive profile and cliff face are clearly visible.

Directions

Smithgall Woods, Dukes Creek Conservation Area is located along GA Alt. 75, which leads from GA 75 at Robertstown to US 129 a few miles north of Cleveland.

From Helen travel GA 75 North. Approximately 1.4 miles beyond the Chattahoochee River Bridge in Helen, turn left onto GA Alt. 75, crossing the bridge over the Chattahoochee River in Robertstown. Proceed approximately 2.5 miles on GA Alt. 75, then turn left at the prominent Smithgall entryway. This left turn is just beyond the GA 348 junction.

From the square in Cleveland travel US 129 North for 3.3 miles before turning right onto GA Alt. 75. Proceed 5.6 miles on GA Alt. 75, then turn right into the Conservation Area.

Inside the Conservation Area, the road quickly comes to a junction. Continue straight at this junction, then immediately turn left into a field. This large, railed field is the parking area for both the trail and nearby visitor center.

Park officials ask that all hikers check in at the visitor center before walking the trail.

Note: Smithgall Woods, Dukes Creek Conservation Area is open to the public on Wednesday, Saturday, and Sunday, sunrise to sunset. Park Passes must be purchased. The area does not have a campground.

EBR
Raven Cliffs
Dukes Creek
Recreation Area

Features
Streams, waterfall

Distance
1.1 miles

Difficulty Rating
Easy to moderate

County
White

Nearest City
Helen

Map
Cowrock
Quadrangle, GA

Blazes
Blue

Ranger District
Chattooga

Dukes Creek Falls Trail

The old Dukes Creek Trail has been given an expensive, glamour-magazine makeover. Two observation decks were built; the first 0.7 mile was completely rerouted. The new trail is slightly easier and more scenic, reduces erosion, and has a wheelchair-accessible observation deck at 0.1 mile.

Beginning at 2,120 feet, this wide, easily walked trail passes the first observation deck, then swings parallel to cascading Dukes Creek. The treadway descends easily well above that stream to 0.7 mile, where the new path ties into the old, looping route. Two-tenths of a mile farther, the wide walkway turns sharply to the right onto a narrower path. The remaining distance makes an easy descent to the boardwalk and large observation deck above where the two creeks— Dukes and Davis—converge at 1,760 feet.

The observation deck is a great spot to view or photograph Dukes Creek Falls. The waterfall—actually on Davis Creek—is estimated to be around 250 feet high. The water cascades down a wide, rocky course, which dilutes the power of the falls, especially at low water levels. One prominent, rectangular piece of bedrock is still perched in the middle of the falls; a few eastern hemlock and rosebay rhododendron grow right on the rock. This waterfall is spectacular when the sun shines immediately after heavy rains.

Highlights
Trailhead: Overlook into the creek valley with picnic tables and benches.
Mile 0.1: Wheelchair-accessible observation deck at end of paved segment offering a clear view of the falls and gorge.
Mile 1.1: Dukes Creek Falls, a wide, 250-foot cascading drop.

Directions

Take GA 75 North from the Chattahoochee River Bridge in Helen, travel approximately 1.4 miles, and turn left onto GA Alt. 75 South, crossing the bridge over the Chattahoochee River in Robertstown. Continue on GA Alt. 75 South for 2.3 miles, then turn right onto Richard B. Russell Scenic Highway (GA 348 North). Travel 1.7 miles on Richard B. Russell Scenic Highway; the large sign for Dukes Creek Recreation Area is on the left.

The Dukes Creek Falls approach road remains open all year. It may be inaccessible during winter storms when Richard B. Russell Highway is closed.

Notes

84

Features
Stream, scenic
views, waterfalls,
rock outcrops, cliffs

Distance
2.5 miles

Difficulty Rating
Easy to moderate
to the cliffs

County
White

Nearest City
Helen

Map
Cowrock
Quadrangle, GA

Blazes
Blue

Ranger District
Chattooga

Raven Cliffs Trail

Beginning near where Dodd Creek mingles its water with and loses its name to Dukes Creek, this popular trail follows Dodd Creek and its valley upstream into the mountains. Alternating between creek level and hillside, the gently sloping trail threads its way along the cascading stream, rarely leaving the sound of the rushing water.

In 1986, The Georgia Wilderness Bill incorporated Raven Cliffs Scenic Area within the 9,115-acre Raven Cliffs Wilderness. Although protected from mechanical intrusion, this trail's beauty, its location near Helen, and its short, easily walked length make it attractive to many people, both backpackers and day hikers. Please stay on the trail and help keep this part of the wilderness from being loved to death. At present, campsites are too numerous and too worn along this overly popular trail. A self-imposed camping moratorium or, better yet, a permit system imposed by the Forest Service may help the area heal.

Raven Cliffs lives up to its former designation almost everywhere you look. Within the first 1.3 miles the trail passes beside numerous cascades and two waterfalls. Beside the path watch for the Fraser magnolia, a deciduous magnolia whose large leaves— 10 to 12 inches long and 6 to 7 inches wide— emanate from the stem in a whorled arrangement, and look for the sweet birch, whose twigs have the distinctive fragrance of wintergreen. From mid-May through early June, Vasey's trillium blooms underneath its characteristic three leaves. The rich carmine flowers of this trillium are often 4 inches in diameter. In late June, the dense thickets of rosebay rhododendron turn the stream borders into narrow bands of white.

From the parking lot, a short path begins with a steel marker. Steps lead immediately to a camping area with trash cans and a Forest Service information board. As you descend into the camping area, Dukes

Creek is on the left. The path continues into the forest, crosses a small rivulet, and turns right to a sign-in post. At 0.1 mile the trail ascends slightly, then levels near the first of several cascades on Dodd Creek at 0.3 mile. By mile 0.6 it descends into a boggy area, marked by numerous campsites. The first waterfall appears at mile 1.1 and pours from a height of 10 feet onto a conveniently placed boulder. Soon the forest becomes dominated by hardwoods. At mile 1.3 a 35-foot waterfall drops into a shallow plunge pool. Rock outcrops, the same color as the cliffs, dot the steep slope above the path.

Continuing to parallel the cascading creek and passing through two fern fields, the path arrives at the base of Raven Cliffs at mile 2.5. Even in summer the massive rock face is visible from a distance through the veil of trees. The cliff walls, some of them amazingly smooth, tower nearly 125 feet above creek level at their highest point.

Highlights
Mile 1.1: 10-foot-high waterfall.
Mile 1.3: Wide, 35-foot-high waterfall.
Mile 2.5: Raven Cliffs and upper and lower Raven Cliffs Falls. The lower falls, called Raven Cliffs Grotto, is a 40-foot waterspout surrounded by cavelike walls.

Directions
Take GA 75 North from the Chattahoochee River Bridge in Helen, travel approximately 1.4 miles, and turn left onto GA Alt. 75 South, crossing the bridge over the Chattahoochee River in Robertstown. Continue on GA Alt. 75 South for 2.3 miles, then turn right onto Richard B. Russell Scenic Highway (GA 348 North).

After traveling 1.7 miles on Richard B. Russell Scenic Highway, you will come to the sign for Dukes Creek Recreation Area. Proceed 1.3 miles past this sign until the highway crosses Dukes Creek. Immediately beyond Dukes Creek look for a parking area marked with a trail sign to the left. From the parking area, walk downstream on the closed road along the creek. Approximately 145 yards down the road, a rivulet flows into the creek; cross the tiny stream, turn right, and follow the blue-blazed trail to Dodd Creek.

EBR
Raven Cliffs
Raven Cliffs Wilderness

Features
Stream, historic turnpike, AT approach

Distance
1.9 miles

Difficulty Rating
Moderate to strenuous

County
White

Nearest Cities
Cleveland (SE), Dahlonega (SW)

Map
Cowrock Quadrangle, GA

Blazes
Blue

Ranger District
Chattooga

Logan Turnpike Trail

The Logan Turnpike Trail, routed entirely within the Raven Cliffs Wilderness, follows a short but historic section of the first road to lead southward out of Union County. Historical accuracy about the route is elusive. The accounts of Logan Turnpike differ not in the main points but in specific details, such as dates, from the others.

In 1821, the Union Turnpike company received a state charter to construct a toll road that would join existing roads north and south of Tesnatee Gap. Completed by 1840, the Union Turnpike was the final link of a continuous road—the forerunner of US 129—that stretched from Gainesville to Cleveland and over the mountains to Blairsville. Shortly after it was finished, Major Francis Logan bought the rights to operate the turnpike. He built his home, a lodge, and a tollgate 0.8 mile south of the Kellum Valley trailhead, near the house with the "Toll Gate" sign. In 1871 Major Logan bought 220 acres, which included a segment of the turnpike north of his tollgate, in western White County. It is probable that the road took his name then. The toll road remained under Logan family management until it was abandoned in 1922, the year the state completed the highway over Neels Gap.

The section of road that became known as Logan Turnpike was roughly 10 miles long, from near Loudsville through Tesnatee Gap to Ponder. *Tesnatee* is the Cherokee word for turkey, and Ponder was located in a valley the Cherokee had named *Choestoe,* "Land of the Dancing Rabbits." The story of rabbits dancing, told by Indians and heard by pioneers, was no doubt thought to be mythological—a wonderful folklore image handed down from an old tribal legend or mountaintop vision. To the Cherokee, however, the story represented special knowledge gained from observation of natural phenomena. In its text describing the eastern cottontail, *The Audubon Society*

Field Guide to North American Mammals states: "On midwinter nights, groups of cottontails have been seen frolicking on crusted snow; as they are not mating aggregations, they may be purely playful gatherings to provide release after periods of forced inactivity."

In its day, Logan Turnpike was one of the major north-south roads through the mountains of North Georgia. Wagon trains loaded with produce rumbled south to Gainesville, then returned to the mountains full of merchandise. The turnpike served as a mail route, and the stagecoach that traveled from Athens, Tennessee, to Augusta, Georgia, crossed over Tesnatee Gap. Over the years a colorful parade of travelers—Confederate soldiers; gold prospectors; famous politicians; drivers of turkey, cattle and hogs; chestnut hunters; early photographers, and organ grinders with tame bears or monkeys—passed by Major Logan's tollgate.

John Muir, who walked alone, quickly and quietly, was probably among the turnpike travelers in the early fall of 1867. The journal he kept of his adventures later became the source for his book *A Thousand Mile Walk to the Gulf*. Muir tells us he passed through Blairsville during the morning of September 21. The next day, perhaps in the early afternoon, he reached "the last mountain summit" on his way to Florida. That last climb was probably to Tesnatee Gap. After crossing this last summit, Muir states that he walked downhill "in the wake of three poor, but merry mountaineers—an old woman, a young woman, and a young man—who sat, leaned, and lay in the box of a shackly wagon that seemed to be held together by spiritualism, and was kept in agitation by a very large and a very small mule." He spent the night of September 22 at Mount Yonah, which is about eight miles due east of Loudsville. By nightfall of the next day John Muir, who would later gain fame as an explorer, naturalist, conservationist, and writer, had reached Gainesville, Georgia.

The Logan Turnpike Trail has either-end access. The lower, southern access point is in Kellum Valley; the upper, northern access point is Tesnatee Gap. This description starts at the Kellum Valley trailhead (approximately 1,960 feet) and ends at Tesnatee Gap (3,138 feet).

Immediately beyond the yellow "Wildlife Management Area" signs, the trail follows a blue blaze left of the old toll road past the first set of dirt mounds, then crosses over the right side of the road before the next set. After the second set of mounds, the trail drops to the middle of the roadbed, where it remains for another 1.1 miles. The turnpike trail soon parallels Town Creek, here near its undisturbed headwaters a clear, cold mountain stream rushing noisily around rocks luxuriant with moss. This thick moss is a sign of health. During high water, silt from upstream erosion can scour the moss from the rocks. In general, the bigger, faster, and muddier the stream, the less moss on its rocks.

The mountains to either side of the trail have long funneled travelers, including the Cherokee whose path the road followed, up the cove to the gap in the ridge. To the left or west is Cowrock Mountain; its highest point is 3,852 feet. Cowrock's cliffs are visible from the trail in winter. To the right is Wildcat Mountain.

At 0.6 mile the trail starts to gain elevation, alternating between easy and moderate grades. The old roadbed, which is often rocky and wet, continues beside Town Creek and its linear forest of eastern hemlock. Where the road cut turns to the right at 1.2 miles, the trail continues straight ahead, uphill. Here it really begins to climb, becoming increasingly steep as it rises toward the gap. The last 0.3 mile, which seems twice as long, gains elevation quickly; it is one of the most rugged sections of trail in Georgia.

Near the gap, the trail links back up with the turnpike. Although the former road was not quite as steep as the last 0.8 mile of the trail, it sloped enough to present special problems to those going either up to or down from Tesnatee Gap. Wagoners, and later auto drivers, often had to tie logs to the backs of their vehicles to help brake them down the mountain. This braking was crucial to the wagoner, for if there wasn't enough dragging weight behind the wagon on a downhill pitch, it could run over the animals in front of it. Before cars had fuel pumps, drivers who started up to the gap with less than half a tank of gas often had to drive their Model T's in reverse to gravity-feed the fuel. On their return trip, they frequently backed down the steep section to avoid damaging their brakes.

Highlights
Throughout: Mature forest with a canopy often 80–100 feet high. Eastern hemlock are common at the lower elevations along Town Creek; tuliptrees dominate the upper cove.
Mile 1.8: Headwaters of Town Creek. The growing creek on the lower end has small cascades, too numerous to count.

Directions
   To the southern, lower elevation, Kellum Valley trailhead: From the Cleveland square, take US 129 North for about 7.7 miles, then turn right onto Kellum Valley Road. Watch for the road sign after you crest the hill past the bridge at Town Creek. After the Kellum Valley Road becomes dirt at approximately 1.2 miles, proceed straight ahead another 0.9 mile to where the road splits just before the "Toll Gate" house on the right.

Continue on the narrow dirt lane past the house for approximately 0.8 mile. The trail begins at the yellow "Wildlife Management Area" signs and the blue blaze. You don't have to worry about missing the trailhead or driving too far: less than 50 yards beyond the trailhead, the road, which becomes the trail, is blocked by dirt mounds and felled logs. Sections of the last 0.8 mile are rough, rocky and often wet, but the road is still passable. High clearance vehicles fare better on this road.

To the northern, upper elevation, Tesnatee Gap trailhead: Take GA 75 North from the Chattahoochee River Bridge in Helen, travel approximately 1.4 miles, and turn left onto GA Alt. 75 South, crossing the bridge over the Chattahoochee River in Robertstown. Continue on GA Alt. 75 South for 2.3 miles, then turn right onto Richard B. Russell Scenic Highway (GA 348 North).

Proceed slightly more than 7.0 miles to the road's high point at Hogpen Gap. Tesnatee Gap's paved parking area, on the south side (left if you are heading north) of the highway, is a few tenths of a mile downhill from Hogpen Gap. The white-blazed path is the Appalachian Trail. With your back to the highway, you will see the beginning of the Logan Turnpike Trail in the ravine to the left of the parking area.

Notes

Notes

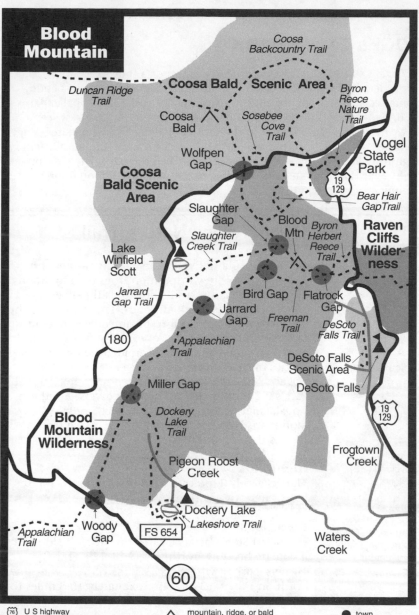

Blood Mountain

Coosa Bald Scenic Area

Coosa Backcountry Trail

Duncan Ridge Trail

Coosa Bald

Coosa Bald Scenic Area

Sosebee Cove Trail

Byron Reece Nature Trail

Wolfpen Gap

Vogel State Park

Slaughter Gap

Blood Mtn

Byron Herbert Reece Trail

Raven Cliffs Wilderness

Slaughter Creek Trail

Lake Winfield Scott

Bear Hair Gap Trail

Jarrard Gap Trail

Bird Gap

Flatrock Gap

Jarrard Gap

Freeman Trail

DeSoto Falls Trail

180

Appalachian Trail

DeSoto Falls Scenic Area

DeSoto Falls

Miller Gap

Frogtown Creek

Blood Mountain Wilderness

Dockery Lake Trail

19 129

Pigeon Roost Creek

Appalachian Trail

Woody Gap

Dockery Lake

Lakeshore Trail

FS 654

Waters Creek

60

---

76 U S highway	⋀ mountain, ridge, or bald	● town
60 Georgia state highway	∿ stream, creek, or river	⌁ campground
FS 654 Forest Service road	┄┄ marked trail	● mountain gap

VOGEL STATE PARK

Vogel's size (280 acres) is not nearly as important as its location. Federally owned national forest land offering a wide range of additional recreational opportunities surrounds the park. The Appalachian Trail, two national forest wildernesses, and three national forest scenic areas are nearby. In addition to the entirely federal recreation sites, Vogel manages three trails of its own—all of them loop trails and all of them beginning and ending at the same place within the park. The two longer trails, Bear Hair Gap and Coosa Backcountry, traverse national forest land for much of their lengths.

EBR
Blood Mountain
Vogel State Park

Features
Diverse forest, interpretive nature trail

Distance
0.4 mile

Difficulty Rating
Easy

County
Union

Nearest Cities
Blairsville (N),
Cleveland (SE),
Dahlonega (S)

Maps
Coosa Bald
Quadrangle, GA;
trail map available at
visitor center

Byron Reece Nature Trail

Named for a native Union County farmer and poet who drew inspiration from the mountains, Byron Reece Nature Trail showcases the diversity of the Southern Appalachian forest. The richness of the Southern Appalachian forest is unequaled over most of the world's temperate zone. Along this short trail alone, an observant walker can identify over twenty species of trees. More types of trees grow within Vogel's 280 acres than within Yellowstone National Park's 2.2 million acres. The most diverse Southern Appalachian forest, the one in Great Smoky Mountains National Park, has more native tree species than all of Europe.

Highlights
Throughout: Interpretive signs describing the forest's most interestng features.

Directions
   Vogel State Park is located on the west side (left if you are heading north) of US 19–129. From Turners Corner, where US 19 joins US 129, continue north on US 19–129 for approximately 10.5 miles to the park sign and entrance road.

From the Blairsville square, travel south on US 19–129 for approximately 10.3 miles to the park sign and entrance. Because trailhead parking is very limited, park rangers ask that hikers park at the visitor center and walk the short distance to the trailhead.

Blazes
White

Campsites
Available with reservation in park campground

To reach the Vogel State Park access trail, turn left immediately after the visitor center. Just before the road forks, look for a set of stone steps and the Nature Trail sign to the right. Follow the green-blazed access trail 0.1 mile from the first trail sign, past a wooden overlook, to the second sign. All of the park's trails begin and end here.

Notes

EBR
Blood Mountain
Vogel State Park

Features
Small streams, view, diversity, wilderness

Distance
3.6 miles (loop)

Difficulty Rating
Moderate

County
Union

Nearest Cities
Blairsville (N),
Cleveland (SE),
Dahlonega (S)

Maps
Coosa Bald
Quadrangle, GA;
trail map available at
visitor center

Blazes
Orange

Campsites
Available with
reservation in park
campground

Bear Hair Gap Trail

The Bear Hair Gap Trail is blazed so that it can be followed in either direction. If you want to follow the signs, turn right onto the road and hike the loop in a counterclockwise direction. If you wish to walk in the opposite direction, continue on the blazed path straight across the road. To the right, counter-clockwise, is the easier way to walk the trail. Traveled in that direction, it is uphill for 1.4 miles, then pre-dominantly level or downhill the rest of the way. Hiked clockwise, the trail has several steep ascents between miles 1.0 and 2.0.

Although Bear Hair Gap Trail alternates between road and path, there is no need for a turn-by-turn description. The trail is well blazed, well signed and easily followed. If a road doesn't have orange blazes, you probably missed a turn onto a path. As always, a double blaze means watch out for a sudden turn.

At mile 1.3 (going counterclockwise) the loop comes to a sign that points to a green-blazed trail to the left. This spur trail, which forms a loop after slightly less than 0.2 mile, climbs gradually to an overlook. Its round-trip distance is 0.5 mile.

The overlook offers a beautiful unobstructed view of Vogel's Lake Trahlyta, named for a legendary Cherokee princess. On a clear day, you can see Brasstown Bald, the highest point in Georgia.

Bear Hair Gap Trail is excellent for beginning hikers of all ages. It is short enough to be walked leisurely in a morning or afternoon, yet long and dif-ficult enough, especially hiked clockwise, to be chal-lenging. All trails are nature trails, this one especially so. Bear Hair Gap Trail encompasses as great a variety of habitats—dry ridges, moist hillsides, moister coves, damp streamsides—as its 3.6-mile length will allow.

Near the end of the loop, going counterclock-wise, there are several large stumps and bleached gray boles lying on the forest floor. These are slow-rotting monuments, grave markers for the magnificent stands of mature American chestnuts that once dominated many areas of North Georgia. Before the blight, they grew best and reached their largest dimensions—often 15 to over 20 feet in circumference—in sheltered coves throughout the Southern Appalachians. Today, chestnut saplings still survive along the trail; occasionally they grow large enough to bear a few of their cocklebur-covered nuts before dying.

From approximately mile 1.1 (walked counterclockwise) and continuing to where the path reenters Vogel State Park, the Bear Hair Gap Trail winds through the 7,800-acre Blood Mountain Wilderness.

Highlights
Throughout: Diverse habitats. Abundant mountain laurel blooming throughout most of May.
Mile 1.3: Spur trail leads to overlook view of Lake Trahlyta and Brasstown Bald (approximately 12 miles northeast).

Directions
(See page 92 of Byron Reece Nature Trail for directions to the Vogel State Park access trail.) Both Bear Hair Gap and Coosa Backcountry Trails turn left at the end of the access trail at 0.1 mile and follow Burnett Branch. The trails soon cross the branch and arrive at a sign next to a road. Here, at 0.3 mile, the loops of both trails begin and end.

Notes

EBR
Blood Mountain
Vogel State Park

Features
Diverse flora, Coosa
Bald, wilderness,
scenic area

Distance
12.4 miles (loop)

Difficulty Rating
Strenuous

County
Union

Nearest Cities
Blairsville (N),
Cleveland (SE),
Dahlonega (S)

Maps
Coosa Bald and
Neels Gap
Quadrangles, GA;
trail map available at
visitor center

Blazes
Yellow

Water Sources
Mile 0.4: Burnett
Branch; mile 3.2:
West Fork Wolf
Creek; mile 6.1:
rivulet; no water
from mile 6.1 to
beyond mile 9.9 (see
description); the final
descending section
back to the park has
plentiful water

Coosa Backcountry Trail

Coosa Backcountry is a challenging day hike for experienced walkers. But beginning hikers, especially hikers unaccustomed to the roller-coaster elevation changes of the mountains, should follow the advice of the rangers at Vogel State Park, who strongly recommend this trail as a backpacking trip, not as a day hike. A further recommendation: beginning backpackers who have not developed the strength to lug packs up long, steep grades should not attempt this trail. Both backpackers and day hikers need a permit, available at park headquarters, to walk the Coosa Backcountry.

Like the shorter Bear Hair Gap Trail, Coosa Backcountry is a loop blazed so it can be walked in either direction. And because it is a loop, the trail gains and loses exactly the same amount of elevation—3,480 feet up and 3,480 feet down—hiked in either direction. Thus the location and steepness of the ascents and descents become the most important consideration when choosing your direction. Following the loop counterclockwise gives you a chance to warm up and make a few easy miles before the long climb to Coosa Bald begins. A clockwise direction, however, forces you to climb 1,820 feet to near the top of Slaughter Mountain, drop 860 feet to Wolfpen Gap, then climb another 880 feet to near the top of Coosa Bald—all within the first 5.4 miles.

The loop section of Coosa Backcountry Trail begins at 0.3 mile. If you want to walk in the easier direction, turn right onto the road. If you want to go against the flow and do it the hard way, continue straight across the road. This description follows the easier, counterclockwise route.

Less than 0.1 mile after turning onto the road, the trail bears right at a sign, quickly crosses Burnett Branch, then follows an easy-to-moderate upgrade through a largely deciduous forest to GA 180 and Burnett Gap at 0.9 mile. Coosa Backcountry, which

began at an elevation of 2,320 feet, crosses the high- | **Campsites**
way at 2,800 feet and continues, after a turn to the | Within Vogel State
right, on an old logging road. The loop descends grad- | Park, camping not
ually along slopes dominated by tuliptree to 2,020 | permitted along the
feet, where it crosses the West Fork of Wolf Creek on a | trail
log bridge at mile 3.2.

After crossing the creek, the trail turns right onto FS 107, Wolf Creek Road, then turns immediately back left into the woods. Here the path climbs steeply for the first time. Once atop the hill at mile 3.5, the trail winds along the steep slopes of Ben Knob, gradually gaining elevation to Locust Stake Gap (2,540 feet) at mile 4.5. From Locust Stake Gap the trail continues level or upward to another gap, Calf Stomp (3,100 feet) at mile 5.8. The steady and often strenuous 1,060-foot climb to near the top of Coosa Bald (4,160 feet) begins here across Calf Stomp Road. Along the way, a rivulet to the right and below the trail (mile 6.1) is the last source of water on the way to Coosa Bald (mile 6.9) and beyond to the final descending section, which begins at mile 9.9.

After the loop crosses a nearly level section of Coosa Bald's broad crown, it ties into the blue-blazed Duncan Ridge Trail at an old road. If you want to finish the walk to the mountain's highest point (4,271 feet), turn right onto the road and follow Duncan Ridge Trail for 0.2 mile. The "Coosa" bench mark embedded in a knot of protruding rock pinpoints the exact spot.

Coosa Backcountry turns left onto the old road and joins Duncan Ridge. Together they descend sharply, first by rocky road, then by rocky, switchbacking path. At mile 7.4 the trail turns left onto Duncan Ridge Road (FS 39), follows it for 30 yards, then returns to the woods on the left side of the road. Here the treadway ascends a moderate, 0.3-mile grade to the top of Wildcat Knob before continuing its rugged descent to Wolfpen Gap (3,260 feet) at mile 8.3.

At Wolfpen Gap the trail crosses GA 180 onto a dirt road, then immediately turns left onto the path. The loop's next 0.9 mile rises to the upper slopes (approximately 4,140 feet) of Slaughter Mountain. The first 0.5 mile of this climb is the trail's steepest grade. After 0.7 mile of easy walking on the moist mountainside, Coosa Backcountry turns 90 degrees to the left and begins a 1,820-foot descent to Vogel State Park. This turn is marked by a sign and double yellow blaze at mile 9.9. (Duncan Ridge continues straight ahead to Slaughter Gap.) The trail's final segment makes switchbacks through an area of lush ferns, small streams, and big boulders. At mile 11.0 the path turns right and completes the loop on a treadway shared with Bear Hair Gap Trail.

Coosa Backcountry traverses botanically rich areas—moist, rocky slopes, hardwood coves, the Coosa Bald mountaintop. The section of the loop from Calf Stomp Gap across Coosa Bald is a wild garden. The Forest Service has designated Coosa Bald Cove as a Botanical Natural Area. This 244-acre tract preserves and protects the cove's unique plant communities. A short segment of the trail wanders through the southeastern corner of the botanical area.

North Georgia's most beautiful spring-blooming wildflowers can be found along the trail. The showy orchis, which has small purple and white bi-colored blooms, is fairly common. This orchid usually flowers from mid-April through early May.

The corridor of the Coosa Backcountry Trail is now almost totally protected. North of GA 180 the trail makes a half circle through the 7,100-acre Coosa Bald National Scenic Area. After it crosses to the south side of GA 180 at Wolfpen Gap (walked counterclockwise), most of the remaining mileage is within the 7,800-acre Blood Mountain Wilderness.

Note: Because much of this trail is routed outside of Vogel's boundaries, its regulations differ from those for other state park backcountry trails. Here there are no reservations, no designated campsites, and no fees associated with camping along the trail. However, you must still obtain a permit for both day hiking and backpacking at the visitor center, and you must still pay all necessary Park Pass fees.

Highlights
Miles 5.8–7.1: Good wildflower displays in spring and early summer.
Mile 6.9: Top of Coosa Bald.

Directions
(See page 92 of Byron Reece Nature Trail for directions to the Vogel State Park access trail.) Both Coosa Backcountry and Bear Hair Gap Trails turn left at the end of the access trail at 0.1 mile and follow Burnett Branch. The trails soon cross the branch and arrive at a sign next to a road. Here, at 0.3 mile, the loops of both trails begin and end.

Sosebee Cove Trail

Sosebee Cove is known primarily for two features: its army-strong stand of tuliptrees and its luxuriously abundant wildflower displays. Although the 175-acre cove hardwood forest may look like virgin timber, most of the cove is actually second-growth. The tract was logged in the early 1900s and has not been substantially altered since that time.

The trail serves as a memorial to US Forest Service Ranger Arthur Woody, who negotiated the purchase of this cove by the Forest Service. You'll see a memorial sign describing his life and achievements.

Near where the loop trail heads to the left (counterclockwise), the largest tuliptree in the area stands 15 yards to the right and down from the big signs. It has a girth of 16 feet 5 inches measured 4 feet 6 inches from the ground, making it the third largest tree near the trails described in this guide. While not as big around as the Sosebee Cove champion, hundreds of other maturing tuliptrees—actually deciduous members of the magnolia family—have reached heights of more than 100 feet. Their gradually tapering gray trunks are free of limbs for much of that distance.

Near the end of the loop back near the road, the path passes beside a yellow buckeye that is gigantic for its species. At 4 feet 6 inches from the ground, the mossy-boled tree measures 15 feet 4 inches in circumference—making it the second largest yellow buckeye in Georgia, only slightly smaller than the current state record holder.

One sign states that Sosebee Cove is "A Botanist's Paradise." It's true. To give even a cursory account of the cove's bewildering diversity would require a small pamphlet. In addition to those listed on the sign, numerous other wildflowers grace the cove from late March through September. There are almost always members of the lily family in sight.

EBR
Blood Mountain
Sosebee Cove
Scenic Area

Features
Two large trees, outstanding wildflower display

Distance
0.3 mile (loop)

Difficulty Rating
Easy

County
Union

Nearest Cities
Blairsville (N), Cleveland (SE), Dahlonega (S)

Map
Coosa Bald Quadrangle, GA

Blazes
None; none needed

Ranger District
Brasstown

They include false hellebore, yellow mandarin, Solomon's seal, false Solomon's seal, trout lily, Turk's-cap lily and three species of trillium—large-flowered, sessile, and Vasey's. The three members of the barberry family—blue cohosh, umbrella-leaf, and mayapple—can be easily identified by their distinctive leaves. There are mints such as crimson bee-balm and wild bergamot; orchids such as rattlesnake plantain and showy orchis. Purple-flowering raspberry, leather flower, and wild columbine bloom in the sunshine of the power cut. Sourgrass, wild geranium, and giant chickweed thrive there along with meadow rue and rue anemone; white baneberry (doll's-eyes), foamflower, spring beauty, and sweet cicely also take turns adding to the cove's beauty.

It seems that no matter when you visit an area during spring, your timing is off: something better than what is blooming is always either in bud or has already blossomed the week before. There is no guaranteed schedule for wildflowers. But from March 25 through May 15 at least one new wildflower species will open every three or four days. And there really are those good days when you time the flowers just right, when you find orchids and trilliums and many other showy species blooming simultaneously along the same path.

Many people leave Sosebee Cove somewhat frustrated, wishing they could have identified more of the plants they found. Knowledge of the following three wildflowers, which are large, distinctive, and common in Sosebee Cove, will at least provide a start for beginners. Uncommon throughout the mountains of North Georgia, the umbrella-leaf is abundant along the rocky seepage slopes of the cove. The nonflowering stems produce a single huge leaf, 1–2 feet across, with jagged, deeply cut edges. The flowering stems produce two somewhat smaller leaves. Throughout much of May, the plant holds a single cluster of relatively small white flowers well above its tropical-looking leaves. The umbrella-leaf is endemic to the Southern Appalachians. An almost identical species lives in the mountains of Japan.

The plant with the broad, fern-like leaves is sweet cicely. Its tiny white flowers bloom in a sparse cluster in early May. Sweet cicely received its name from its aromatic roots, which have a licorice-like scent when bruised.

The Turk's-cap lily is a perennial herb that reaches 9 to 10 feet in height. This splendid wildflower commonly grows 6 to 8 feet tall in Sosebee Cove. Its lanceolate leaves emanate from the stem in whorls about 10 inches apart, giving the plant a distinctive, tiered appearance. This lily's orange to orange-red flowers (with reddish-brown, freckle-like spots) most often nod toward the ground at an angle similar to that of a showerhead. Their long, exposed stamens point downward away from the plant. Their 2- to 3-inch petals, however, flare into a reflexed arc—out from, up from, then back above the point of attachment. The Turk's-cap lily usually blooms from about mid-July to mid-August.

Sosebee Cove has two short interconnected loop trails. The main trail—a loop about 0.2 mile in length—begins at the foot of the steps below the parking area. The second trail, which is less than 0.1 mile in length, crosses through the center of the loop.

Sosebee Cove is a special place, and it is protected as a National Forest Scenic Area. Its plants are not portable. It is against the law to pluck or pull up any flower or plant, even the tiny ones that you think no one will miss. If, as is often said, ignorance is no excuse for breaking the law, then certainly arrogance is no excuse either.

Most of the scenic area's 175 acres have been incorporated into the 7,800-acre Blood Mountain Wilderness, which lies to the south of GA 180.

Highlights
Throughout: Maturing hardwoods and lush spring and summer wildflower displays.

Directions
The trailhead is located on the north side (right if you are heading west) of GA 180. From Turners Corner, where US 19 joins US 129, continue north on US 19–129 for slightly less than 11.0 miles (0.4 mile past Vogel State Park), then turn left onto GA 180. Proceed 3.1 miles on GA 180 until you reach Sosebee Cove's paved parking area on the right.

From the Blairsville square, travel on US 19–129 South for approximately 10.0 miles to GA 180. Follow GA 180 to the Sosebee Cove parking area.

Notes

EBR
Blood Mountain
Lake Winfield Scott
Recreation Area

Features
AT approach,
wilderness

Distance
1.2 miles

Difficulty Rating
Easy to moderate

County
Union

Nearest Cities
Blairsville (N),
Dahlonega (S)

Maps
Neels Gap
Quadrangle, GA;
Appalachian Trail
map

Blazes
Blue

Campsites
Available in recre-
ation area camp-
ground; North Loop
remains open all
year

Ranger District
Brasstown

Jarrard Gap Trail

Jarrard Gap Trail is an easy-to-follow, easily walked approach to the Appalachian Trail. Slaughter Creek Trail shares the trailhead and the first 0.2 mile of the treadway. After 0.1 mile of level walkway at 2,890 feet near Slaughter Creek, the trail turns left immediately before a footbridge. The path continues through rose-bay rhododendron beside the creek, then crosses it on a single split log. On the other side of the creek, the path quickly reaches a wide dirt road, where the trails split. Slaughter Creek continues straight across the road; Jarrard Gap turns right and follows the road for 0.2 mile to a three-way intersection. The trail angles across the road that enters the intersection from the right, returning to the woods on an old single-lane road blocked by boulders. The road's entrance is marked with a double blaze and a trail sign.

For the next 0.4 mile the trail follows Lance Branch up its ravine. Most often, it remains on the hardwood slopes above the Slaughter Creek tributary. This section gains elevation gradually; its steepest grade is short and only moderately difficult.

At 0.8 mile the path crosses the branch. The re-mainder of the trail, still a combination of roadbed and path, rises to the gap. Again, the steepest grade is short and only moderately difficult. The trail turns right onto a single-lane dirt road 35 yards before its end at Jarrard Gap (3,300 feet) on the Appalachian Trail. This road provides access to nearby private property.

If you want to take a longer day hike from Lake Winfield Scott, Jarrard Gap can be walked as the first leg of a 6.2-mile loop beginning and ending at the lake. Once you've reached Jarrard Gap, turn left onto the white-blazed Appalachian Trail and continue 2.3 miles to Slaughter Gap, where you turn left onto Slaughter Creek Trail.

The final 0.3 mile of this trail is within the

7,800-acre Blood Mountain Wilderness. (See page 294 for campfire regulations pertaining to the Blood Mountain Wilderness.)

Highlights

Miles 0.5–1.2: Hardwood forest. Trail enters Blood Mountain Wilderness at 0.9 mile.

Directions

Lake Winfield Scott Recreation Area is located on the east side of GA 180 between GA 60 and US 19–129.

From Dahlonega, drive north on GA 60. At Stonepile Gap, where US 19 and GA 60 split, continue left on GA 60. At the GA 60–GA 180 junction in Suches, turn right onto GA 180 East and travel for slightly less than 4.5 miles. Turn right onto paved Lake Winfield Scott Road (FS 37) and into the entrance of Lake Winfield Scott Recreation Area. The trailhead sign and pull-off parking area are just beyond the bridge at the south end of the lake. (There is also a parking lot for hikers to the left before the lake.)

From the US 19–129–GA 180 junction (0.4 miles north of Vogel State Park entrance) travel approximately 6.8 miles on GA 180 West to the left turn onto Lake Winfield Scott Road (FS 37). This road is 0.7 mile beyond the first left turn into the recreation area.

Notes

104

Features
AT approach, small
streams, wilderness

Distance
2.7 miles

Difficulty Rating
Easy to moderate

County
Union

Nearest Cities
Blairsville (N),
Dahlonega (S)

Maps
Neels Gap
Quadrangle, GA;
Appalachian Trail
map

Blazes
Blue

Water Sources
At frequent intervals

Campsites
Available in
recreation area
campground;
North Loop remains
open all year

Ranger District
Brasstown

Slaughter Creek Trail

Slaughter Creek and Jarrard Gap Trails share the
same treadway for their first 0.2 mile. Like Jarrard
Gap and all other approaches to the Appalachian
Trail, Slaughter Creek is blue blazed. And also like
Jarrard Gap, Slaughter Creek trail is composed of a
series of old roadbeds connected by constructed
paths.

Slaughter Creek gains 1000 feet in elevation, but
does so gradually over its 2.7-mile length. There are
no grades that would be considered strenuous. Most
of the ascent is accomplished by easy-to-moderate
grades, which often alternate with sections that are
level or dip slightly to stream crossings.

Where Slaughter Creek and Jarrard Gap Trails
split, Slaughter Creek Trail continues straight ahead
across the road. Back into the evergreen thickets of
rosebay rhododendron and mountain laurel, the
path quickly rises to the slopes above the creek,
where it remains until it dips to a junction at 0.7
mile. Here the trail turns right at the intersecting
roadbeds and continues to follow Slaughter Creek up
its watershed. Beyond this turn, in winter, you can
see the prominent rock slabs that extend up
Slaughter Mountain's southwestern flank.

At mile 1.7 the trail angles onto a rocky old logging road that closely follows Slaughter Creek up a
hardwood cove. After the heath thickets disappear,
the stream becomes much more visible, the forest
more open. Stumps from past logging days still dot
the cove. Those stumps and logs bleached light gray
are vestiges of the chestnut blight.

The trail crosses its namesake creek, the last of
many stream crossings, at mile 2.2. Forty-five yards
farther, it turns uphill toward the gap. The final 0.3
mile climbs a moderately difficult slope that supports
a forest increasingly dominated by oaks.

Slaughter Gap is a major trail junction. The

Appalachian Trail enters the gap, then turns 90 degrees to the right. The gap is also the eastern end of the Duncan Ridge Trail, which quickly leads to Vogel State Park's Coosa Backcountry Trail.

For a longer day hike from Lake Winfield Scott Recreation Area, connect Slaughter Creek Trail with a 1.0-mile segment of the Appalachian Trail to reach the top of Blood Mountain. If you want to walk toward Blood Mountain and its superb vistas, do not turn right onto the Appalachian Trail. Instead, walk Slaughter Creek Trail almost straight across the opening and follow the white-blazed trail after it has turned right.

The trail from Slaughter Gap to the crest of Blood Mountain is surprisingly easy, considering that Blood Mountain (4,461 feet) is one of Georgia's highest peaks. While the trail does wind steadily uphill, there are no long, uninterrupted steep grades. Actually, after you have reached Slaughter Gap—at 3,860 feet a very high gap in Georgia—much of your elevation gain is behind you.

If you plan to continue walking from the end of Slaughter Creek Trail, you may want to remember that the last source of easily obtainable water is at mile 2.2, where the trail crosses Slaughter Creek.

Because of excessive rutting and erosion on the old-road segments of this trail, the Forest Service has rerouted most of those segments onto new footpath. While the mileage has changed very little, the trail itself is much improved.

Beyond the 1.8-mile mark, the trail remains within the 7,800-acre Blood Mountain Wilderness. (See page 295 for campfire regulations pertaining to the Blood Mountain Wilderness.)

Highlights
Mile 1.8: Trail enters the Blood Mountain Wilderness and ascends through a mature hardwood forest.

Directions
(See page 103 of Jarrard Gap Trail for directions to the Lake Winfield Scott Recreation Area.) The Slaughter Creek trailhead starts at its sign at the south end of Lake Winfield.

Helton Creek Falls Trail

Features
Two waterfalls,
outstanding forest

Distance
0.1 mile

Difficulty Rating
Easy

County
Union

Nearest Cities
Blairsville (N),
Cleveland (SE),
Dahlonega (S)

Map
Coosa Bald
Quadrangle, GA

Blazes
None; none needed

Ranger District
Brasstown

Flanked by towering eastern hemlocks, this short but scenic trail gently descends to a pair of waterfalls on Helton Creek. The first waterfall—really a waterslide—is about 30 feet high. The second, a short distance upstream, is wide and approximately 50 to 55 feet high. Its twin cascades spill into a dark green wading pool.

Directions

Helton Creek Road, which leads to Helton Creek Falls, is located on the east side (right if you are heading north) of US 19–129. From Turners Corner, where US 19 joins US 129, continue north on US 19–129 for 9.5 miles (1.6 miles past Neels Gap), then turn right onto paved Helton Creek Road (FS 118). Travel 2.3 miles on Helton Creek Road (the pavement ends after 0.7 mile) to the railed, pull-in parking area just past the trailhead sign to the right.

From the Blairsville square, head south on US 19–129 for slightly less than 11.5 miles (1.1 miles past Vogel State Park) to Helton Creek Road.

Byron Herbert Reece Trail

EBR
Blood Mountain
Blood Mountain Wilderness

This trail, formerly known as the Blood Mountain Spur Trail, has been renamed the Byron Herbert Reece Trail. Because of its new name, it might be confused with the Byron Reece Nature Trail in Vogel State Park, a short, interpretive loop trail. Both memorialize the same man, a native Union County poet and farmer who was born in Choestoe in the shadow of Blood Mountain. This is the trail to take if you want to walk the Appalachian Trail to the west, toward the Freeman Trail and Blood Mountain.

The Byron Herbert Reece Trail quickly tunnels through a thicket of mountain laurel and rosebay rhododendron, crosses one of the headwater forks of Shanty Branch, then gently rises beside the other fork. At 0.2 mile the path (at a double blaze) curls away from the stream and begins the first of two switchbacks that climb to an old roadbed at 0.4 mile. After a gentle 0.1 mile, the spur angles away from the road and ascends moderately through a forest with a predominantly oak canopy and white pine understory. Byron Herbert Reece soon dead-ends at the Appalachian Trail, forming a three-way T-intersection on the Blood Mountain side of Flatrock Gap (3,420 feet). To the left it is 1.0 mile to Neels Gap; to the right, it is 1.5 miles and 1,040 feet up to the top of Blood Mountain (4,461 feet), the highest peak on the AT in Georgia.

The Georgia Appalachian Trail Club built the Byron Herbert Reece Trail, and they did an excellent job; the trail is wide, well marked and easily followed. The GATC constructed this spur trail to alleviate car and hiker congestion at Neels Gap. They urge Blood Mountain and Freeman Trail day hikers to begin their walk at the Byron Reece Picnic Area (3,040 feet) rather than at Neels Gap. The Byron Herbert Reece Trail is shorter and only slightly steeper than the AT from Neels Gap (3,109 feet).

Features
Wilderness, AT approach

Distance
0.7 mile

Difficulty Rating
Easy to moderate

County
Union

Nearest Cities
Blairsville (N),
Cleveland (SE),
Dahlonega (S)

Maps
Neels Gap
Quadrangle, GA;
Appalachian Trail
Map

Blazes
Blue

Ranger District
Brasstown

The Byron Herbert Reece Trail is entirely within the 7,800-acre Blood Mountain Wilderness. (See page 294 for campfire regulations pertaining to the Blood Mountain Wilderness.)

Directions

The Byron Herbert Reece Memorial Picnic Area is located on the west side (left if you are heading north) of US 19–129. From Turners Corner, where US 19 joins US 129, continue north on US 19–129 for approximately 8.3 miles (0.5 mile past Neels Gap), then turn onto the second road downhill from the gap. The parking area is halfway around a one-way loop; the unmistakable trailhead is slightly farther along the loop.

From the Blairsville square, travel south on US 19–129 for approximately 12.5 miles to the memorial loop.

Do not park at the Walasi-Yi Center and hike the AT from Neels Gap; parking in front of the store is for customers only.

Notes

Freeman Trail

EBR
Blood Mountain
Blood Mountain
Wilderness

Unlike other AT approach trails, which begin at a trailhead and lead to the AT, the Freeman Trail has both of its ends joined to the AT, making a loop. Starting at Flatrock Gap (3,420 feet), Freeman Trail often follows the contours along the southern flank of Blood Mountain. In winter, you can see Blood Mountain's uppermost slopes towering above the trail.

The path winds through a second-growth oak-hickory forest with occasional large trees. While the trail is not steep, gaining only 240 feet to Bird Gap, the treadway and trailside are rocky. It is this rock—boulder jumbles, protruding outcrops, large slabs—that gives this trail its distinctive, rugged scenery.

The western end of the footpath follows an easy upgrade to Bird Gap (3,660 feet). Turn right onto the white-blazed AT to complete the loop over Blood Mountain. The three-trail loop—Byron Herbert Reece to Flatrock Gap, Freeman from Flatrock Gap to Bird Gap, the AT from Bird Gap back to Flatrock Gap, and Byron Herbert Reece again from Flatrock Gap to the parking area—is 6.7 miles.

The Freeman Trail is entirely within the 7,800-acre Blood Mountain Wilderness. (See page 294 for campfire regulations pertaining to the Blood Mountain Wilderness.)

Features
Wilderness, AT approach, rock outcrops

Distance
1.9 miles

Difficulty Rating
Easy to moderate

County
Lumpkin

Nearest Cities
Blairsville (N), Cleveland (SE), Dahlonega (S)

Maps
Neels Gap Quadrangle, GA; Appalachian Trail map

Blazes
Blue

Water Sources
Miles 0.2, 1.4: seasonal seeps

Ranger District
Brasstown

Highlights
Throughout: steep, rocky, scenic slopes.

Directions
(See page 108 of Byron Herbert Reece Trail for directions to its trailhead.) Freeman is an interior trail. To reach the AT junction from the nearest trailhead, walk the 0.7-mile Byron Herbert Reece Trail (formerly known as Blood Mountain Spur Trail) to its junction with the AT at Flatrock Gap. Turn right onto the AT toward Blood Mountain. Freeman's sign and entering treadway are to the left 25 yards away.

DeSoto Falls Scenic Area

Features
Streams, waterfalls

Distance
(See description)

Difficulty Rating
Lower Falls: easy to moderate; Middle Falls: easy

County
Lumpkin

Nearest Cities
Cleveland (SE), Blairsville (N), Dahlonega (S)

Map
Neels Gap Quadrangle, GA

Blazes
Signs with arrows; no blazes needed

Campsites
No camping permitted on the trail; campsites available seasonally at the recreation area campground

Ranger District
Brasstown

DeSoto Falls Trail

The falls and the 650-acre scenic area got their name from mountain folklore. Early settlers—so the legend goes—found a piece of Spanish armor in the vicinity of the falls and believed it was left behind by Hernando DeSoto or one of his men as they wandered about the southeast looking for treasure.

Like several other scenic areas, DeSoto Falls combines with a National Forest Recreation Area bearing the same name. Access to the scenic area and trail is gained through the recreation area on US 129. The trail begins across the bridge over Frogtown Creek; a sign with arrows and distances to the falls marks the path.

If you hike to both waterfalls—from the trailhead (elevation 2,080 feet) to the Lower Falls, from the Lower Falls past the trailhead to the Middle Falls, then back to the trailhead—you will walk 1.9 miles.

The Lower Falls spill and splash 30 to 35 feet. Nine-tenths mile away, the Middle Falls drop in four stages—close to 90 feet altogether. Both have large observation decks.

Note: The trail that once continued from the Middle Falls to the Upper Falls is now closed.

Highlights
Lower Falls, 30 feet high.
Middle Falls, 90 feet high.

Directions
DeSoto Falls Recreation and Scenic Areas are located on the west side (left if you are heading north) of US 19–129. From Turners Corner, where US 19 joins US 129, continue north on US 19–129 for slightly more than 4.0 miles to the recreation area sign and entrance.

From the Blairsville square, travel south on US 19–129 for approximately 16.5 miles to the recreation area sign and entrance.

Once inside the recreation area, follow the loop to the right (as the sign directs) past the signed trailhead to the DeSoto Falls Trail Parking Area, which is marked with a stick-figure hiker sign.

The recreation area campground is closed seasonally. A large parking area near the campground entrance is now open year-round.

Notes

EBR
Blood Mountain
**Dockery Lake
Recreation Area**

Features
Dockery Lake,
mountain views

Distance
0.5 mile (loop)

Difficulty Rating
Easy

County
Lumpkin

Nearest City
Dahlonega

Map
Neels Gap
Quadrangle, GA

Blazes
None; none needed

Campsites
Available seasonally
in the recreation
area campground

Ranger District
Brasstown

Lakeshore Trail

From the trailhead, the path quickly winds through the small picnic area down to an A-frame picnic shelter, where it becomes a loop circling the 6-acre lake. At 2,388 feet, Dockery is a mountain lake, cold and clear enough for trout habitat.

Along the way, numerous short side paths lead to small, concrete-reinforced platforms at the water's edge. These platforms were built primarily as fishing sites, but they also serve as lakeside vantage points for walkers. Halfway around the lake the trail crosses over the dam and its outlet stream, an unnamed tributary of Waters Creek.

Dockery Lake is an excellent and easily accessible site for the entire family to enjoy picnicking, camping, walking, and mountain scenery. Lakeshore— easy, short, and partially graveled—is one of the best national forest trails for children.

Highlights
Throughout: Dockery Lake.

Directions
From Stonepile Gap, where US 19 splits from GA 60 north of Dahlonega, continue on GA 60 North. Slightly more than 3.6 miles beyond the gap, turn right onto unpaved FS 654 across the highway from the large Dockery Lake sign. Proceed straight ahead on FS 654 for approximately 1.0 mile, then turn left where the road forks and follow the sign for picnicking, fishing, and hiking to the picnic area parking lot.

Lakeshore Trail starts next to the information board.

Dockery Lake Trail

EBR
Blood Mountain
**Dockery Lake
Recreation Area**

Starting at about 2,420 feet, Dockery Lake Trail ascends 200 feet through a predominantly oak-pine forest in the first 0.3 mile, then turns left and slants off the ridge into a cove. Carolina silverbells, also known as snowdrop trees, abound in the cove. Look for small, often stooped trees that have elliptical leaves and longitudinal yellowish streaks on their small branches. Drooping, bell-shaped white flowers open in mid-April. Blooming later, through most of May and into early June, flame azaleas are common in the surrounding forest. Their blossoms vary from pale yellow to fiery orange-red.

The wide, well-marked trail continues to descend, often beside small tributary streams of Waters Creek, to mile 1.1. Almost as soon as it stops going down, it goes up. Across a small stream at mile 1.2, the climb to Miller Gap and the Appalachian Trail begins at about 2,040 feet. The next 0.5 mile, which follows a moderate-to-strenuous gradient, is the most difficult part of the ascent. At mile 2.0 the path rises above a small cascade on a feeder stream flowing toward Pigeon Roost Creek. To the right, especially in winter, there is an excellent view of the upper Waters Creek watershed, its valley wild and completely forested. The highest mountains visible to the east are Buck Knob, Pigeon Roost, and Columbia Ridge.

As you pass through forest that includes red maple, eastern hemlock, eastern white pine and Fraser magnolia, the path steadily works its way up to a gap at mile 2.8, then curls to the left onto a former roadbed. The remainder of Dockery Lake Trail ascends gently to its upper end at Miller Gap (3,005 feet) on the white-blazed Appalachian Trail. This trail junction occurs along Section 2 of the Appalachian Trail between Woody and Neels Gaps. The stretch of trail from approximately mile 1.2 to Miller Gap lies within the 7,800-acre Blood Mountain Wilderness.

Features
AT approach, wilderness, small streams, view

Distance
3.4 miles

Difficulty Rating
Moderate to strenuous

County
Lumpkin

Nearest City
Dahlonega

Maps
Neels Gap Quadrangle, GA; Appalachian Trail map

Blazes
Blue

Water Sources
At frequent intervals for first 2.5 miles

Campsites
Available seasonally in the recreation area campground

Ranger District
Brasstown

Highlights

Mile 0.4: Trail enters a cove with many Carolina silverbells and flame azaleas.
Mile 2.0: View of adjacent ridges.
Mile 3.2: Trail follows a ridge crest with winter views of adjacent ridges.

Directions

(See page 112 of Lakeshore Trail for directions to the Dockery Lake Recreation picnic area.) Dockery Lake Trail starts behind its trailhead sign at the back of the Dockery Lake picnic area parking lot.

Notes

Eyes On Wildlife Trail

In 1986 a fire burned over 30 acres on the lower eastern slope of Rocky Mountain. After salvage logging and a prescribed burn, the slope was replanted with eastern white pine saplings. Money from the salvage sale was used to create this trail, which was cooperatively developed by the Blue Ridge Mountain Hikers and the Forest Service in 1993.

This easily walked trail begins by crossing a bridge over Tom Jones Branch. Fifty yards beyond its marble monument sign, the trail reaches its loop junction. This description follows the slightly easier grades and the directional arrow to the left, clockwise around the flattened loop.

The roadbed, which is the lower limit of the burn and salvage cut, continues above Tom Jones Branch. Eastern white pines—tall maturing trees and recently planted saplings—dominate the slope above the trail. If all goes according to plan, the eastern white pine saplings will make wood very quickly. A tall, chainsawed blowdown had grown to 25 inches in only 46 years.

At 0.4 mile the trail turns up and to the right away from the branch. One-tenth mile farther, it turns right again onto a logging road that leads through the burn and salvage cut area. For the next few years, until the pines block the views and the road grasses in, you will still be able to see the charred snags on the upper slope, mountains to the northeast, and plenty of animal tracks—mostly deer, bobcat, and fox.

An American chestnut relative, the Allegheny chinquapin is common along the upper road bank. The chinquapin varies from a large shrub to a small tree up to 40 feet high. Here they are shrubby in size and form. Their deciduous leaves are similar to but noticeably smaller than those of the American chestnut, and their burrs are smaller but every bit as prickly.

EBR
Duncan Ridge
Cooper Creek
Recreation Area

Features
Streams, winter views

Distance
1.6 miles (loop)

Difficulty Rating
Easy to moderate

County
Union

Nearest Cities
Blairsville (N),
Dahlonega (S)

Maps
Mulky Gap
Quadrangle, GA;
description and map
available from
ranger district

Blazes
None; directional
arrows on carsonite
signs

Campsites
Available seasonally
at recreation area
campground

Ranger District
Toccoa

With 0.5 mile remaining, the walkway turns down and to the right at a small wildlife opening. This final section descends through a moist, unburned, second-growth forest above Cooper Creek. Along the way there are views through rosebay rhododendron and eastern hemlock to the stream.

Highlights
Miles 0.7–1.0: Winter views to the northeast.
Mile 1.4: Views down to Cooper Creek.

Directions
From Dahlonega, travel north on GA 60 (also US 19). At Stonepile Gap, where GA 60 and US 19 split, continue north (to the left) on GA 60 for approximately 15.0 miles. Turn right onto paved Cooper Creek Road (FS 33) at the Cavendar Gap and Cooper Creek Recreation Area signs.

From the GA 60–Cooper Creek Road junction, follow paved Cooper Creek Road (FS 33) for 0.8 mile before turning left onto FS 236 at the Coopers Creek WMA* and Cooper Creek Recreation Area signs. Proceed 2.3 miles on dirt-gravel FS 236 to the large parking area on the right just before the bridge over Cooper Creek. The loop begins at its fancy marble trailhead sign across the road from the parking lot.

The US Army regularly conducts training exercises in the Coopers Creek Wildlife Management Area. Although there is little threat of physical harm, army training complete with aircraft, marching soldiers, and small arms fire can quickly shatter the solitude you may be seeking. To avoid such noisy encounters, phone Camp Frank D. Merrill in Dahlonega and check the schedule before planning your hike. The number is (706) 864-3367, extension 114.

Notes

Yellow Mountain Trail

The Yellow Mountain Trail begins on the western edge of Cooper Creek Scenic Area. From the trailhead it rises to the northeast until it reaches the ridge top of Yellow Mountain, which is the scenic area's northern border. Near the end of the ridge the trail forks. The left fork, the green-blazed Shope Gap Trail, heads northward away from the scenic area. The Yellow Mountain Trail heads southeastward, back into the scenic area, where it remains until after it crosses Bryant Creek.

The hike starts with an easy-to-moderate climb through a stand of eastern hemlock. Above this shady grove, the trail enters an open oak-pine forest on Yellow Mountain's dry southern slopes. Shortleaf pine are common and can be identified by their needles—three to five inches long in clusters of two to three—and by their bark, which is broken into irregularly shaped plates and covered with thin reddish scales.

After its initial ascent, the path rises easily to the ridge crest and its junction with blue-blazed Cooper Creek Trail at 1.0 mile. Cooper Creek angles downhill and left, serving as a 0.4 mile connector to Mill Shoals Trail. Yellow Mountain Trail continues easily uphill with the ridge crest to the level top of its namesake mountain (2,963 feet). Large green blazes mark the scenic area's boundary. At mile 1.6 the treadway reaches another trail junction.

To the left (north) green-blazed Shope Gap Trail descends moderately, then more gently through a mixed oak-pine forest. After slightly less than 0.5 mile, the path comes to a rough, single-lane road. Shope Gap Trail ends at Shope Gap on Duncan Ridge Road (FS 39) slightly over 0.1 mile to the left on the single track road. If you want to complete the counterclockwise Yellow Mountain–Shope Gap–Mill Shoals loop, turn left onto FS 39 at Shope Gap, and

EBR
Duncan Ridge
**Cooper Creek
Scenic Area**

Features
Forest

Distance
3.0 miles

Difficulty Rating
Moderate

County
Union

Nearest Cities
Blairsville (N),
Dahlonega (S)

Map
Mulky Gap
Quadrangle, GA

Blazes
Yellow

Water Sources
Bryant Creek crossing at mile 2.6

Campsites
Available seasonally
at Cooper Creek
Recreation Area
campground

Ranger District
Brasstown

follow the orange-blazed Mill Shoals Trail.

The Yellow Mountain Trail continues gently downhill through a forest where chestnut sprouts are frequent. Beyond a young forest at mile 2.2, it switchbacks steadily down a steep slope through mature eastern white pine. Please watch for the blazes so you don't unintentionally cut across the switchbacks.

The footpath crosses Bryant Creek, a Cooper Creek tributary, on a foot log with handrails at mile 2.6. The treadway continues gradually uphill, through a forest cut in the late 1970s, to a narrow road. Eighty yards beyond the first road, the trail ends at Bryant Creek Road (FS 33-A) in Addie Gap.

Highlights

Mile 1.6: Just past the Shope Gap junction, look for metamorphic rock and granite tinged with black and pink at the trail's highest elevation, 2,963 feet.

Throughout: Ample wildflowers. In early April, look for trailing arbutus, dwarf iris, plantain-leaved pussytoes, pipsissewa, hawkweed, cinquefoil, partridgeberry, and huckleberry. A native orchid, rattlesnake plantain, blooms with a white spike in midsummer.

Directions

(See page 116 of Eyes on Wildlife Trail for directions to Cooper Creek Road.) From the GA 60–Cooper Creek Road junction, follow paved Cooper Creek Road (FS 33) for 0.8 mile before turning left onto FS 236 at the Coopers Creek WMA* and Cooper Creek Recreation Area signs. Proceed 2.3 miles on dirt-gravel FS 236 to the large parking lot on the right just before the bridge over Cooper Creek.

If you are not planning to camp at the recreation area (0.3 mile farther on FS 236), leave your vehicle at the scenic area parking lot. Yellow Mountain Trail begins across Cooper Creek, a short 300-yard walk farther along FS 236 toward the recreation area. The yellow-blazed, signed trailhead begins to the right of the road.

*The US Army regularly conducts training exercises in the Coopers Creek Wildlife Management Area. Although there is little threat of physical harm, army training complete with aircraft, marching soldiers, and small arms fire can quickly shatter the solitude you may be seeking. To avoid such noisy encounters, phone Camp Frank D. Merrill in Dahlonega and check the schedule before planning your hike. The number is (706) 864-3367, extension 114.

Mill Shoals Trail

Mill Shoals Trail has been rerouted. It now ends on FS 39 (Duncan Ridge Road) at Shope Gap and forms a loop with Shope Gap Trail (former left fork of the Yellow Mountain Trail) and Yellow Mountain Trail.

Mill Shoals Trail quickly gains elevation through a forest dominated by eastern white pine and several species of oak, including southern red oak. The path starts out easy, then becomes progressively steeper as it skirts the northwestern edge of Cooper Creek Scenic Area up long, steady switchbacks. Its most difficult sustained upgrade, however, is no harder than moderate. At 0.7 mile Mill Shoals Trail reaches the top of a spur ridge, where a sign marks its junction with the blue-blazed Cooper Creek Trail. This 0.4-mile connector follows an old logging road to the right and rises easily to its Yellow Mountain junction, 1.0 mile from the Yellow Mountain trailhead.

Mill Shoals continues straight ahead, down onto the upper slopes of a hardwood cove. The American chestnut stumps in the cove are still bigger around than the trees that have supplanted them. At 0.9 mile the path, now out of the scenic area, dips to an old roadbed. Here the treadway turns right onto the road, then almost immediately slants down and to the left, off the road and into the rosebay rhododendron.

The path remains level or slightly downhill until it reaches Mill Shoals Creek tumbling over moss-covered rocks at mile 1.4. Along the way the trail crosses two of the creek's feeder streams and winds through pockets of tall eastern white pine and moist, lower-slope areas of eastern hemlock and rosebay rhododendron. After it crosses Mill Shoals Creek, the trail turns right onto another old roadbed, then quickly works its way up to Duncan Ridge Road (FS 39) at mile 1.5 where there is a good view of Cliff Ridge and Beebait Knob to the west.

EBR
Duncan Ridge
Cooper Creek Recreation Area

Features
Forest, stream

Distance
2.5 miles

Difficulty Rating
Easy to moderate

County
Union

Nearest Cities
Blairsville (N),
Dahlonega (S)

Map
Mulky Gap
Quadrangle, GA

Blazes
Orange

Water Sources
Miles 1.0-1.4:
two rivulets and
Mill Shoals Creek

Campsites
Available seasonally
at recreation area
campground

Ranger District
Brasstown

The route turns right and follows FS 39 for 1.0 mile to Shope Gap at the junction of FS 39 and an old woods road. To complete the three-trail, clockwise loop, turn right onto the woods road and follow green-blazed Shope Gap Trail.

Highlights
Mile 1.4: Mill Shoals Creek.

Directions
(See page 116 of Eyes on Wildlife Trail for directions to Cooper Creek Road.) From the GA 60–Cooper Creek Road junction, follow paved Cooper Creek Road (FS 33) for 0.8 mile before turning left onto FS 236 at the Coopers Creek WMA* and Cooper Creek Recreaton Area signs. Proceed 2.3 miles on dirt-gravel FS 236 to the large parking lot on the right just before the bridge over Cooper Creek.

If you are not planning to camp at the recreation area (0.3 mile farther on FS 236), you may want to leave your vehicle at the scenic area parking lot. Mill Shoals Trail begins across Cooper Creek, nearly 0.3 mile farther along FS 236 toward the recreation area. The orange-blazed, signed trailhead begins to the right of the road. The Forest Service requests that only campers park in the recreation area; pull-off parking along FS 236 is very limited.

The US Army regularly conducts training exercises in the Coopers Creek Wildlife Management Area. Although there is little threat of physical harm, army training complete with aircraft, marching soldiers, and small arms fire can quickly shatter the solitude you may be seeking. To avoid such noisy encounters, phone Camp Frank D. Merrill in Dahlonega and check the schedule before planning your hike. The number is (706) 864-3367, extension 114.

Notes

Old-Growth Forest Trail

EBR
Duncan Ridge
Cooper Creek
Scenic Area

This unofficial trail, actually a combination of old roads, descends easily toward Mark Helton Creek. Fifty-five yards before the road fords the creek, the route turns left and uphill onto a narrower woods road at 0.2 mile. Continue to the left and uphill at the fork 60 yards beyond the turn.

High above the shoals on Cooper Creek at 0.4 mile, you will start to see a few mature tuliptrees in the 11- to 13-foot circumference range. Mature tuliptrees develop very deeply furrowed bark that sloughs off in large chunks, starting from the bottom, as the trees age. The tops of nearly all old, forest-grown tuliptrees have been blown down by storms.

The roadbed rises easily through a predominantly hardwood forest with old-growth sweet birch, sassafras, northern red and white oak, blackgum, and a few eastern white pine. The first tuliptree lunker—15 feet 9 inches in circumference—is just to the left of the walkway at 0.7 mile. A tall, hollowed-out giant with a girth of 15 feet 3 inches is downslope a short distance past the first large tree.

Two-tenths of a mile past the first large tuliptree, the trail curls to the left and down over a low ridge. Here in the "Valley of the Giants" large, old-growth white oaks and tuliptrees are common. Their wide crowns of large branches are particularly noticeable when the leaves are off the trees.

At mile 1.1 the trail passes close beside the great-granddaddy—the thickest tree in the Chattahoochee National Forest. This topped-out old tuliptree is 18 feet 3 inches around, measured 4 feet 6 inches from the ground, the standard measurement height. The deadfall-blocked roadbed continues.

This unmaintained route leads into the 1,240-acre Cooper Creek Scenic Area. Because it is not officially maintained, you can expect the number of deadfalls to increase the farther you walk.

Features
Stream, impressive old-growth tuliptrees, excellent spring wildflower display

Distance
1.1 miles

Difficulty Rating
Easy to moderate

County
Union

Nearest Cities
Blairsville (N), Dahlonega (S)

Maps
Suches and Mulky Gap Quadrangles, GA

Blazes
None; none needed

Ranger District
Toccoa

Highlights
Throughout: Excellent spring wildflower display from mid-April through early May.
Miles 0.4–1.1: Forest with many old-growth trees, the largest having a circumference of 18 feet 3 inches.

Directions
(See page 116 of Eyes on Wildlife Trail for directions to Cooper Creek Road.) From the GA 60–Cooper Creek Road junction, follow paved Cooper Creek Road (FS 33) straight ahead for 2.8 miles. After 2.4 miles, at the Cooper Creek Road–Grady Grizzle Road junction, the road turns to gravel. Continue on Cooper Creek Road approximately 0.4 mile to the gated, one-lane old road angling sharply downhill to the left. The trail begins behind the gate.

Note: The US Army regularly conducts training exercises in the Coopers Creek Wildlife Management Area. Although there is little threat of physical harm, army training complete with aircraft, marching soldiers, and small arms fire can quickly shatter the solitude you may be seeking. To avoid such noisy encounters, phone Camp Frank D. Merrill in Dahlonega and check the schedule before planning your hike. The number is (706) 864-3367, extension 114.

Notes

AMICALOLA FALLS
STATE PARK

Nestled along the southernmost edge of the Blue Ridge Mountain chain, this 1,440-acre park is primarily known for three features: its waterfall, its trail, and its lodge. Sliding and falling in stages, Amicalola Falls, a 729-foot drop, is the highest in Georgia. The 8.1-mile approach to the southern terminus of the Appalachian Trail at Springer Mountain begins behind the visitor center. One and one-half miles of the approach trail are within park boundaries.

Plentiful wildflowers and the usual high volume of "Amicalola"—the Cherokee's tumbling waters—make April and May ideal times to enjoy the park.

Trail to Base of Falls

The sound of rushing water accompanies you on this trail as it crosses and then follows Little Amicalola Creek up the hill. Benches for resting, occasional switchbacks, and rough pavement make the climb possible for just about everyone. Rock stairs and handrails help you negotiate the few short, steep spots as you wind through a cove hardwood forest along the cascading creek. Several large tuliptrees tower over the trail.

The view of the falls is worth the trip, even on a cloudy day. Take your time along the trail to look for a wide variety of wildflowers in this hardwood cove. Twelve interpretive stations located along the trail and near the reflection pool offer information about the wildlife of the area.

Highlights
Mile 0.3: Amicalola Falls—a spectacular 729-foot cascade—the highest waterfall in Georgia.

Directions
Amicalola Falls State Park is located on the

WBR
Springer Mountain
Amicalola Falls
State Park

Features
Highest waterfall in Georgia, stream, interpretive signs

Distance
0.3 mile

Difficulty Rating
Easy to moderate

County
Dawson

Nearest Cities
Dahlonega (E),
Ellijay (NW),
Dawsonville (SE)

Maps
Nimblewill
Quadrangle, GA;
park map available
at visitor center

Blazes
None; none needed

Campsites
Available with
reservation in park
campground

north side of GA 52 between Dahlonega and Ellijay. The park can be accessed from many different directions; the three easiest routes, however, are from Dahlonega, Dawsonville, and Ellijay. There are numerous park signs to direct you.

From the Ellijay square travel GA 52 East approximately 21.0 miles.

From the Dahlonega square travel GA 52 West approximately 18.0 miles.

From the Dawsonville square travel GA 53 West and GA 183 North before turning right onto GA 52 East. The distance to the park entrance is approximately 15.0 miles.

After entering the park, continue straight ahead on the main road past the visitor center, picnic shelters, and cabins. The parking area for the trailhead is on the road's turnaround loop. The trail begins near the reflection pool.

Notes

West Ridge Trail

WBR
Springer Mountain
Amicalola Falls State Park

The West Ridge Trail is actually a network of footpaths that totals 1.7 miles. The park map labels each of the network's four segments with its own name, and each of the four segments has its own blaze color. If you start and end across the road from the visitor center and walk all of the labeled segments, you will walk approximately 2.3 miles.

Three trails form the loop: The Creek Trail (yellow blazes), the Lower West Ridge Trail (red blazes), and the Upper West Ridge Trail (green blazes). The Creek Trail begins at a wooden bridge across the road from the visitor center and ascends 80 to 100 feet above Little Amicalola Creek. After about 0.2 mile, it ties into the Lower West Ridge Trail. Bear right to follow the loop in a counterclockwise direction. Follow this fairly flat trail through sparse patches of mountain laurel, Virginia pine, oak, and blackgum trees until it meets the Upper West Ridge Trail. Bear right again and ascend gradually through a series of laurel-covered switchbacks to an intersection with the West Ridge Spring Trail (orange blazes), a 0.3-mile spur trail that takes you to a spring and picnic area. The considerable number of downed trees you'll see in this area are the result of the blizzard in March 1993. To continue along the loop bear right and follow the green blazes as the trail descends back toward the creek where it meets the Creek Trail to close the loop.

During the winter, you can see the Burnt Mountain system from several locations on the trail. On the forest floor near the path, several kinds of wildflowers may catch your eye. Galax is common, and small patches of trailing arbutus and wild ginger thrive here and there beneath the trees.

Features
Stream, forest

Distance
1.7 miles (loop)

Difficulty Rating
Easy to moderate

County
Dawson

Nearest Cities
Dahlonega (E),
Ellijay (NW),
Dawsonville (SE)

Maps
Nimblewill and
Amicalola
Quadrangles, GA;
park map available
at visitor center

Blazes
Four different colors
for the entire
network

Campsites
Available with
reservation in park
campground

Highlights
Winter views from several locations along the trail.

Directions

(See page 124 of Trail to Base of Falls for directions to the Amicalola Falls State Park entrance.) This trail has multiple access points. The visitor center has a pamphlet that describes the park's trails. This description of the West Ridge Trail begins at the access point across the road and field from the visitor center, which is on the main (lower) park road.

Notes

Amicalola Wildlife Interpretive Trail

B ecause three of the facts stated in this description differ from what you will see at the trailhead, an explanation is necessary. The trail distance (2.5 miles) given here was wheel measured. The stream is signed Amicalola River at the bridge, but named Amicalola Creek on the topo sheet, in the DNR fishing regulations pamphlet, and in a prominent canoeing guide. And finally, the name for this trail comes from its interpretive pamphlet rather than the longer name on the trailhead sign.

The construction of the Amicalola Wildlife Interpretive Trail was a cooperative effort between DNR and the Boy Scouts. Located in the hilly Dahlonega Upland District of the uppermost Piedmont, this trail has thirty-five interpretive signs. The signs and trailhead pamphlet describe a wide range of human and natural history subjects. These interpretive stations identify trees and wildlife foods, point out some of the many wildlife boxes (including a box for overwintering butterflies), demonstrate wildlife management practices, and much more. DNR makes an effort to keep the pamphlets available at the trailhead.

The beginning 35 yards of the trail descend sharply on rocks to the canoe launch site on Amicalola Creek. Here, not far from its end at the Etowah River, mountain-born Amicalola Creek is river width and perhaps the most scenic stream in the Piedmont. The creek is scenic because it looks just like a mountain stream: green where it is deep and slow, clear where it is shallow and gliding, white and gray where it is fast through rock.

The first segment of the trail closely parallels the wide creek through a forest and understory resembling low-elevation stream-corridor forests further north. The footpath passes beside Edge of the World rapid at 0.3 mile. This Class IV rapid has a horizon

Piedmont
Dawson Forest Wildlife Management Area
Amicalola Tract

Features
Interpretive signs, Amicalola Creek, views

Distance
2.5 miles (loop)

Difficulty Rating
Easy to moderate

County
Dawson

Nearest Cities
Dawsonville (E), Marblehill (W)

Map
Juno Quadrangle, GA

Blazes
Blue

Campsites
Camping is not permitted along the trail; primitive camping opportunities exist elsewhere on the Dawson Forest WMA

line from bank to bank: to the approaching canoeist the creek drops from sight, creating a strong urge to stop and scout. During high water this rapid is impressively powerful.

One-tenth mile beyond Edge of the World, the treadway turns uphill and away from the creek at the arrow and double blaze. Here it enters an oak-pine forest which closely resembles typical upland Piedmont stands to the south. Eastern white pine and chestnut oak are evidence of the transitional nature of the forest.

Seldom level for long, this well-blazed, easily followed loop winds in and out of small rivulet hollows divided by low ridges. Most of the grades are easy or easy to moderate.

The footpath comes to the first of its three surprises at mile 1.4. To the right there is a man-made view of a straight stretch of the shoaling creek, sparkling silver on sunny days. A short distance beyond the view, the treadway reaches a small opening with a concrete picnic table and a monument for a young Boy Scout who died in 1991. At mile 2.2, as the trail starts to descend from the highest ridge along the loop, an interpretive sign informs you that the view to the north is of Springer Mountain (3,782 feet).

Highlights
Mile 0.3: Class IV Edge of the World rapids.
Mile 1.4: Long-distance view of a straight run of Amicalola Creek.
Mile 2.2: View of Springer Mountain to the north.

Directions
The trailhead sign and pull-off parking area are located on the southeastern side of the GA 53 bridge over Amicalola Creek. This bridge spans the wide creek on the segment of GA 53 between Dawsonville and Tate.

From the GA 53–GA 108 junction in Tate, travel GA 53 East for 13.0 miles to the bridge.

From the Dawsonville square continue 6.5 miles on GA 53 West to the bridge.

Notes

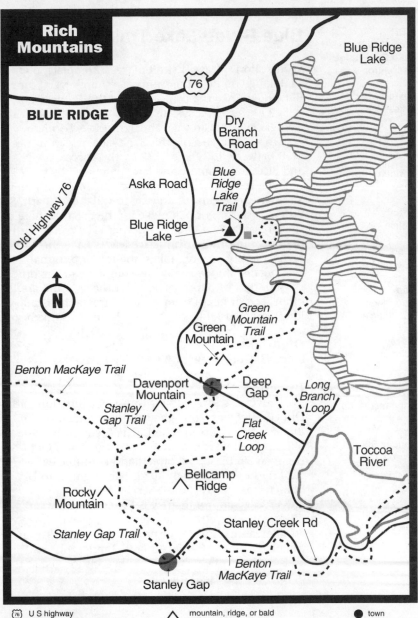

Rich Mountains

Blue Ridge Lake

76

BLUE RIDGE

Dry Branch Road

Old Highway 76

Aska Road

Blue Ridge Lake Trail

Blue Ridge Lake

N

Green Mountain Trail

Green Mountain

Benton MacKaye Trail

Davenport Mountain

Deep Gap

Long Branch Loop

Stanley Gap Trail

Flat Creek Loop

Toccoa River

Bellcamp Ridge

Rocky Mountain

Stanley Creek Rd

Stanley Gap Trail

Benton MacKaye Trail

Stanley Gap

76	U S highway	⋀	mountain, ridge, or bald	●	town
⑩	Georgia state highway	∿	stream, creek, or river	⏃	campground
FS 654	Forest Service road	⋯	marked trail	●	mountain gap

WBR
Rich Mountains
**Lake Blue Ridge
Recreation Area**

Features
Lakeshore

Distance
0.6 mile (loop)

Difficulty Rating
Easy

County
Fannin

Nearest City
Blue Ridge

Map
Blue Ridge
Quadrangle, GA

Blazes
None; none needed

Campsites
Available seasonally
in the recreation
area campground

Ranger District
Toccoa

Blue Ridge Lake Trail

This short, pleasant stroll makes a complete loop, taking you near the scenic lakeshore several times. Blue Ridge Lake is a component of the Tennessee Valley Authority, a system of impoundments in North Georgia, North Carolina, and Tennessee. Formerly known as Lake Toccoa, this 3,290-acre reservoir was built between 1929 and 1932 by the Toccoa Power and Electric Company and later purchased by the TVA.

The trail passes through a mixed forest of pines and hardwoods and is an easy-to-walk, level path. Six different species of oak make up the greatest share of the larger hardwoods. The southern red oak is particularly common. Its distinctive leaves have three to seven sharply pointed lobes; the top or terminal lobe is elongated and very narrow compared to the others.

Pileated woodpeckers inhabit the area and are often seen or heard drumming on trees. Their call—a loud, irregular kik-kik-kik-kik-kik!—may also be heard.

Highlights
Mile 0.3: Good view of Blue Ridge Lake.

Directions
Travel GA 515–US 76 North to its junction with Old US Highway 76 in the southwestern corner of Blue Ridge. At this junction, which currently has a blinking yellow traffic light, turn right onto Old US Highway 76 (East First Street) and continue eastward 3.3 miles to Dry Branch Road. Turn right onto Dry Branch Road at the Forest Service sign.

Proceed approximately 2.1 miles (the last 0.6 mile is dirt-gravel) to the paved entrance of the recreation area. Just inside the entrance, turn left toward the picnic area. After less than 0.2 mile, this road ends at a parking area. The trailhead is located at the back end of the parking lot.

Green Mountain Trail

WBR
Rich Mountains
Aska Trails Area

Green Mountain's unusual configuration makes it a modern trail—full of features and options. It has three trailhead access points, two trailheads, one loop, one out and back linear segment, and one connector. From its Deep Gap end the trail forms a 1.9-mile loop with both ends of the loop on Aska Road, 40 yards apart. At the top of the loop the linear segment stretches 2.8 miles to the northeastern trailhead at Blue Ridge Lake. Along the way a connector ties into another trail—Long Branch Loop.

The following description starts slightly below Deep Gap (2,200 feet) and follows the signed entrance of the loop, the one to the left across Aska Road. The trail enters the oak-pine forest on a cut-in path. Although the hardwoods dominate as usual, eastern white, shortleaf, and Virginia pines are common along this trail. As is almost always the case beneath the south-slope, oak-pine forests of this region, mountain laurel is often abundant.

The treadway alternates short, steep ridge climbs with longer, easier grades on the southeastern slope. The route rises onto the ridge crest of Green Mountain, the highest elevation (2,520 feet) on the trail, at 0.6 mile. It then dips 0.2 mile to its signed junction at a roadbed.

If you want to walk only the loop portion of the trail, curl down and to the right onto the roadbed. The remainder of the loop follows the very easy grades of the woods road 1.1 miles back down to Aska Road.

The linear segment of the trail continues straight ahead from the junction. The first 0.5 mile alternates short, moderate, downridge runs with longer, easier grades on east-facing slopes. At mile 1.3 (mileage continuing from Deep Gap) the treadway passes the signed junction for the 0.5-mile connector to the Long Branch Loop.

Features
Winter views, Blue Ridge Lake

Distance
(See description)

Difficulty Rating
Moderate

County
Fannin

Nearest City
Blue Ridge

Maps
Blue Ridge Quadrangle, GA; Aska Trails Area pamphlet available from ranger district

Blazes
White

Water Sources
Mile 2.4: wet weather spring; mile 2.5: permanent branch; mile 2.8: permanent rivulet

Ranger District
Toccoa

Beyond the connector the trail—again a cut-in path—loses elevation gradually on winding, moister slopes. At mile 1.7 the path rounds a tulip-tree hollow with a good spring wildflower display. The broad white flowers of bloodroot appear on the forest floor in early spring.

Continuing to the northeast, the path descends again on a low spur ridge where the damage from Hurricane Opal is obvious and extensive. The now-cleared route ties into an old roadbed at mile 2.3. The roadbed descends to and then winds through an area of springs and small streams near lake level. By mile 2.6 the trail begins to follow the shoreline of Blue Ridge Lake (1,720 feet).

Most of the remaining trail undulates on easy grades close to the lake. Here there are many winter and close-range year-round views of the green water. At mile 3.1 the roadbed rises over a low ridge, descends, then angles to the right onto blazed path. The final 0.2 mile curls around two hollows where a number of large white oaks were blown down by the hurricane in 1995. These large trees will be cleared with a salvage cut.

Highlights

Miles 0.2–1.2: Winter views of a long string of named knobs and mountains to the east.

Miles 0.6–3.4: Numerous winter views of Blue Ridge Lake.

Miles 2.6–3.4: Occasional year-round views of Blue Ridge Lake.

Directions

From the GA 5–US 76 junction in Blue Ridge (where GA 5 heads north to McCaysville at the McDonald's) travel US 76 East for 0.7 mile to Windy Ridge Road (the first right past the Wendy's). Turn right onto Windy Ridge Road and continue a short distance to a three-way intersection. Turn left at this intersection and continue 0.1 mile before turning right onto signed Aska Road across from Harmony Baptist Church.

To the southwestern, Deep Gap trailhead: Travel Aska Road for approximately 4.5 miles to the Deep Gap parking area. This parking area is to the right of the road just past Deep Gap, the road's highest point. The Green Mountain Trail begins across Aska Road at the trail sign to the left.

To the northeastern, Blue Ridge Lake trailhead: Travel Aska Road for approximately 2.4 miles before turning left onto signed Campbell Camp Road. Proceed 0.7 mile (past private property), then turn left onto FS 711, marked with a brown carsonite sign. Continue 1.5 miles (stay right at the fork) to the parking area to the right and the trailhead bulletin board on the left.

Flat Creek Loop

WBR
Rich Mountains
Aska Trails Area

Walked in a counterclockwise direction, the loop follows the southeastern slopes of Davenport Mountain to the headwaters of Flat Creek. After crossing the creek the first time, the route traverses the lower north-facing slopes of Bellcamp Ridge before crossing the creek again. The remainder of the trail winds along the lower southeastern slopes of Davenport Mountain, where hollows and ridge spurs are more defined. By changing elevation and expo-sure—and by paralleling the creek—this loop takes full advantage of the area's diversity.

Flat Creek is surrounded by the Blue Ridge and its spurs. Here the Blue Ridge is also the Tennessee Valley Divide. Flat Creek flows west to east to the Toccoa River. The Toccoa heads north into Tennessee where its name changes to the Ocoee, a well-known white-water river.

After less than 0.1 mile, Flat Creek comes to its first signed fork. The northern end of the white-blazed Stanley Gap Trail is to the right. Rising easily on a for-mer logging road, Flat Creek reaches the signed begin-ning of its loop at 0.5 mile. This description heads to the right (counterclockwise). One-tenth mile past the loop's beginning, a signed, green-blazed connector leads up and to the right 0.1 mile to the Stanley Gap Trail.

Beyond the connector walking is easy on the woods-road through an oak-pine forest. Virginia pine is especially common on spur ridges and portions of the upslope to the right. At mile 2.3 both the trail and forest change. Here the route descends through a young hardwood forest dominated by sweet birch, tuliptree, and white oak. The rocky seepage slope to the left supports a good stand of spring wildflowers.

By mile 2.6 the downgrade parallels Flat Creek through a green passageway of eastern hemlock and rosebay rhododendron. Farther down and away from

Features
Streams, winter views

Distance
5.8 miles (loop)

Difficulty Rating
Easy to moderate

Counties
Fannin and Gilmer

Nearest City
Blue Ridge

Maps
Blue Ridge Quadrangle, GA; Aska Trails Area pamphlet available from ranger district

Blazes
Green and white circles

Water Sources
At frequent intervals

Ranger District
Toccoa

the stream the trail—a cut path—snakes through hardwood saplings regenerating from logging. Back on roadbed, the route curls left onto path (marked by a carsonite sign) and crosses Flat Creek—shallow and less than 15 feet wide in high water—at mile 4.2. This unbridged stream is a rock-step crossing in warm, dry weather.

The remaining 1.1 miles of the loop heads uphill, on easy or easy-to-moderate grades, on roadbed and cut path. Here the forest varies from dry oak-pine to moister hardwood hollows dominated by tuliptree.

Highlights

Miles 0.5-2.1: Occasional winter views, primarily of Bellcamp Ridge to the left, south.

Mile 2.4: Rocky seepage slope with a good spring wildflower display under hardwoods.

Mile 2.7: Long cascading run on Flat Creek.

Directions

(See page 132 of Green Mountain Trail for directions to Aska Road.) Travel Aska Road for approximately 4.5 miles to the Deep Gap parking area. This parking area is to the right just past Deep Gap, the road's highest point.

The trailhead is at the back of the parking area.

Notes

Stanley Gap Trail

WBR
Rich Mountains
Aska Trails Area

While Stanley Gap is a new trail, much of its treadway is not. This ridge and upper-slope segment of trail, from Deep Gap to Stanley Gap, was part of the old Rich Mountain Trail, which no longer exists by that name. Stanley Gap Trail has either-end vehicular access. Because its Deep Gap end is easily reached by paved road, this description starts at Deep Gap and ends at Stanley Gap.

Walked as it is described, this trail heads southwest on Davenport Mountain and its ridges for roughly half its length. The route then bends to the southeast, climbing Rocky Mountain before descending with its ridges to the gap. Once it bends to the southeast, the trail follows the famous Blue Ridge and the Tennessee Valley Divide.

From the trailhead parking area slightly below Deep Gap (2,200 feet), walk the Flat Creek Loop for 0.1 mile to the signed beginning of the white-blazed Stanley Gap Trail, which leads up and to the right. The path winds through hardwood hollows as it rises to the upper southern slopes of Davenport Mountain, a Rocky Mountain spur. The route continues to ascend as it passes below Davenport's crown and rises to the ridge top between Davenport and the unnamed (yet higher) peak further to the southwest. At 0.8 mile a green-blazed connector leads down and to the left 0.1 mile to Flat Creek Loop.

Instead of following the ridge top up and over each crest, the trail works its way up gradually, alternating between ridge top and upper slope. Where the ridge rises sharply, the path angles off it and ascends more slowly on the slope.

Continuing from the connector, the treadway climbs steadily with the ridge before slabbing to the left onto upper slope and hollow. The trail continues to ascend through an oak-pine forest with occasional dense stands of Virginia pine and mountain laurel

Features
Winter views, spring wildflowers

Distance
4.9 miles

Difficulty Rating
Moderate

Counties
Gilmer and Fannin

Nearest City
Blue Ridge

Map
Blue Ridge Quadrangle, GA; Aska Trails Area pamphlet available from ranger district

Blazes
White

Water Sources
Miles 0.0–0.8: rivulet tributaries of Flat Creek; mile 3.5: trail passes 50 feet above a seasonal spring

Ranger District
Toccoa

thickets. The white-diamond-blazed Benton MacKaye Trail ties in at mile 2.3 (approximately 3,160 feet) and shares the route.

Turning to the southeast, the two trails ascend toward the top of Rocky Mountain (3,442 feet) before angling onto its eastern flank. The route passes approximately 120 feet below Rocky Mountain's crown as it begins its 1000-foot descent to Stanley Gap. At mile 4.3 the Benton MacKaye splits away to the left. On its own again the path descends, occasionally through stands of pine. The trail's final stretch follows a woods road to Stanley Gap (2,320 feet).

Highlights

Miles 1.0–4.6: Good winter views of Blue Ridge Lake, the city of Blue Ridge, Aska Road Valley, and ridges in all directions. South of Rocky Mountain there are winter views to the south and southwest of Big Bald (4,081 feet, south) and Cold Mountain (3,846 feet, southwest) only 3.0 miles away. Beyond those two mountains are the high peaks of the Rich Mountain Wilderness.

Miles 1.0–3.8: An open, mature, predominantly hardwood forest.

Directions

(See page 132 of Green Mountain Trail for directions to Aska Road.)

To the northern, Deep Gap trailhead: Travel Aska Road for approximately 4.5 miles to the Deep Gap parking area. This parking area is to the right just past Deep Gap—the road's highest point. The Stanley Gap–Flat Creek Loop junction is 0.1 mile from the trailhead at the back of the parking area.

To the southern, Stanley Gap trailhead: From Blue Ridge travel Aska Road for approximately 8.0 miles (3.5 miles past the Deep Gap parking area), then turn right onto signed Stanley Creek Road, also marked with a large Rich Mountain Wildlife Management Area sign. Proceed straight ahead on this wide, dirt-gravel road.

After approximately 3.2 miles you will pass pull-off parking on the right for the Benton MacKaye Trail (white diamond blazes). Continue another 0.8 mile to Stanley Gap (the road's highest point), where a sign marks the road to the right that leads immediately to the trailhead parking area and bulletin board.

Long Branch Loop

Much of this logging-road loop winds through a recent shelterwood cut. Many of the tall trees that were left standing, however, were blown down by Hurricane Opal in 1995. A year later, the area was just beginning its regeneration process. In a few years stump sprouts and saplings will create a shrubby habitat preferred by many songbirds. A sapling thicket will form in five to ten years. If the trail is not well maintained, briers will be a problem until the saplings shade them out.

The trail reaches its signed loop at 0.2 mile. The following mileages follow the loop down and to the right in a counterclockwise direction. At 0.9 mile a signed connector leads 0.5 mile to the Green Mountain Trail. This blazed path rises through forest and affords winter views of Blue Ridge Lake.

One-tenth mile beyond the connector, the route crosses Long Branch—a long step wide—and ascends easily to the upper hill slope of the cut. The remainder of the loop winds through the regenerating area.

Directions

(See page 132 of Green Mountain Trail for directions to Aska Road.) Travel Aska Road for approximately 6.0 miles before turning left onto paved Shady Falls Road. (If the road sign is missing, look for Flat Creek Road, the next left past Shady Falls Road.) Continue slightly less than 0.2 mile on Shady Falls Road, then turn left onto the first road to the left. The road's left fork quickly ends at the trailhead parking area.

WBR
Rich Mountains
Aska Trails Area

Features
Stream

Distance
2.3 miles (loop)

Difficulty Rating
Easy to moderate

County
Fannin

Nearest City
Blue Ridge

Maps
Blue Ridge
Quadrangle, GA;
Aska Trails Area
pamphlet available
from ranger district

Blazes
Green and white
circles

Ranger District
Toccoa

COHUTTA WILDERNESS

Officially designated on January 3, 1975, the Cohutta Wilderness now encompasses 36,977 acres—35,268 acres within Georgia and the remainder in Tennessee. The Georgia portion of the wilderness is located northeast of Chatsworth, primarily in Fannin and Murray counties.

The Georgia Wilderness Bill of 1986 added 2,940 acres, all within the Chattahoochee National Forest, to the Cohutta Wilderness. This new designation extended the Cohutta to the northeast, from Dally Gap along FS 22 to the Tennessee line.

Although much of this wilderness was logged earlier in the century, the forest has returned, healing the scarred land and obliterating all but the smallest traces of man's past exploitation. With continued wilderness designation and the passage of time, the forest will slowly regain much of its former magnificence.

A network of fifteen trails totaling 87 miles penetrates this rugged wilderness, where elevations range from 950 to 4,200 feet. All but three of these trails lead to or follow the scenic Jacks and Conasauga Rivers, whose headwaters are protected by National Forest land in and around the wilderness. These two rivers are among the few larger streams in North Georgia that still offer quality wild-trout fishing.

Tennessee's 8,082-acre Big Frog Wilderness in the Cherokee National Forest is contiguous with the Cohutta Wilderness along the Cohutta's northern border.

Note: Trails in the Cohutta Wilderness are organized east to west downstream along the Jacks River and Conasauga River watersheds. East Cowpen Trail cuts through the center of the wilderness and runs along the Cohutta Mountain ridge that divides the two watersheds.

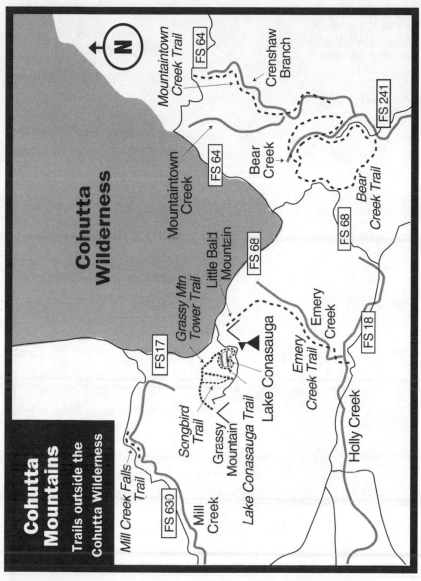

Cohutta Mountains

Trails outside the
Cohutta Wilderness

Cohutta Wilderness

Mountaintown Creek Trail

FS 64

Crenshaw Branch

FS 241

Mountaintown Creek

FS 64

Bear Creek

Little Bald Mountain

FS 68

Bear Creek Trail

Grassy Mtn Tower Trail

FS 68

Lake Conasauga

FS 17

Emery Creek

FS 18

Songbird Trail

Emery Creek Trail

Grassy Mountain

Lake Conasauga Trail

Mill Creek Falls Trail

Mill Creek

FS 630

Holly Creek

76 U S highway
60 Georgia state highway
FS 654 Forest Service road

mountain, ridge, or bald
stream, creek, or river
marked trail

town
campground
mountain gap

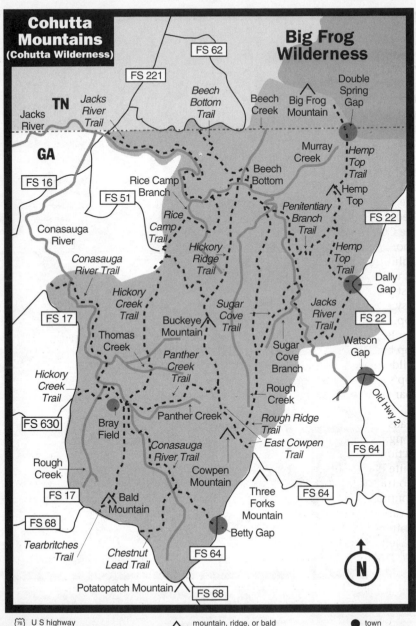

Cohutta Mountains
(Cohutta Wilderness)

Big Frog Wilderness

FS 62

FS 221

TN

Jacks River

Jacks River Trail

GA

Jacks River

FS 16

FS 51

Rice Camp Branch

Conasauga River

Conasauga River Trail

Rice Camp Trail

Hickory Ridge Trail

Beech Bottom Trail

Beech Creek

Beech Bottom

Double Spring Gap

Big Frog Mountain

Murray Creek

Hemp Top Trail

Hemp Top

FS 22

Penitentiary Branch Trail

Hemp Top Trail

Dally Gap

Hickory Creek Trail

FS 17

Thomas Creek

Buckeye Mountain

Sugar Cove Trail

Jacks River Trail

FS 22

Panther Creek Trail

Sugar Cove Branch

Watson Gap

Hickory Creek Trail

FS 630

Bray Field

Panther Creek

Rough Creek

Rough Ridge Trail

East Cowpen Trail

Old Hwy 2

FS 64

Rough Creek

FS 17

FS 68

Conasauga River Trail

Cowpen Mountain

Bald Mountain

Three Forks Mountain

FS 64

Tearbritches Trail

Chestnut Lead Trail

Betty Gap

FS 64

Potatopatch Mountain

FS 68

N

76 U S highway
60 Georgia state highway
FS 654 Forest Service road

⋀ mountain, ridge, or bald
〜 stream, creek, or river
▬ ▪ marked trail

● town
⌇ campground
● mountain gap

Hemp Top Trail

WBR
Cohutta Mountains
Cohutta Wilderness

This trail and the mountain it climbs over are named for a local crop that was once important for both the Cherokee and European settlers. Cherokee women wove their hemp into rope, fishnets, and cloth. Hemp, the kind made into rope, was listed as one of Fannin County's major cash crops in 1860.

Hemp Top is primarily an upper slope and ridge trail, which makes it a good winter view walk. The old Hemp Top, which was 2.1 miles long, began at the former trailhead atop Hemp Top Mountain. The Georgia Wilderness Bill of 1986 added 2,940 acres to the Cohutta Wilderness, all within the Chattahoochee National Forest. This addition extended the Cohutta to the northeast, from Dally Gap along FS 22 to the Tennessee line. The new Hemp Top Trail's first 4.1 miles follow the wide, level treadway and easy grades of former FS 73, from Dally Gap to Hemp Top.

Beyond the Penitentiary Branch junction, Hemp Top becomes the least traveled trail in the Cohutta Wilderness. Walked alone during the week, Hemp Top's woods can become big and lonely. Bear and boar spoor are common.

Starting at Dally Gap (2,578 feet), Hemp Top heads north through a second-growth oak-pine forest along the Blue Ridge and the Tennessee Valley Divide. Section 10 of the Benton MacKaye Trail, marked with white diamonds, ties into Hemp Top at 0.9 mile. The two trails share the same treadway to Big Frog Mountain in Tennessee. Hemp Top continues to gain elevation on easy grades to its signed junction with Penitentiary Branch Trail, which drops down and to the left, at mile 2.3.

The forest becomes increasingly hardwood, dominated by the oaks as usual, as the trail gains elevation. Shagbark hickories are relatively common here. At mile 4.1 the route arrives at the former trailhead

Features
Wilderness,
Big Frog Mountain,
winter views

Distance
6.2 miles

Difficulty Rating
Moderate to
strenuous

Counties
Fannin, GA and
Polk, TN

Nearest Cities
Blue Ridge (E),
Ellijay (S)

Maps
Hemp Top
Quadrangle, GA-TN;
Cohutta Wilderness
map

Blazes
White

Water Sources
Mile 5.4: Double
Spring Gap—a
seasonal seepage
spring, sometimes
boar-wallowed—to
either side of gap;
mile 6.2: seasonal
spring 0.4 mile to the
left (west) on Licklog
Trail

Ranger District
Cohutta

and former fire tower site—the crown of Hemp Top Mountain (3,580 feet). Atop the mountain the trail turns left and down onto a path that quickly descends to an old woods road. Except for three uphill grades along the way—two short and easy, the other longer and moderate—the treadway steadily descends to Double Spring Gap (3,220 feet) at mile 5.4.

Double Spring Gap is located at the intersection of an east-west running political boundary and a north-south running geographical boundary. The political border separates states, national forests, counties, and wildernesses. The geographical boundary is the Tennessee Valley Divide, which separates major watersheds.

Less than 100 yards above Double Spring Gap, a sign welcomes you to Tennessee and the Cherokee National Forest. Beyond that sign, Hemp Top serves as the boundary between Tennessee's 8,082-acre Big Frog Wilderness on the right and the Cohutta Wilderness on the left. It is also beyond that sign that Hemp Top begins its strenuous, uninterrupted climb up Big Frog Mountain. There are no switchbacks to decrease exertion; the old road ascends straight up—and up.

Hemp Top meets Licklog Trail (4,040 feet) at a right angle along the Cohutta–Big Frog Wilderness boundary. If you turn left (northwest) onto Licklog Trail toward the high point of Big Frog Mountain, you will come to a seasonal spring after 0.4 mile. Licklog Trail ends at its junction with Wolf Ridge and Big Frog Trails atop Big Frog Mountain (4,200 feet) slightly more than 0.1 mile beyond the spring.

Highlights
Throughout: Winter views.
Mile 6.2: Big Frog Mountain, the highest peak (4,200 feet) in the combined Cohutta-Big Frog Wilderness.
Mile 6.2: Dark orange-red flame azalea display that peaks in June atop Big Frog Mountain.

Directions
From the US 76–GA 5 intersection just north of Blue Ridge, travel north on GA 5 toward McCaysville for 3.7 miles. Turn left onto Old GA 2 at the "Old State Route 2" sign and small Watson Gap sign. Continue on this road for approximately 10.5 miles (the pavement ends at mile 9.0) to the major Forest Service intersection at Watson Gap. Turn hard right at the gap onto FS 22 (one lane) and drive approximately 3.6 miles to the trailhead at Dally Gap. Standing in the gap, Hemp Top Trail is up and to the right, behind its locked gate and sign. (Jacks River Trail is down and to the left.)

Jacks River Trail

WBR
Cohutta Mountains
Cohutta Wilderness

The Jacks bears the name of the obviously stout Cherokee who, for a small fee, ferried travelers across the river on his back in Alaculsy Valley. The Jacks River Trail is the longest and wettest (forty-two fords) in the Cohutta Wilderness. The river it follows and crosses is also the most popular destination in the wilderness. A network of seven trails leads day hikers and backpackers directly to this trail and its river, so expect to have plenty of company on weekends and holidays (but don't expect Jack to help you across the fords).

If you are interested in walking Jacks River Trail from end to end, you may want to start at its southeastern (upstream) Dally Gap Trailhead (2,578 feet). This route travels downriver and downhill, losing about 1,050 feet to Beech Bottom at mile 8.6 and slightly more than 1,600 feet to its end in Alaculsy Valley.

The trail follows a wide, easily walked old road from Dally Gap. For the most part, this first section is a gentle downhill stroll through hardwood forest to the Jacks River and its tributary, Bear Branch. Along the way, where the white-blazed Benton MacKaye Trail ties into the Jacks River Trail for a very short distance, there are two large eastern hemlocks to the left. The larger of the two—13 feet 2 inches in circumference and 133 feet in height—is the most recent of the last three state record eastern hemlocks found in the Cohutta Wilderness.

Although it parallels Bear Branch from the gap, the trail does not approach closely enough for a view until mile 1.6. Three-tenths of a mile farther, the trail trades streams and follows the Jacks as it winds toward the northwest. This turn is only a few hundred yards from where the river enters the wilderness.

At mile 2.3 the trail crosses the Jacks—the first of twenty fords to the falls. As on the Conasauga River Trail, a blaze usually guides the trail's return to dry

Features
Wilderness, Jacks River Falls, cascades, pools, and bluffs

Distance
16.7 miles

Difficulty Rating
From Dally Gap downstream to northwestern trailhead in Alaculsy Valley: easy to moderate; from Alaculsy Valley upstream to trailhead at Dally Gap: moderate

Counties
Fannin and Murray

Nearest Cities
Blue Ridge (E), Ellijay (S), Chatsworth (SW)

Maps
Hemp Top and Tennga Quadrangles, GA-TN; Cohutta Wilderness map

Blazes
Orange

Water Sources
Jacks River and its tributaries

Ranger District
Cohutta

land across the river from each ford. These blazes, however, are not always easy to spot. Part of the challenge of Jacks River Trail is figuring out where the fords begin and end. Often you need to angle downstream while fording the river to locate the blaze and worn spot on the opposite bank. Just remember that the trail, even on islands, always heads downriver. (See page 162 of the Conasauga River Trail, also in the Cohutta Wilderness, for further descriptions of the fords and their potential dangers.)

Much of today's trail, including some of the fords, follows the path of a former logging railroad used to transport timber out of the mountains during the early 1930s. In places, parallel rows of the slowly rotting ties are still visible. You may still find hand-forged railroad spikes of several different sizes. If you are walking in an aisle-like section—straight, level and wide—you are probably on the former railroad bed. It was flattened by horse-drawn scrapes and, later, by steam shovel. Logging along the Jacks River began in 1929. By 1937 the railroad had been dismantled.

Along the riverbanks near many of the fords, look for the piled-rock buttresses that mark the location of the trestles that once spanned the river. A flood washed these bridges away nearly 60 years ago.

The high shoals below the second ford begin the river's most turbulent stretch. For nearly a mile the river, especially during high water, is one long ricocheting cascade, more white than not. Here the Jacks exhibits the steep-sided, V-shaped profile of a youthful river cutting into mountain. Where the Jacks descends, so does the trail. It may climb a hillside, but it always drops back to the river.

Starting with the fourth crossing at mile 4.6, you wade the river fifteen times in 2.5 miles. These fords come in quick succession, most only 0.1 or 0.2 mile apart. The trail remains nearly level and parallel to the river between crossings to its eighteenth ford at mile 7.1. The Penitentiary Branch Trail junction is in the campsite across from this ford.

Beyond the next (nineteenth) ford, the trail climbs a short distance up and away from the river, then descends to cross Rough Creek at mile 8.0. Rough Ridge Trail ties into the Jacks River Trail immediately across the creek. If you turn left and follow the creek upstream, you will be on Rough Ridge Trail. Jacks River Trail turns right and closely parallels the creek downstream before swinging to the left, above and then away from the river. Once it leaves the Jacks, the trail gently ascends to a ridge, then slopes down to its twentieth and final ford before the falls. The section of trail between the nineteenth and twentieth fords twice appears to lead up and away from the river. But it is actually the river that twice meanders away from the trail. And both times, instead of following the river, the trail takes the short cut straight across the gap.

Beyond the twentieth crossing, the Jacks River Trail reaches two junctions, one right after the other at mile 8.6. The first, to the left, is yellow-blazed Hickory Ridge. The second, to the right 45 yards farther downstream, is unblazed Beech Bottom. The end of Hickory Ridge has been rerouted since it was drawn on the Cohutta Wilderness map. If you are walking the Jacks River Trail downstream toward the falls, you will reach the Hickory Ridge junction before you reach the Beech Bottom junction.

The trail continues to follow the river downstream to the cliffs above Jacks River Falls at mile 9.2. Dropping in stages at the head of a wide gorge, this waterfall is the most scenic and most visited single feature in the Cohutta Wilderness. It is also the most powerful falls in the North Georgia backcountry. The dark-pink blooms of the Piedmont rhododendron usually peak from May 15th through June 5th, adding to the beauty of the Jacks River Falls area and other rocky, open areas along the river corridor.

If you would like to see and hear Jacks River Falls at its frothing, roaring best, wait until winter or early spring, after several days of heavy rains. Then, on a sunny day, the waterfall becomes one long, crashing, upwelling run of brilliant white water. Beech Bottom Trail enables you to reach the falls without having to ford the river.

Beyond the falls, the trail follows an obvious railroad cut down to the river's edge. It reaches the twenty-first ford, the first in 1.8 miles, at mile 10.3. Here the pattern of crossing and paralleling the river begins again. Only this time the trail remains level or slightly downhill between crossings.

Downstream from the start of the twenty-sixth ford, you will see the first of several tall bluffs along the lower Jacks. The gap at the top of this bluff is Horseshoe Bend Overlook. If you want a good look at the sheer rock around the bend, keep walking down the bank after the crossing. Beyond the forty-second and final ford at mile 14.8, the last section of trail remains close to the river, occasionally close enough for long-range views. Here, as it flows toward its meeting with the Conasauga River just outside the wilderness boundary, the Jacks becomes wider and less turbulent, its pools longer and deeper.The Jacks River Trail ends next to a bridge in Alaculsy Valley (966 feet).

Starting from its southeastern terminus at Dally Gap, the distances to the Jacks River Trail's junctions are as follows: Benton MacKaye Trail, 0.9 mile; Sugar Cove, 3.9 miles; Penitentiary Branch, 7.2 miles; Rough Ridge, 8.0 miles; Hickory Ridge, 8.6 miles; Beech Bottom, 8.7 miles; Rice Camp, 10.4 miles.

Highlights

Miles 2.6, 3.6: Excellent views of the Jacks River as it cascades through the mountains.

Mile 9.2: Jacks River Falls—an impressive 80-foot, two-tier waterfall.

Mile 11.8: Bluffs along the western side of the river at Horseshoe Bend.

Directions

To the northwestern trailhead in Alaculsy Valley: From the GA 52–US 411 intersection in Chatsworth, travel US 411 North approximately 13.4 miles, past Eton toward Tennga, to the community of Cisco. In Cisco, turn right onto the paved road immediately before the Cisco Baptist Church, which is also on the right. This road, once Highway 2, is now known as Old Highway 2; it is also called FS 16. Continue on FS 16 (follow the pavement until it ends; stay to the right at the fork; pass Hopewell Church; cross the Conasauga River; continue straight ahead where FS 51 turns right) for approximately 8.7 miles to the suspension bridge over the Jacks River. The Jacks River Trail parking lot is to the right, across the river in Tennessee.

To the southeastern trailhead at Dally Gap: From the US 76–GA 5 inter-section just north of Blue Ridge, travel north on GA 5 toward McCaysville for 3.7 miles. Turn left onto Old GA 2 at the "Old State Route 2" sign and small Watson Gap sign. Continue on this road for approximately 10.5 miles (the pavement ends at mile 9.0) to the major Forest Service intersec-tion at Watson Gap. Turn hard right at the gap onto FS 22 (one lane) and drive approximately 3.6 miles to the trailhead at Dally Gap.

Notes

Sugar Cove Trail

WBR
Cohutta Mountains
Cohutta Wilderness

One of five interior trails in the Cohutta Wilderness, Sugar Cove requires a 2.5-mile walk—0.4 mile on East Cowpen and 2.1 miles on Rough Ridge—just to reach its upper elevation junction. But if you are interested in hiking this trail, don't let the additional distance discourage you. The 2.5 miles are easily walked and quickly completed.

Beginning at about 3,600 feet, Sugar Cove Trail immediately plunges into a beautiful, steep-sided cove. The upper portion of the cove has an open hardwood forest, allowing largely unobstructed views of 50 to 60 yards. Past the beginning patches of sweet shrub, the forest floor is often covered with arching fern fronds. The rich soil also makes this cove a great place to see wildflowers in the spring. By mid-May during a rainy year, the lush display seems almost tropical.

As you descend, the forest becomes more dense and the individual trees grow taller and thicker. Here, beside the normally dry headwater streamed of Sugar Cove Branch, the second-growth cove hardwoods— black cherry, yellow buckeye, sweet birch, sugar maple, and tuliptree—have grown to larger dimensions than along any other trail in the Cohutta Wilderness.

The abundance of sugar maple—a tree at the southern limit of its range—is the cove's most distinctive feature and the obvious origin of its name. These maples occur less and less frequently from west to east in the Georgia mountains. Although fairly common from the Cohuttas westward, sugar maples are rare in the trailside forests of north central and northeastern Georgia.

Near the bottom of the cove, the largest sugar maple along the trail is 10 feet 9 inches in circumference and perhaps 110 feet tall. Quite possibly a state record, it has a blackened base and is located a few feet to the right of the trail at 0.8 mile. The sugar maple leaf has smooth margins, is dark green above

Features
Wilderness, unusual cove forest, Jacks River

Distance
2.2 miles

Difficulty Rating
From Rough Ridge Trail to Jacks River Trail: moderate; from Jacks River Trail to Rough Ridge Trail: strenuous

County
Fannin

Nearest Cities
Ellijay (S), Blue Ridge (E)

Maps
Hemp Top Quadrangle, GA-TN; Cohutta Wilderness map

Blazes
White

Water Sources
Sugar Cove Branch beginning at mile 1.1

Ranger District
Cohutta

and usually has five long, pointed lobes. If you have seen the Canadian flag, you have seen the shape of the sugar maple leaf.

During its first 1.2 miles, the trail loses nearly 1,100 feet. The beginning 0.3 mile drops sharply. Beyond that plunge, the downgrades become less severe as the trail slopes down to its first crossing of Sugar Cove Branch at mile 1.1. After crossing the branch, the path crosses a tributary, then returns to and crosses the branch a second time.

Immediately after it crosses Sugar Cove Branch for the fifth time at mile 1.5, the trail veers left and climbs, steeply at first, a hillside high above Jacks River. The path scarcely levels before beginning its slow, winding, 0.5 mile descent to the river.

The trail crosses the Jacks (elevation about 1,880 feet), then quickly reaches its lower-end sign where it meets the orange-blazed Jacks River Trail. To the right and upstream, it is 3.9 miles to Dally Gap, the southeastern trailhead of the Jacks River Trail.

Highlights
Throughout: Lush wildflower displays during spring months.
Mile 0.8: Record-size sugar maple for Georgia.
Mile 2.2: Jacks River.

Directions
(See page 160 of East Cowpen Trail for directions to its southern trailhead at Three Forks.) Sugar Cove is an interior trail that has its southwestern (upper elevation) end on Rough Ridge Trail and its northeastern (lower elevation) end on Jacks River Trail.

To reach Sugar Cove's upper elevation end, start at the southern trailhead of East Cowpen Trail and walk 0.4 mile to Rough Ridge Trail. Hike 2.1 miles on Rough Ridge, an easy walk, to the prominent, usually signed junction where Sugar Cove Trail begins on the right. This junction is further marked by a flat rock big enough to sit on, a worn resting place around the sign, and Sugar Cove's descending, bare-dirt treadway.

Notes

Penitentiary Branch Trail

WBR
Cohutta Mountains
Cohutta Wilderness

Features
Wilderness,
Jacks River

Distance
3.6 miles

Difficulty Rating
From Hemp Top
Trail to Jacks River
Trail: easy to moder-
ate; from Jacks
River Trail to Hemp
Top Trail: moderate

County
Fannin

Nearest Cities
Blue Ridge (E),
Ellijay (S)

Maps
Hemp Top
Quadrangle, GA-TN;
Cohutta Wilderness
map

Blazes
White

Water Sources
Mile 3.2:
Penitentiary Branch,
mile 3.6: Jacks River

Ranger District
Cohutta

In the early decades of the 1900s, there was a remote logging camp near what is now Penitentiary Branch. The loggers worked long hours six days a week. When their one day off finally came, there was no place the men could go on Sunday and still be back in time for work at daybreak Monday morning. So they were stuck—in what must have felt like a prison.

An interior trail, Penitentiary Branch requires a 2.3-mile walk on Hemp Top Trail to reach its upper elevation junction. The hiking is easy—it gains approximately 470 feet on a former Forest Service road, now Hemp Top Trail.

Like the other trails leading to the Jacks River, Penitentiary Branch loses elevation along the way. But even though it loses 1,370 feet, compared to most of the others, especially Rough Ridge and Hickory Ridge, the descent is mild. The trail, beginning at 3,050 feet, is wide and easily walked. As long as you stay on the former jeep road and ignore the side paths, you should have no difficulty following the trail down to the river.

For most of the first 3.0 miles a canopy of oak, hickory, maple, and Virginia pine shade the trail. Underneath these taller trees, a great variety of herbaceous plants, ferns, shrubs, and smaller trees form a dense understory. Against this solid, hedge-like background of green, the remaining clusters of bright-orange flame azaleas are especially showy in mid-June at higher elevations. May is the peak month, however, for flame azalea along lower elevation trails such as Penitentiary Branch.

Scattered alongside the trail, Virginia pines thrive in pockets of dry, rocky soil as they do throughout much of North Georgia. Often they grow on granite ledges where no other tree can. Usually 30 to 50 feet high and somewhat scraggly in appearance, Virginia pines are readily identified. Their yellow-green needles—two to the sheath, 1 to 3 inches long and twisted—are shorter than those of any other native pine in the mountains. Also characteristic of the Virginia pine is the reddish-brown bark which is broken into small scales.

After 3.2 miles, the trail rock-steps across the normally inches-deep Penitentiary Branch and follows it toward the river. In the moist coves near Jacks River, the composition of the forest abruptly changes. Here tall eastern hemlock, American beech, basswood, sweet birch, and tuliptree shade the trail. Penitentiary Branch ties into the orange-blazed Jacks River Trail at a large campsite clearing. To the right (downstream) it is two river crossings and 2.0 miles to Jacks River Falls; to the left (upstream) it is 7.2 miles to Dally Gap, the southeastern terminus of the Jacks River Trail.

Highlights
Miles 0.5–3.0: Mixed hardwood and pine with varied, dense understory. In May and June, mountain laurel and flame azalea bloom.
Miles 3.2–3.6: Trail crosses then follows Penitentiary Branch through diverse cove forest.
Mile 3.6: Jacks River.

Directions
(See page 142 of Hemp Top Trail for directions to its Dally Gap trailhead.) Penitentiary Branch is an interior trail that has its eastern (upper elevation) end on Hemp Top Trail and its western (lower elevation) end on Jacks River Trail. To reach the upper elevation end of Penitentiary Branch, walk 2.3 miles on Hemp Top Trail starting from its Dally Gap trailhead. A prominent junction sign usually marks Penitentiary Branch's descending treadway to the left.

Notes

Rough Ridge Trail

A long Rough Ridge Trail, as well as throughout the Cohuttas, you may notice patches of earth that look like they have been tilled for planting. These areas have not been roto-tilled; they are the work of wild hogs that have been rooting for food. These nonnative, feral animals compete with bear and deer for mast, and their rooting harms the mountain flora, especially wildflowers.

Unlike domestic swine, the hog has a heavy, bristly coat which varies in color from reddish-brown to black. And while domestic swine are usually heavy through the hindquarters, the wild hog has massive shoulders and a mane of bristles running along the back of the neck, giving the animal a humped appearance. The mane stands up when the hog is excited or angry. Their young, looking much like giant chipmunks, have horizontal stripes and blotches of brown and yellow on their sides. Both sexes have tusks.

Where living close to humans, hogs are usually nocturnal, but in remote areas like the Cohutta Wilderness, they often become active during the day. Keep in mind that these wild hogs are large and formidable animals; the larger, solitary males range from 300 to over 400 pounds. Do not molest or antagonize them or their young in any way.

Blue- and white-blazed Rough Ridge is the longest of the seven Jacks River lead-in trails. Starting along East Cowpen Trail at 3,760 feet and ending at 1,620 feet, it also loses more elevation than the other Jacks River approaches. Most people who have carried a heavy pack up or down this trail agree that the ridge it follows is aptly named.

The trail stays on or near the crest of Rough Ridge for much of its length. For the first 4.0 miles it often follows wide, grassy roadbeds. But soon after beginning its series of steep descents, the trail narrows to forest path, often winding and occasionally rocky.

WBR
Cohutta Mountains
Cohutta Wilderness

Features
Wilderness, views of Big Frog Mountain, Jacks River

Distance
7.0 miles

Difficulty Rating
From East Cowpen to Jacks River: moderate to strenuous; from Jacks River to East Cowpen: strenuous

County
Fannin

Nearest Cities
Blue Ridge (E), Ellijay (S), Chatsworth (SW)

Maps
Hemp Top Quadrangle, GA-TN; Cohutta Wilderness map

Blazes
Blue or white

Water Sources
Mile 0.3: seasonal spring; Rough Creek and Jacks River at trail's end

Ranger District
Cohutta

For the first 2.1 miles, to the Sugar Cove junction, Rough Ridge Trail gently undulates through a hardwood forest with witch-hazel, sassafras, and a deciduous holly common in the understory. Oaks—white, chestnut, scarlet, black, and northern red—dominate the ridge top. Most are second-growth trees from 60 to 70 years old. Beyond the Sugar Cove sign the trail descends, alternating nearly level stretches with moderate downgrades for 1.6 miles. At mile 3.7, it climbs moderately for less than 0.2 mile, levels off, then drops below the ridge.

The trail becomes rocky and narrow as it continues to descend into a flat hardwood cove. Here you cross two shallow streams at mile 4.4, and then start the second and last climb—a sharp 0.1-mile ascent back to the ridge top. From here, Rough Ridge Trail becomes a downhill roller coaster, alternating level stretches or easy downgrades with steep pitches to mile 6.3, where it enters a cove dominated by eastern hemlock. Along this last section you may catch glimpses of Big Frog, a 4,200-foot mountain three or four miles to the northeast in Tennessee.

After reaching the cove, the path turns left and dips to a tributary of Rough Creek. It parallels both the feeder stream and creek before crossing Rough Creek at mile 6.7. The remainder of the trail closely follows the creek downstream to a sign which marks its lower junction on the orange-blazed Jacks River Trail. Rough Ridge Trail does not cross Rough Creek a second time; it ends where the Jacks River Trail crosses Rough Creek. To the left and downriver, it is 1.2 miles and one ford to Jacks River Falls.

Highlights
Throughout: Remote area, less used than most Cohutta trails. Beautiful in late spring when the flame azalea blooms. Several good winter views.
Mile 5.8: View of Hickory Ridge.
Mile 7.0: Jacks River.

Directions
(See page 160 of East Cowpen Trail for directions to its Three Forks Mountain trailhead.) Rough Ridge is an interior trail that has its southern (upper elevation) end on East Cowpen Trail and its northern (lower elevation) end on Jacks River Trail. To reach the upper elevation end of Rough Ridge, walk 0.4 mile on East Cowpen Trail starting from its southern end at Three Forks Mountain. Rough Ridge Trail's sign and beginning treadway are to the right.

Hickory Ridge Trail

WBR
Cohutta Mountains
Cohutta Wilderness

Hickory Ridge starts at 3,200 feet on the shoulder of Buckeye Mountain, deep within the Cohutta Wilderness. To reach its closest junction, you must walk 2.6 miles on East Cowpen Trail.

Hickory Ridge Trail is easy to describe. The lightly used path starts out level, then descends to another level stretch, then descends again. The rest of the trail, alternating between nearly level sections and downridge pitches of varying length and steepness, repeats this pattern down to the Jacks River. Hickory Ridge leads uphill half a dozen times, but these upgrades are so short and easy that by Cohutta Wilderness standards, they are hardly noticeable.

On your way down the trail, the higher ridge a mile to the east (to your right) is Rough Ridge. When the leaves are off the hardwoods, there are views of 4,200-foot Big Frog Mountain to the northeast.

Although these ridges have an unusually high number of mockernut and pignut hickories for this North Georgia region, the oaks (northern red, scarlet, black, white, and chestnut) still dominate the trailside forest for most of its length. Chestnut oaks, preferring the dry, rocky soils of ridges and mountainsides, are especially plentiful along the upper portion of the trail. These slow-growing oaks are the thickest trees on Hickory Ridge. They have dark-brown, deeply furrowed bark; large, often twisted limbs; and leaves with numerous wavy, rounded teeth or lobes. Many of them are starting to hollow. A grove of shortleaf pine is located about halfway down the ridge on the driest stretch of trail.

At mile 3.2 the trail descends through a belt of rosebay rhododendron and eastern hemlock, turns parallel to a small stream, then drops quickly down to the Jacks River (1,560 feet) by way of the streambed. If it has not been blazed recently, the last 0.2 mile of Hickory Ridge, from where it first reaches the river to

Features
Wilderness, Jacks River

Distance
3.6 miles

Difficulty Rating
From East Cowpen to Jacks River Trail: easy to moderate; from Jacks River Trail to East Cowpen Trail: strenuous

County
Fannin

Nearest Cities
Chatsworth (SW), Ellijay (S), Blue Ridge (E)

Maps
Hemp Top Quadrangle, GA-TN; Cohutta Wilderness map

Blazes
Yellow

Water Sources
None except for lower elevation end at Jacks River

Ranger District
Cohutta

its end, can be confusing. Once you come to the river, turn right and follow the Jacks upstream. After you duck under rhododendron, walk over a rocky, washed-out section of shoreline, and pass a path that angles to the left into deep water, you will again find the trail's treadway. Make the ford where you see the worn bank and yellow blaze.

Hickory Ridge ends at its junction sign on the Jacks River Trail. Jacks River Falls is 0.6 mile to the left, downstream.

Highlights

Mile 3.4: Jacks River.
Mile 3.6: From the Hickory Ridge–Jacks River junction, it is 0.6 mile downstream to Jacks River Falls.

Directions

(See page 160 of East Cowpen Trail and page 146 of Jacks River Trail for directions to their trailheads.) Hickory Ridge is an interior trail that has its southern (upper elevation) end on East Cowpen Trail and its northern (lower elevation) end on Jacks River Trail. Its Jacks River access point is 8.6 miles from the Jacks River Trail's southeastern trailhead at Dally Gap. Its East Cowpen access point is 4.4 miles from East Cowpen's southern trailhead at Three Forks Mountain, and 2.6 miles from East Cowpen's northern trailhead at the end of FS 51.

If its initial blaze has become faint or if its sign has been vandalized, Hickory Ridge's East Cowpen junction can be difficult to find. You will find Hickory Ridge Trail in the middle of a horseshoe curve that almost doubles back on itself. On the outside of the curve, where East Cowpen's old roadbed widens, look for the treadway.

Notes

Beech Bottom Trail

WBR
Cohutta Mountains
Cohutta Wilderness

Beech Bottom, really an old road blocked to vehicular traffic, is the most easily walked trail in the Cohutta Wilderness. It is also the only trail that leads to the most scenic single feature in the wilderness—the wildly churning Jacks River Falls—without forcing hikers to ford the Jacks at least once. These two facts predictably account for another: Beech Bottom is the most heavily used trail in the Cohuttas.

Starting in Tennessee's Cherokee National Forest, the easily followed trail heads southeastward, entering the Cohutta Wilderness and Georgia's Chattahoochee National Forest (0.3 mile) in quick succession. The old road, which remains in the Chattahoochee National Forest, gradually loses elevation as it winds around steep ravines to mile 1.0, where it crosses an unnamed branch. Across the first branch, the trail follows another upstream. Along this section of trail, there are two large, slow-growing trees—an American beech and an eastern hemlock—that escaped the logging earlier in the century. Beech Bottom continues level or gently uphill to mile 2.4, where it begins its gradual descent to the Jacks River. The middle of the trail often winds along dry ridges where the forest changes to oak and Virginia pine.

At mile 3.3 the trail turns sharply to the right, then quickly crosses Beech Creek. To the right before Beech Creek, the clearing (quickly returning to forest) is the former site of a hunting lodge. This structure, once owned by the Jacks River Game and Fish Preserve, Inc., was torn down in the early 1980s. The intertwining rocky paths across the creek all head in the same direction. After they come together, continue through Beech Bottom—a flat floodplain area just east of where Beech Creek joins the Jacks River—on the dirt path to the left.

Beech Bottom is now wilder than it has been for over a hundred years. The Forest Service has a photo-

Features
Wilderness, streams, Jacks River, Jacks River Falls

Distance
4.0 miles

Difficulty Rating
Easy to moderate walked in either direction

Counties
Fannin, GA and Polk, TN

Nearest City
Chatsworth

Maps
Hemp Top Quadrangle, GA-TN; Cohutta Wilderness map

Blazes
None; none needed

Water Sources
At frequent intervals

Ranger District
Cohutta

graph of a sawmill operating in the bottoms in the early 1890s. In the late 1920s and early 1930s, Beech Bottom was the site of a logging camp. After the logging the bottoms were cleared more extensively, fenced, and farmed. Spring-blooming daffodils now mark the former sites of two old homes, which were also torn down in the early 1980s.

Continue straight ahead on the path until it meets the orange-blazed Jacks River Trail. To the right, downstream, it is 0.6 mile to the cliffside overlook above Jacks River Falls.

Highlights
Mile 4.0: Jacks River. Jacks River Falls is 0.6 mile to the right and downstream.

Directions
(See page 146 of Jacks River Trail for directions to its northwestern trailhead in Alaculsy Valley.) From the Jacks River trailhead in Alaculsy Valley, continue farther into Tennessee on Forest Route 221. Slightly more than 1.0 mile past the suspension bridge over the Jacks River, where FS 16 enters Tennessee and becomes FR 221, make a sharp right turn onto FR 62. Continue approximately 4.5 miles on FR 62, then turn into the large graveled parking area above and to the left of the road.

During bad winter weather FR 62 is gated.

Notes

Rice Camp Trail

WBR
Cohutta Mountains
Cohutta Wilderness

Rice Camp Trail follows the clear, cold, often sliding water of small streams for the first half of its length. Almost from its beginning at 1,740 feet, the wide and always wet trail parallels a tributary of Rice Camp Branch. After crossing this headwater rivulet for the third time at mile 1.1, the trail trades streams and follows Rice Camp Branch.

After nine Rice Camp Branch crossings and 1.9 miles of nearly level terrain, the path turns left away from the stream and ascends moderate and more gradual upgrades on an old roadbed until it opens into a white oak flat, once the site of a logging camp and sawmill. At mile 2.7 the trail makes a short, sharp drop to a muddy rivulet. Look for the smooth, light-gray bark of the last few large beech trees still standing beside the small stream.

The remainder of Rice Camp traverses a succession of low, dry ridges through a predominantly oak-pine forest. The resulting ups and downs are easy or moderate. The land beside the trail often slopes away gradually on small spur ridges or falls away suddenly into moist ravines on either side of the ridge top.

The wilderness path descends through a belt of rosebay rhododendron and eastern hemlock to 1,350 feet, where it ends at the orange-blazed Jacks River Trail above a normally shallow tributary. Jacks River Falls is one ford and 1.2 miles to the right, east and upstream, on the Jacks River Trail.

Highlights
Mile 1.1: A small 8- to 10-foot-high waterfall.
Mile 3.9: Jacks River.

Directions
From the GA 52–US 411 intersection in Chatsworth, travel US 411 North approximately 13.4 miles, past Eton toward Tennga, to the community of Cisco. In Cisco, turn right onto the paved road

Features
Wilderness, streams, Jacks River

Distance
3.9 miles

Difficulty Rating
Easy to moderate walked in either direction

County
Fannin

Nearest City
Chatsworth

Maps
Hemp Top Quadrangle, GA-TN; Cohutta Wilderness map

Blazes
Yellow

Water Sources
At very frequent intervals for first 2.7 miles

Ranger District
Cohutta

immediately before the Cisco Baptist Church, also on the right. Once part of GA 2, this road is now known as Old GA 2. This road is also FS 16. Continue on FS 16 (the pavement ends; stay to the right at the fork; pass Hopewell Church; cross the Conasauga River) for approximately 7.9 miles, then turn right onto FS 51. Proceed about 4.8 miles, making two fords. The fords may require a utility vehicle in wet weather. You will find the Rice Camp trailhead, bulletin board, and parking area on the left. As you approach, Rice Camp Trail is to the left and East Cowpen Trail is straight ahead into the wilderness.

Notes

East Cowpen Trail

WBR
Cohutta Mountains
Cohutta Wilderness

At one time East Cowpen Trail was a state road, old GA Highway 2. Even after the area was officially declared wilderness in 1975, the highway remained open to the public. After long negotiations, the road was permanently closed to vehicles in September 1987, and now is gradually acquiring the look of a trail.

East Cowpen serves as the main artery through the middle of the wilderness, leading directly to five trails and indirectly to the entire trail system. For most of its length, the trail runs the ridge crest of Cohutta Mountain, which separates the two watersheds of the wilderness. Starting at its southern trailhead at Three Forks Mountain (3,500 feet), East Cowpen Trail follows an easy-to-moderate upgrade to 4,100 feet near the top of Cowpen Mountain at mile 1.3.

At 4,149 feet, Cowpen Mountain is the highest peak in Georgia's much larger share of the Cohutta Wilderness. The remainder of the trail, except for two or three easy uphill grades, is level or downsloping all the way to its northern trailhead at the Rice Camp Trail parking area (1,760 feet). Beyond its first 3.5 miles, East Cowpen makes numerous sharp descents. At mile 6.7 the trail leaves the wilderness and follows a woods road the remaining distance to the Rice Camp Trail parking area.

Starting at its southern end at Three Forks Mountain, the distances to East Cowpen's trail junctions are as follows: Rough Ridge, 0.4 mile; Panther Creek, 2.3 miles; Hickory Ridge, 4.3 miles; Hickory Creek, 6.9 miles; Rice Camp, 7.0 miles.

The upper elevation end of East Cowpen—from Three Forks to the Panther Creek junction—is botanically significant. Here the cucumbertree, a deciduous magnolia that is usually only a minor forest component, is found frequently. In addition to the graceful fern fields, lily-of-the-valley colonies are common along this segment, as they are on the broad-topped,

Features
Wilderness, highest ridge in Georgia's portion of the wilderness

Distance
7.0 miles

Difficulty Rating
From Three Forks Mountain to its northern trailhead on FS 51: easy to moderate; from FS 51 to its southern trailhead at Three Forks Mountain: strenuous

County
Fannin

Nearest Cities
Blue Ridge (E), Ellijay (S), Chatsworth (SW)

Maps
Hemp Top Quadrangle, GA-TN; Cohutta Wilderness map

Blazes
None; none needed

Water Sources
Ridge trail, only a few seasonal springs

Ranger District
Cohutta

rich-soiled, high-elevation ridges throughout the Cohutta Wilderness. There is also an excellent native azalea display, usually peaking from May 20 to June 20, that includes hybrids in many hues from almost white to the customary orange of flame azalea.

Highlights
Miles 0.0–2.3: Excellent springtime azalea display that features hybrids of various hues.

Directions
To the northern trailhead: The directions to East Cowpen's northern trailhead are exactly the same as those for Rice Camp Trail, also in the Cohutta Wilderness. East Cowpen is the trail that continues straight ahead where FS 51 ends at the Rice Camp Trailhead. (See page 157 of Rice Camp Trail for further directions.)

To the southern, Three Forks trailhead: From the Ellijay square travel GA 52 West for 9.5 miles to the Lake Conasauga Recreation Area sign. Turn right onto FS 18 and continue 3.5 miles on that road before turning right onto FS 68. Once on FS 68, continue straight ahead, uphill. After traveling approximately 6.0 miles on FS 68, you will reach the three-way FS 68–64 junction near Potatopatch Mountain. Turn right onto FS 64 and proceed 4.4 miles to the large East Cowpen parking area to the left in the middle of a sharp curve.

Alternate route to the southern, Three Forks trailhead: From Blue Ridge follow the directions to Jacks River Trail (page 146), also in the Cohutta Wilderness. From the four-way intersection at Watson Gap, turn left with FS 64 (opposite FS 22) and drive approximately 8.5 miles before turning right into East Cowpen's large graveled parking area.

The one-way shuttle distance between trailheads around the western side of the wilderness is approximately 28.5 dirt-road miles.

Notes

Conasauga River Trail

WBR
Cohutta Mountains
Cohutta Wilderness

Features
Wilderness, bluffs, boulders, cascades, and pools along the Conasauga River

Distance
13.1 miles

Difficulty Rating
From Betty Gap downstream to northwestern trailhead at FS 17-B: easy to moderate; from FS 17-B upstream to southeastern trailhead at Betty Gap: moderate

Counties
Gilmer, Fannin, and Murray

Nearest Cities
Ellijay (SE), Chatsworth (SW)

Maps
Dyer Gap Quadrangle, GA; Hemp Top and Tennga Quadrangles, GA-TN; Cohutta Wilderness map

Blazes
Yellow

Water Sources
Conasauga River and its tributaries

Ranger District
Cohutta

Arising from the southwestern corner of the Cohutta Wilderness, the Conasauga is without doubt one of Georgia's most beautiful rivers. The origin of its name, however, is ambiguous. *Conasauga* is settler-spelling for the Cherokee word for strong horse, and *kahnasaugh* is the Cherokee word for grass. A flooded mountain river is definitely a strong horse, but the Cherokee didn't see their first horse until well after they moved to the Southern Appalachians.

The origin of the southeastern trailhead's name is less mysterious. During the logging days, a widow named Betty sold meals and lodging to travelers. Her home was in a gap halfway across the Cohutta Mountains.

Starting at Betty Gap (3,040 feet), the initial 0.2 mile descends very sharply, the first of only two difficult grades on this predominantly level trail. A small spring-fed stream—the first of many—emerges beneath a stand of large eastern white pine near the top of the descent. For the first 1.3 miles, until it reaches the river, much of the trail wanders through a maze of gathering rivulets, headwaters of the Conasauga. Especially after a rain, this upper section of the trail is part water, closely following, crossing, and rock-hopping down the middle of the many shallow, intertwining streams.

To the left along this same segment stands the thickest eastern hemlock in Georgia—15 feet 8 inches in circumference measured 4 feet 6 inches from the ground. A former state record holder, this tree was dethroned by a very close neighbor, which has since died. The current Georgia champion is one of two large eastern hemlocks towering together along the Jacks River Trail. (The state record blackgum—10 feet 4 inches in circumference and 124 feet tall—is located to the left of the trail near the surviving hemlock.)

The eastern hemlock is a slow-growing, long-living tree. The record age, rings actually counted, is nearly 1,000 years. The Conasauga River giant is at least four or five centuries old.

Once it reaches the river, the trail fords the Conasauga thirty-eight times—eighteen to Bray Field, and twenty beyond. Most of the fords are shallow and present no danger other than slipping and getting wet. But in winter and early spring before the leaves bud out, when the river normally has its strongest flow, the current can reach mid-thigh depth and become surprisingly powerful. Do not plan to hike the Conasauga River Trail immediately after heavy rains or when heavy rains are predicted. Steep-sided mountain rivers, like the Conasauga and Jacks in the Cohuttas, rise rapidly following a substantial rainfall and quickly become too dangerous to ford, leaving hikers stranded between crossings.

Usually a blaze marks the trail's return to dry land across the river from each ford. These guiding blazes, however, are not always easily found. You must often angle downstream while fording the river to locate the blaze and worn spot on the opposite bank. And occasionally, at an apparent ford, you have to walk 20 or 30 yards downstream along the bank before spotting the trail across the river. Just remember that the trail, even on islands, always heads downriver.

At mile 1.9 Chestnut Lead Trail meets the Conasauga River Trail. A large, worn campsite helps mark the junction. Beginning here you may notice evidence of the railroad ties that were part of a narrow gauge railroad constructed along the river when the area was logged. The earliest extensive logging occurred along this trail in 1912, and continued in the area through most of the 1930s. You may still occasionally find a hand-forged spike.

The generally level trail closely follows the scenic Conasauga River between fords. This crystalline mountain stream, dropping over 100 feet per mile to Bray Field, is a rocky succession of white shoals and green pools. By midmorning the fast-flowing riffles beside the shaded path are sparkling silver.

As soon as the air above the Conasauga warms in the spring, tiger swallowtails begin their daily flutterings up and down the river corridor. Below these colorful yellow and black butterflies, rainbow trout face upstream to feed, holding steady in the slowed currents of the pools.

After its eighteenth ford at mile 4.9, the trail climbs up and over a hill, descends to and crosses Tearbritches Creek, then enters Bray Field (1,920 feet). A former cabin site and now a grassy, often congested camping area, it is the most important trail junction in the western half of the wilderness. Tearbritches Trail ends here; two trails, Conasauga and Hickory Creek, pass through the small clearing, and the lower access point of a fourth trail, Panther Creek, is nearby. Possibilities for extended hikes from Bray Field are numerous.

From Bray Field at mile 5.4 the trail continues downstream another 7.7 miles and another twenty fords. In the middle of the field the trail, turning to the left away from the river on an old jeep road, becomes contiguous with the white-blazed Hickory Creek Trail. Follow the road as it winds around a beaver pond, then returns to the river. The trails split 1.3 miles from Bray Field; Hickory Creek Trail turns left with the road, Conasauga River Trail continues straight ahead on the path. Here the river fords begin again.

Watch carefully for the trail blazes on the second crossing below Bray Field. As you ford the river from right to left, look for a gap in the rocks a few feet in from the bank. The trail cuts through the gap at a right angle away from the river.

A short climb to the top of the bluff on the west bank of the Conasauga gives you a beautiful view of the cascades. From this vantage point you can also see a long, straight vein of quartz running through the last third of the long pool just below the falls.

The path continues its pattern of crossing, then paralleling the river until the thirty-eighth ford at mile 11.9. Here, at approximately 1,260 feet, the trail leaves the Conasauga River. Twenty-five yards beyond this last ford, the trail turns 90 degrees to the left and begins to climb. The remaining 1.2 miles are predominantly level or uphill, with several moderate grades and one short, steep pitch near the end. After it levels out, the trail turns left onto an old road, then ends in the gravel parking lot (1,640 feet) on FS 17-B.

The Conasauga has the cleanest, clearest water of any river its size in Georgia. Its clarity—like wilderness rivers out west—gives it the illusion of being shallower than it is. Below Bray Field the sluices, slides, shoals, boulders, bluffs, and pools are continuous along the lower Conasauga.

Starting from its southeastern trailhead at Betty Gap, the distances to Conasauga River Trail's junctions are as follows: Chestnut Lead, 1.9 miles; Panther Creek, 4.9 miles; Tearbritches, 5.4 miles; Hickory Creek, 5.4 miles; Hickory Creek, 6.7 miles.

Highlights

Throughout: Bluffs, huge boulders, cascades, and pools.

Mile 7.0: Long, sliding cascade just below the confluence of Rough Creek and the Conasauga. A bluff on the west side of the river provides a good view.

Directions

To the southeastern trailhead at Betty Gap: From the Ellijay square travel GA 52 West for 9.5 miles to the Lake Conasauga Recreation Area sign. Turn right onto FS 18 and continue 3.5 miles on that road before turning right onto FS 68. Once on FS 68, continue straight ahead, uphill. After traveling approximately 6.0 miles on FS 68, you will reach the three-way FS 68–FS 64 junction near Potatopatch Mountain. Turn right onto FS 64 and proceed 1.4 miles to the Conasauga River Trail sign and parking area.

To the northwestern trailhead at FS 17-B: From the GA 52–US 411 intersection in Chatsworth, travel US 411 North approximately 13.4 miles, past Eton toward Tennga, to the community of Cisco. In Cisco, turn right onto the paved road immediately before the Cisco Baptist Church, which is also on the right. This road was once part of GA 2 and is now known as Old Highway 2. This road is also called FS 16. Continue on FS 16 (the pavement ends; stay to the right at the fork) for approximately 3.2 miles, then turn right onto FS 17 at the Lake Conasauga sign. Proceed straight ahead (17-A turns right) on FS 17 for approximately 3.6 miles before turning left onto FS 17-B at the Conasauga River Trail sign. After 0.2 mile FS 17-B ends at the Conasauga River parking area and trailhead.

To arrange a shuttle, leave a vehicle at the northwestern trailhead, then follow FS 17 southward 7.8 miles to its junction with FS 68. Turn left onto FS 68 and continue straight ahead on FS 68, then FS 64, 5.5 miles to the trailhead at Betty Gap.

Notes

Chestnut Lead Trail

WBR
Cohutta Mountains
Cohutta Wilderness

Chestnut Lead is the shortest trail in the Cohutta Wilderness and is the second easiest of the four Conasauga lead-in trails. It starts at 3,280 feet and, like the others, drops steadily to the river. But compared to Tearbritches and Panther Creek Trails, which lose 2,000 feet in elevation, the grades of Chestnut Lead lose only 1000 feet and almost seem easy to hike.

The trail's first 0.5 mile follows a ridge crest through a second-growth hardwood forest, probably the origin of the trail's name—a lead is a local term for ridge. While none of the trees are massive, some good-sized ones tower over an understory of bracken fern, sassafras, and blackberry bushes. The sweet birch, the original source of wintergreen flavoring, is abundant. You can recognize it by its dark brown trunk whose smooth surface fissures into scaly plates. The leaves are elliptical, saw-toothed, and often notched at the base. The familiar wintergreen aroma comes from scratched or split twigs. Other tree species include tuliptree, white and scarlet oak, sourwood, American holly, and American beech. Look for chestnut saplings on the ridge or in the cove below.

American chestnut trees—once the dominant tree of cove hardwood forests below 5,000 feet—rarely mature today. Like their ancestors, saplings quickly fall victim to the chestnut blight, a fungus that wiped out mature stands throughout eastern North America after 1904 when it was accidentally introduced in New York City. But because American chestnut wood resists rot, the massive trunks of fallen trees remain. After you spot the trunks, look for saplings growing from the old roots. You can distinguish the American chestnut's elliptical leaves from those of the chestnut oak by their sharp, curved, and elongated teeth.

As you near 0.5 mile, eastern hemlock appear

Features
Wilderness, outstanding forest, spring wildflower display, Conasauga River

Distance
1.7 miles

Difficulty Rating
From trailhead to Conasauga River Trail: easy to moderate; from Conasauga River Trail to trailhead: moderate

Counties
Gilmer and Fannin

Nearest Cities
Ellijay (SE), Chatsworth (SW)

Maps
Dyer Gap Quadrangle, GA; Cohutta Wilderness map

Blazes
Blue

Water Sources
Chestnut Creek and Conasauga River

Ranger District
Cohutta

among the tuliptrees and the trail descends steadily into a cove of wild-flowers. Sugar and striped maples, basswoods, yellow buckeyes, and black cherry trees are common in the moist cove.

The trail turns left at 0.9 mile, descending more sharply until it nears Chestnut Creek on the left. Rosebay rhododendron grow along the creek banks; wildflowers are plentiful and varied. Gradually, the trail levels and crosses the creek several times as it nears the Conasauga River. The trail ends on the other side of the river at its junction with the Conasauga River Trail. To the left, downstream, it is 3.5 miles on the yellow-blazed Conasauga River Trail to Bray Field.

Highlights
Throughout: A wake robin with white blossoms is abundant near the beginning of the trail. This trillium usually blooms during late April and early May. A partial list of other spring-blooming wildflowers includes: large-flowered trillium, Catesby's trillium, mayapple, jack-in-the-pulpit, yellowroot, Solomon's seal, false Solomon's seal, foamflower, rue anemone, and dwarf iris. Rosebay rhododendron blooms along Chestnut Creek in June. Late summer and fall flowers include lush displays of orange-spotted jewelweed and its yellow cousin, touch-me-not, as well as cardinal flower.
Mile 1.7: Conasauga River.

Directions
From the square in Ellijay, take GA 52 West 9.5 miles. At the Lake Conasauga Recreation Area sign, turn right onto FS 18 and continue 3.5 miles to FS 68 (the pavement ends after 1.3 miles). Turn right onto FS 68 and continue uphill. After traveling approximately 6.0 miles on FS 68, you will reach the three-way FS 68–FS 64 junction near Potatopatch Mountain. Turn left toward Lake Conasauga (still following FS 68) and proceed 2.0 miles to the Chestnut Lead Trail sign and parking area on your right.

Notes

Panther Creek Trail

WBR
Cohutta Mountains
Cohutta Wilderness

The first 30 yards of this heavily used scenic trail ford the Conasauga River at approximately 1,940 feet. Once across, this interior trail follows Panther Creek upstream to its headwaters high in the mountains, crossing the stream frequently along the way. For the first 1.1 miles the trail gradually rises beside Panther Creek, but after crossing the brook to the left below a long cascade, the trail suddenly changes.

Here it becomes not only steep but also rocky as it ascends to the falls through a boulder field. This is the most rugged section of trail in the Cohutta Wilderness.

You can easily walk down to the bottom of Panther Creek Falls. Above, the wide waterfall drops, then slides 60 to 70 feet. The sun-faceted water glistens intensely in contrast to the deep green of the surrounding forest. Below, the creek hurtles down the mountainside, twisting and tumbling, splitting and rejoining in a continuous cascade hundreds of feet in length.

From near a giant eastern hemlock, the trail curls upward to the left beneath Panther Bluff to the top of the falls at mile 1.4. Here, where Panther Creek disappears over the brink, rock ledges provide the only trailside vista within the Cohutta Wilderness. There are no roads, houses, or smokestacks in sight. Miles of unbroken wilderness stretch out in front of these isolated falls.

If you intend to hike farther up the mountain, walk near the left side of Panther Creek until you find a blaze or see a muddy gap in the rosebay rhododendron where the trail crosses the stream. For the next 0.5 mile, the path gradually ascends Panther Creek's cove-like valley. Although it doesn't open to the north, this fertile cove supports an unusually diverse forest: sweet birch, yellow buckeye, black cherry, Carolina silverbell, sugar maple, and four

Features
Wilderness,
streams, cascades,
waterfall, bluff,
scenic view

Distance
3.4 miles

Difficulty Rating
From Conasauga
River Trail to East
Cowpen Trail: strenuous; from East
Cowpen Trail to
Conasauga River
Trail: moderate

County
Fannin

Nearest Cities
Blue Ridge (E),
Ellijay (S),
Chatsworth (SW)

Maps
Hemp Top
Quadrangle, GA-TN;
Cohutta Wilderness
map

Blazes
Blue

Water Sources
Panther Creek for
much of the lower
2.0 miles

Ranger District
Cohutta

species of deciduous magnolia—tuliptree, cucumbertree, Fraser magnolia, and umbrella magnolia.

The trail, which reaches approximately 2,800 feet at the top of the falls, climbs to near 3,800 feet at its eastern junction. At mile 1.9 the path makes a short, very steep ascent, the first, and by far the shortest, of three sharp upgrades that gain much of the remaining elevation to East Cowpen.

During wet years, the uppermost mile of Panther Creek is lush with herbaceous wildflowers, shrubs, and ferns. Sweet shrub and flame azaleas are abundant. This segment and the upper elevation end of East Cowpen Trail have the best fern fields—large, dense patches of primarily New York and hay-scented (a slight, sweet scent) ferns—in the Cohutta Wilderness.

Highlights
Miles 1.2–1.4: Cascade, boulder field, Panther Creek Falls, Panther Bluff, and scenic overlook in quick succession.

Directions
Panther Creek is an interior trail that has its eastern (upper elevation) end on East Cowpen Trail and its western (lower elevation) end on Conasauga River Trail. Its East Cowpen junction is 2.3 miles from East Cowpen's southern trailhead at Three Forks Mountain. Look for Panther Creek's sign and blue blaze to the left. Its Conasauga River junction is 4.9 miles from Conasauga River's southeastern trailhead at Betty Gap. The beginning of the lower end of Panther Creek Trail crosses the Conasauga River over what is usually an island.

The shortest route to reach Panther Creek's lower elevation, Conasauga River Trail junction is to walk Hickory Creek Trail from its western, FS 630 trailhead. (See page 172 of Hickory Creek Trail for directions to its western trailhead.) Follow Hickory Creek Trail to Bray Field, then take the Conasauga River Trail upstream for a short distance. (See East Cowpen, Conasauga River, and Hickory Creek Trails, also in the Cohutta Wilderness, for further information.)

Notes

Tearbritches Trail

WBR
Cohutta Mountains
Cohutta Wilderness

Beginning at 3,606 feet, Tearbritches Trail climbs 0.4 mile—sharply at first, then more moderately—to the broad crown of Bald Mountain (4,005 feet). On top, while you're still breathing hard from the climb, you might recognize a familiar fragrance—the Christmas-tree scent of the spruce-fir forest in North Carolina.

To the left of the trail, in what was a clearing when the Cohuttas became wilderness, there are at least twenty fir and spruce trees, species not native to Georgia. A road once led to the clearing; someone must have planted these trees. There are also a few native yellow birches on top of Bald Mountain. These few trees are extremely close to the western limit of their range across uppermost North Georgia.

Bald Mountain is significant for two reasons: its broad, nearly level crown was once an athletic field for the Cherokee, hence the name Bald (also formerly called Ball) Mountain. The mountain's other claim to fame is geographical. All research to this point has proven that Bald Mountain is the westernmost land-mass over 4,000 feet in elevation in the eastern United States. That is to say that the land west of Bald Mountain does not rise above 4,000 feet again until it reaches the Great Plains, far across the Mississippi River.

The short climb to Bald Mountain is the only upgrade on the way down to Bray Field and the Conasauga River. Tearbritches continues across the eastern side of the mountain's crest, then begins its descent. For the next 2.7 miles, from mile 0.5 to mile 3.2, the trail alternates short, level stretches with longer downslopes that become more abrupt toward the base of the mountain. From mile 2.0 to mile 2.9, the trail makes a particularly steep downridge plunge. Tearbritches loses approximately 2,040 feet along this 2.7-mile section of trail.

Features
Wilderness,
Conasauga River,
Bald Mountain

Distance
3.4 miles

Difficulty Rating
From trailhead to
Bray Field: moder-
ate; from Bray Field
to trailhead:
strenuous

Counties
Murray and Fannin

Nearest Cities
Ellijay (SE),
Chatsworth (SW)

Maps
Crandall and Dyer
Gap Quadrangles,
GA, Hemp Top
Quadrangle, GA-TN;
Cohutta Wilderness
map

Blazes
Orange

Water Sources
Mile 3.2:
Tearbritches Creek

Ranger District
Cohutta

At mile 3.0 the trail splits. Follow the left fork and continue downhill to the level ground beside Tearbritches Creek at mile 3.2. From here, the trail crosses its namesake creek immediately beyond a prominent camping area, then quickly arrives at its signed junction with the Conasauga River Trail on the edge of Bray Field (1,920 feet).

Bray Field is the most important trail junction in the western half of the wilderness. Tearbritches ends at the field; two other trails—Conasauga River and Hickory Creek—pass through it, and the lower access point of a fourth trail, Panther Creek, is nearby.

The upper slopes of Bald Mountain have an open oak forest similar to the high ridge areas on the Appalachian Trail. The broken canopy allows an abundance of sunshine to reach the forest floor. The sun, in turn, encourages an abundance of vegetation—ferns, shrubs, and occasionally, blackberry briers—to crowd the trail. Although there are brier patches along the upper portion of the trail, they are not as bad as the trail's name might suggest.

From early to mid-June, hundreds of Indian pinks bloom along either side of the trail starting at 0.9 mile. These perennial herbs, which often grow two feet tall, descend with the trail for nearly 0.1 mile. The Indian pink's unusual flower resembles a trumpet, red on the outside and bright yellow-green on the inside. At its uppermost end, the throat of the trumpet flares into five narrow, reflexed lobes.

Highlights
Mile 0.4: Summit of Bald Mountain.
Mile 3.4: Conasauga River.

Directions
(See page 166 of Chestnut Lead Trail for directions to the FS 68–FS 64 junction near Potatopatch Mountain.) At the FS 68–FS 64 junction, turn left toward Lake Conasauga (still following FS 68). You will pass the trailhead for Chestnut Lead Trail after 2.0 miles. The Tearbritches trailhead is 1.5 miles later, marked by a kiosk and a trash can.

If you are walking the Conasauga River Trail east to west from Betty Gap, you will find the Tearbritches Trail sign and initial blaze to the left of the trail just after it crosses Tearbritches Creek and begins to enter the upstream edge of Bray Field.

Hickory Creek Trail

WBR
Cohutta Mountains
Cohutta Wilderness

Hickory Creek is the third longest trail in the Cohutta Wilderness, and most people who hike it do not walk its entire length. Instead, they walk from either trailhead to the scenic Conasauga River, which the trail fords. Hickory Creek's western trailhead provides the shortest and easiest route to the Conasauga downstream from Bray Field.

Starting from the western trailhead (2,300 feet), the wide, white-blazed trail (actually an old road known locally as Camp 20 Trail) descends gradually through a predominantly hardwood forest. After the first mile the trail swings to the left beside Rough Creek (there are two Rough Creeks in the Cohuttas). The rocky old road parallels this lively brook until crossing it at mile 1.6. The trail continues 75 yards to the Conasauga River, where it turns right and follows the road upstream beside the river. From this turn and for 1.3 miles to its crossing of the Conasauga at Bray Field, Hickory Creek Trail shares its treadway with the yellow-blazed Conasauga River Trail.

The two trails closely parallel the western bank of the Conasauga for 0.7 mile. This segment affords many largely unobstructed views of this beautiful mountain river. At mile 2.4 the trail slants to the right away from the river and half-circles a chain of beaver ponds. Hickory Creek fords the Conasauga (usually knee deep or lower), through the gap of the former road across Bray Field, at mile 3.0.

Bray Field was once a family farm, a railroad switch, and a logging camp. In the 1920s the Bray family ran a boarding house for logging officials. Now the forest is encroaching on what's left of the clearing. Only campers keep it somewhat open.

The remaining 5.7-mile segment is the Cohutta's easiest long stretch without river crossings. From the Conasauga at an elevation of 1,920 feet, Hickory Creek Trail loses only 120 feet to its northern, East Cowpen trailhead. There are no long, strenuous

Features
Wilderness, streams, Conasauga River

Distance
8.6 miles

Difficulty Rating
Easy to moderate walked in either direction

Counties
Murray and Fannin

Nearest City
Chatsworth

Maps
Hemp Top and Tennga Quadrangles, GA-TN; Cohutta Wilderness map

Blazes
White

Water Sources
Frequent sources along entire trail

Ranger District
Cohutta

grades; however, there are numerous ups and downs, most of them short and easy. These undulations follow a pattern. The trail meanders through a terrain of low, flat-topped ridges frequently notched by streams and gaps. Thus Hickory Creek Trail dips to a stream, rises to the side or top of a ridge, dips to a gap, rises along the next ridge, then dips again to water.

The only potentially confusing point along the trail occurs at mile 4.1, where it crosses a rocky stream, then turns right at a campsite and follows a roadbed. This stream is Thomas Creek, the first large enough for a name since the Conasauga River.

At the Cohutta sign at mile 7.9, the trail leaves the wilderness and follows a closed woods road to the East Cowpen Trail. Evidence of logging activity is noticeable on both sides of the trail (and road) after it exits the wilderness.

The first 4.9 miles to the east of the Conasauga wind through an unbroken, isolated forest. Here oaks, hickories, tuliptrees, and eastern white pines are slowly regaining their former size. There are more stands of tall eastern white pine along this section than on any other trail in the Cohutta Wilderness.

Two deciduous magnolias—Fraser and umbrella—grow in the moist areas near streams. Their leaves, which are larger than those of any other trees in North Georgia, grow from branch ends in a circular, whorled arrangement. The leaf of the Fraser magnolia can be readily identified by its eared (auriculate) base.

Highlights
Miles 1.7–2.4: The Conasauga River—pools, boulders, and shoals.
Miles 2.4–2.6: Beaver ponds.

Directions
To the western trailhead: From the GA 52–US 411 intersection in Chatsworth, travel approximately 7.3 miles on US 411 North, then turn right onto Grassy Street a short distance past the Crandall Post Office. Continue over the railroad tracks before turning right again. After this second right turn, proceed 0.1 mile, then turn left onto FS 630 (Mill Creek Road) toward Lake Conasauga Recreation Area. Stay on FS 630 (it becomes gravel) for approximately 9.0 miles to the FS 630–FS 17 intersection. Continue straight through this intersection on FS 630; the Hickory Creek Trail parking area is 0.3 mile ahead.

To the northern trailhead: Follow the directions on page 157 for Rice Camp Trail. As you approach the trailhead, Rice Camp is to the left and East Cowpen is straight ahead behind its gate. The Hickory Creek Trail junction is 140 yards up East Cowpen Trail to the right.

Bear Creek Trail

Bear Creek has changed dramatically. For years it was a one-way, 0.8-mile trail leading to the massive Gennett Poplar. Now, however, it has been lengthened and changed to a 6.6-mile double loop that is popular with mountain bikers. The first 1.6 miles and the last 0.5 mile are similar to wide hiking trails; the rest of the route follows old woods roads and dirt-gravel Forest Service roads.

The trail, an old woods road, follows Bear Creek upstream, crossing a tributary at 0.2 mile. The evergreen of rosebay rhododendron and eastern hemlock flanks the stream. In the spring, in late April and early May, clumps of dwarf iris grace the trail with their blue-violet blossoms.

At 0.5 mile the trail turns right and crosses Bear Creek; 0.2 mile farther it crosses it again. A short distance (0.1 mile) beyond the second Bear Creek crossing, look for the Gennett Poplar a few yards to the left of the trail. It is hard to miss. This huge tuliptree, its straight trunk looking much like a massive gray column, seems out of place, dwarfing all other trees along the path. Measured 4 feet 6 inches up from the ground, this North Georgia forest giant is 17 feet 9 inches in circumference, making it the second thickest tree in the Chattahoochee National Forest. Even with the last 10 or 20 feet of its top long gone, the surrounding branches reach nearly 100 feet high.

The Gennett Poplar has stopped growing thicker. Its circumference has increased only 1 inch in the last 17 years, none in the last 10.

Those curious parallel rows of small holes encircling the trunk were bored and enlarged by generations of small woodpeckers—yellow-bellied sapsuckers. After tapping the holes, they return to feed on sap and small insects.

The trail continues past the tuliptree to an intersection at mile 1.0. Here you have the option of

WBR
Cohutta Mountains
Bear Creek
Camping Area

Features
Gennett Poplar,
streams, wildlife
openings

Distance
6.6 miles (loop)

Difficulty Rating
Moderate

County
Gilmer

Nearest City
Ellijay

Maps
Dyer Gap
Quadrangle, GA;
trail map and
description available
from ranger district

Blazes
Blue

Water Sources
Eight stream crossings: four in the first
1.6 miles, one at
mile 3.3, and three
more in the last 0.2
mile

Campsites
Primitive camping
available year-round
at Bear Creek campground

Ranger District
Cohutta

turning right to follow the 3.0-mile lower loop back to the trailhead. Bear Creek Trail follows the longer outer loop straight ahead upstream along Bear Creek, crossing it once. The route switchbacks away from the creek at mile 1.6 and ascends on an old roadbed. Continuing upward on the slope around several knobs, the trail curves to the right and reaches a wildlife opening at mile 2.3.

After crossing the opening, the route proceeds along another old roadbed to a gate at mile 2.6. Here the trail makes a signed right turn onto a gravel road, FS 68. The treadway descends on this road, crossing the creek at 3.3 miles. Two-tenths mile after the creek there is another wildlife opening, and a short distance beyond that, another gate. Continue through the gate and turn right with the trail (and road) at mile 3.9. The route soon follows the steep slope above the creek.

There is a signed intersection at mile 4.8. The lower loop is to the right; the outer loop continues straight ahead. The treadway passes the third wildlife opening (an old trail enters from the left) at 5.6 miles. Blue blazes mark the loop where it turns to the right.

The final opening has a directional sign guiding you to the right at mile 6.0. The remainder of the loop follows an old woods road that descends steadily and somewhat sharply to the trailhead. The woods road crosses a tributary stream at mile 6.4 and again at mile 6.5. Shortly after crossing Bear Creek at mile 6.6, the loop returns to the trailhead.

Bear Creek and all of the tributary streams can be crossed dry-shod at normal water levels.

Highlights
Mile 0.8: The Gennett Poplar, the second thickest tree in the Chatta-hoochee National Forest.
Mile 5.7: Winter view from both sides of the trail.

Directions
From the square in Ellijay travel GA 52 West 5.1 miles, then turn right onto an unmarked, paved county road at the Bear Creek Campground sign. Proceed 5.0 miles, crossing Mountaintown Creek, before turning right onto FS 241, a one-lane dirt-gravel road. Continue straight ahead on FS 241 for 2.0 miles (pass the Bear Creek Camping Area spur) until the road ends at a parking area. The trail begins behind the bulletin board.

From the US 411–GA 52 junction in Chatsworth, travel GA 52 East for 19.5 miles to the left turn at the Bear Creek Campground sign.

Mountaintown Creek Trail

WBR
Cohutta Mountains
Cohutta Wildlife
Management Area

This trail, named for the creek that was named for the former Cherokee settlement in the area, is ideal for a two-day backpacking trip. The first day you can walk downhill to the level campsites along Mountaintown Creek, and on the second, after eating a few pounds of your load, you can take your time heading back up the mountain.

This little-used, primitive trail begins on an old roadbed near Rich Knob at about 3,120 feet. Mountaintown Creek follows one old road or another for most of its length. For the first 0.5 mile, until it turns sharply to the left, the trail descends steadily and often steeply. Beyond the turn, it continues on an easy downgrade through a young forest recovering from a cut made around 1977. The trail rock-hops a tributary of Crenshaw Branch, the first of many crossings to come, at mile 1.2.

At mile 1.7 the trail passes a sliding cascade, 25- to 30-feet wide, enough to let the sun in, and perhaps 15 feet high. Two-tenths of a mile farther, Mountaintown Creek makes its steepest descent through its most scenic section. Above and to the right, a bluff lines the path. Below and to the left, a continuous cascade 100 yards or more in length races down the water-carved notch of a miniature, V-shaped gorge. Pinched into narrow, tilted chutes, parts of this entrenched sluiceway resemble the fast, straight runs of commercial waterslides. There is a diverse forest of mature trees on the slope below the trail. Among them are unusually large red maples, tall and shaggy-barked, remarkably different in appearance from the small, smooth-barked red maples so often found in the understory.

Where the downsloping grade ends at mile 2.3, the trail turns left, crosses a side stream, then switches to the main stem of Crenshaw Branch. The path remains level or gradually downhill for the next 1.3

Features
Streams, cascades

Distance
5.6 miles

Difficulty Rating
Moderate to strenuous

Counties
Fannin and Gilmer

Nearest Cities
Ellijay (S),
Blue Ridge (E)

Maps
Dyer Gap
Quadrangle, GA;
Cohutta Wilderness map

Blazes
None; none needed

Water Sources
Many stream crossings, mostly
Mountaintown Creek

Ranger District
Cohutta

miles as it follows the turbulent branch downstream. Tall basswoods—easily distinguished by their large, sharply pointed, heart-shaped leaves—are common beside this section of trail.

At mile 3.6 the trail reaches a cleared camping area at the junction of two old roads. Here, where Mountaintown Creek and Crenshaw Branch flow together, the path changes streams again. Continue straight ahead from the campsite and cross Mountaintown Creek. The final 2.0 miles, nearly level and easily walked, follow this shallow, unusually calm creek, crossing it three more times. The trail ends at a primitive campground (1,660 feet).

Highlights
Mile 0.8: Grassy ridge-line walk.
Miles 1.5–2.5: Cascades and waterfalls.

Directions
From the square in Ellijay, take GA 52 West and travel 9.5 miles. At the Lake Conasauga Recreation Area sign, turn right onto FS 18 and continue 3.5 miles on that road before turning right onto FS 68. Once on FS 68, proceed straight ahead, uphill. After traveling about 6.0 miles, you will reach the three-way FS 68–FS 64 junction near Potatopatch Mountain. Turn right onto FS 64 and drive about 6.9 miles to the trailhead sign on the right side of the road. You can park at a primitive camping area to the left of the road less than 100 yards before the trailhead.

From the GA 52–US 411 intersection in Chatsworth, travel US 411 North approximately 4.2 miles to the town of Eton. Turn right at the stoplight in Eton, following the sign for Lake Conasauga. This route is signed as CCC Road farther away from Eton. Once it becomes gravel and enters FS property, it becomes FS 18, also known as Holly Creek Road. Continue straight on CCC Road for approximately 10.0 miles (after 6.0 miles the pavement ends) to the three-way, FS 18–FS 68 intersection. Turn left onto FS 68, then continue uphill and straight ahead. Once on FS 68, follow the directions from Ellijay.

Notes

Lake Conasauga Trail

Nineteen-acre Lake Conasauga, nestled among the mountains at 3,140 feet, is Georgia's highest elevation lake. Abundant spring wildflowers, fall color, 4,000-foot mountains, and the nearby designated wilderness lure many visitors to the area; beaver ponds, black bear tracks, and a Songbird Management Area are added attractions. The view from the fire tower, cool evenings in July, and water that stays green no matter how hard it rains are all part of everyday life at Lake Conasauga.

The trail completely encircles the lake, connecting fishing spots, picnic areas, and campgrounds. The path, level and very easily walked, becomes a paved road in the camping area. Large eastern hemlock, jungle-like thickets of rosebay rhododendron, and bridges over green coves help offset the lack of solitude on summer weekends.

Highlights
Throughout: High elevation Lake Conasauga and its numerous recreational opportunities.

Directions
From the square in Ellijay, travel GA 52 West for 9.5 miles. At the Lake Conasauga Recreation Area sign, turn right onto FS 18 and continue 3.5 miles to the three-way FS 18–FS 68 intersection.

Turn right onto FS 68 and proceed straight ahead, uphill. After traveling approximately 6.0 miles on FS 68, you will reach the three-way FS 68–FS 64 junction near Potatopatch Mountain. At the Lake Conasauga sign, follow FS 68 as it turns left and drive straight ahead approximately 4.4 miles to the first turn (Camping Loop A) into the recreation area.

If you are not going to camp, please continue 0.9 mile farther on FS 68, past the turn for Camping Loop B, to the turn into the picnicking and swimming area.

WBR
Cohutta Mountains
**Lake Conasauga
Recreation Area**

Features
Beautiful Lake Conasauga, scenic views

Distance
1.2 miles (loop)

Difficulty Rating
Easy

County
Murray

Nearest Cities
Ellijay (SE), Chatsworth (SW)

Maps
Crandall Quadrangle, GA; Cohutta Wilderness map

Blazes
None; none needed

Campsites
Available seasonally in the recreation area campground; overflow camping area at Songbird trailhead (open year-round)

Ranger District
Cohutta

From the US 411–GA 52 intersection in Chatsworth, travel US 411 North approximately 4.2 miles to the town of Eton. Turn right at the stoplight in Eton, following the sign for Lake Conasauga. This route is signed as CCC Road farther away from Eton. Once it becomes gravel and enters Forest Service property, it becomes FS 18, also known as Holly Creek Road.

Continue straight on CCC–Holly Creek Road for approximately 10.0 miles to its three-way, FS 18–FS 68 intersection. Six miles from Eton the pavement ends; sections of the final 2.5 miles curve and climb sharply. Turn left onto FS 68, travel approximately 6.0 miles, turn left at the Lake Conasauga sign, and drive 4.4 miles to the recreation area.

Alternate route from Chatsworth: From the US 411–GA 52 junction in Chatsworth, travel GA 52 East for approximately 15.0 miles. Turn left onto FS 18 at the Lake Conasauga Recreation Area sign.

Notes

Grassy Mountain Tower Trail

The Grassy Mountain Tower Trail ascends from Lake Conasauga, the highest elevation lake in Georgia (3,140 feet), to the spectacular views atop Grassy Mountain (3,692 feet). This is a relatively easy trail that winds through a variety of habitats—a great day hike any time of the year. During migrations, when hawks ride the thermals over the mountains and warblers filter through the Songbird Management Area, it is also one of North Georgia's better birding areas.

The trail starts at the dam on Lake Conasauga where a sign directs you to both the Tower and Songbird Trails. The path through mixed hardwoods and conifers is lined with rosebay rhododendron. After 0.4 mile, the trail emerges at an information sign beside a beaver pond. Follow the path across a footbridge and climb through rhododendron and mountain laurel thickets. The habitat changes as you pass through an area of saplings and shrubs, part of the 120-acre Songbird Management Area.

About 0.2 mile beyond the footbridge the trail forks, the Songbird Trail angles down and to the left, and the Grassy Mountain Tower Trail turns right. The ascent steepens for the next mile as you pass through mixed hardwoods, eastern hemlock, and eastern white pine.

At mile 1.6 the path leaves the woods and emerges onto a gravel road. From this point, it is a short 0.4 mile to the top of Grassy Mountain. You'll walk through a forest dominated by oaks that become shorter and shorter with elevation. Low-branched and wide-crowned, these orchard-like trees have adapted to the fierce wind on the escarpment.

Once you reach the top, you'll want to climb the fire tower steps to the first landing. They take you above the stunted northern red and white oaks to enjoy great views of the Cohutta Wilderness to the

WBR
Cohutta Mountains
Lake Conasauga
Recreation Area

Features
Scenic view, Lake Conasauga, beaver pond

Distance
2.0 miles

Difficulty Rating
Easy to moderate

County
Murray

Nearest Cities
Ellijay (SE), Chatsworth (SW)

Maps
Crandall Quadrangle, GA; Cohutta Wilderness map

Blazes
None; none needed

Campsites
Available seasonally at recreation area campground

Ranger District
Cohutta

northeast and Fort Mountain to the southwest.

This trail has a good spring wildflower display. From early to mid-April, trout lily blooms in abundance. From late April through early May, look for Catesby's trillium near the beginning of the trail and sessile trillium and lousewort higher up near the tower.

Highlights

Mile 0.0: The trail starts at the dam end of Lake Conasauga, a beautiful man-made lake fed by mountain streams.

Mile 0.4: The Grassy Mountain Tower and Songbird Trails follow the edge of a beaver pond, a birding area.

Mile 2.0: A 360-degree vista from the Grassy Mountain Fire Tower. Look northeast for the Cohutta Wilderness and southwest for Fort Mountain and Chatsworth.

Directions

(See page 177 of Lake Conasauga Trail for directions to the recreation area, and see page 182 of the Songbird Trail for directions to its trailhead.) Grassy Mountain Tower could be described as an interior trail. Its official beginning and sign are located at the edge of the dam farthest from the main campground. From the picnic area parking lot, which the Forest Service requests that you use if you are not camping, walk the wide Lake Conasauga Trail to the dam.

If you would rather walk past Songbird Trail's beaver ponds on the way to the Tower Trail, start at the Songbird Trailhead, walk 0.6 mile, then tie into the Tower Trail.

Notes

Songbird Trail

WBR
Cohutta Mountains
Lake Conasauga
Recreation Area

The 120-acre Songbird Management Area provides optimum habitat for songbirds. To the left, where the second-growth forest remains uncut, a branch of Mill Creek parallels the trail. To the right, a dense young stand cut in the late 1970s is maintained by managed burning to keep its vegetation thick and shrubby, a habitat required by many songbirds.

The trail proceeds straight ahead to a fork in the path at a directional sign—at 0.3 mile the loop starts around the beaver pond. Continuing straight ahead, following the loop in a counterclockwise direction, the treadway parallels a beaver pond, the first of a 0.3 mile-long chain. A boardwalk leads out over the pond to an observation platform, offering a perfect spot to sit and watch for wildlife. The beaver lodge and dam are visible.

At mile 0.6 the Grassy Mountain Tower Trail, having come from Lake Conasauga, enters from the right at a bulletin board and directional sign. Both trails share the same treadway at this point. The trail crosses a low bridge, then leads up the hill to the left at a directional sign. After passing through another shrubby opening, the Grassy Mountain Tower Trail continues straight and Songbird Trail branches left. The Songbird Trail crosses three more footbridges before completing the loop.

Over the years the beaver have enhanced this loop. Their ponds have added beauty and increased the diversity of habitat and wildlife. The area supports many bird species. Cavity nesters, such as the flicker, live in the gray snags; the woodcock probes the mud for earthworms; the kingfisher dives for small fish. Watch for wood ducks living in the boxes around the pond or in the cavities of dead trees. Frogs, in one form or another, snakes, and salamanders can be viewed from the water's edge. Colorful dragonflies helicopter to and fro, hawking insects.

Features
Songbird Management Area, beaver ponds

Distance
1.7 miles (loop)

Difficulty Rating
Easy

County
Murray

Nearest Cities
Ellijay (SE), Chatsworth (SW)

Maps
Crandall Quadrangle, GA; Cohutta Wilderness map

Blazes
None; none needed

Campsites
Available seasonally in the recreation area campground; overflow camping area at the Songbird Trailhead (open year-round)

Ranger District
Cohutta

The shoreline mud registers the comings and goings of the local animals. Raccoon, deer, wild hog, and beaver tracks are not difficult to find. If you come upon a large, wide-palmed footprint that isn't human, you have probably found a black bear track.

The best time for birding along this trail is during spring migration. Then the males are both vocal and colorful. Mid-May is usually a good time for bird-watching.

Highlights

Throughout: Good birding area. Many species live in or migrate through the management area.

Mile 0.3: A beaver pond, busy with bird, amphibian, and insect life. Mammal tracks can be seen in the mud.

Directions

(See page 177 of Lake Conasauga Trail for directions to the recreation area.) The Songbird Trail begins at the Overflow Camping Area at Lake Conasauga. To reach the Overflow Camping Area, continue straight ahead on FS 68 approximately 1.2 miles past Camping Loop A (first entrance into the recreation area). The trail starts at the Songbird Management Area bulletin board. Trailhead parking is available across the road from the Overflow Camping Area.

Notes

Emery Creek Trail

WBR
Cohutta Mountains
Cohutta Wildlife
Management Area

Although Emery Creek Trail is primitive—unblazed and usually without signs—it is scenic and now, for the most part, easily followed.

The first 0.2 mile of the trail follows an old road, now closed to traffic, that starts at an elevation of approximately 960 feet, high above Holly Creek. This section of Holly Creek, with its deep pools, cascades, and huge boulders, is beautiful and popular. Soon after it descends to stream level, the trail narrows to a rocky path and reaches the convergence of Holly and Emery Creeks. As you face upstream, Holly Creek is to the right, Emery to the left. The trail continues along the left bank of Emery Creek. You can either cross Holly Creek alone below the fork, or you can cross both just above their confluence. In high water, this crossing becomes a hazardous ford.

Beyond this initial crossing, this path becomes less traveled as it parallels Emery Creek through a forest dotted with tall eastern white and shortleaf pines and thick, uninitialed American beech trees. It becomes more interesting and isolated as it moves farther away from Holly Creek's swimming holes. Shortly after its fifth crossing at mile 1.3, the trail turns right onto a gravel road and then left onto another old road before crossing Emery Creek. Follow trail signs at these junctions.

Forty yards beyond the eighth crossing (most can be made dry-shod) at mile 2.2, a wide spur trail to the left leads 125 yards to the first waterfall. Surprisingly loud and powerful for the stream's size and 45 to 50 feet high, the fall drops from wide ledge to wide ledge to a small green pool at its base. Emery Creek Falls is both higher and longer than you might first guess. Below most of the ledges, the fall slides into a narrow pool which pours over the lip of the next ledge.

To reach the second falls, continue on the main trail as it bends to the left and ascends very sharply

Features
Streams, waterfalls, overlook view

Distance
7.5 miles

Difficulty Rating
Moderate to strenuous

County
Murray

Nearest Cities
Ellijay (SE), Chatsworth (SW)

Maps
Crandall and Dyer Gap Quadrangles, GA; Cohutta Wilderness map; trail map available from ranger district

Blazes
None

Water Sources
Abundant for the first 5.0 miles

Campsites
Mile 7.5: open, grassy meadow at the Group Camping Area

Ranger District
Cohutta

for 0.1 mile. At mile 2.7 the trail comes to a point where you can scramble down the hillside to explore a series of four cascades. The highest of the cascades is a 20- to 25-foot waterfall.

The trail crosses Emery Creek three more times and remains level or slightly uphill to a closed Forest Service road. This road marks the place where the trail used to end. In 1994 it was extended up to Little Bald Mountain during a service project led by Recreational Equipment, Inc. Turn left onto the road, walk about 50 feet, then turn right onto another old woods road. The trail follows this roadbed as it meanders along a main tributary of Emery Creek to about mile 4.5. Here it leaves the roadbed, crosses the creek, and climbs above the creek.

From this point on, the trail becomes strenuous, following a narrow, ascending path as it cuts its way across steep, boulder-strewn slopes in an isolated forest of pines and hardwoods. At mile 7.2 a beautiful overlook opens on the left with a south-southwest view of Fort Mountain. The trail ends at the primitive Group Camping Area, which is essentially a large grassy field on Little Bald Mountain (3,640 feet) just off FS 68. The Cherokee once used this field for tribal games and ceremonies.

Highlights
Mile 2.2: Spur trail to Emery Creek Falls, a 50-foot, two-ledge drop.
Mile 2.7: Hillside scramble down to a four-tiered cascade.
Mile 7.2: Overlook with a south-southwest view of Fort Mountain.

Directions
To the southern trailhead at Holly Creek: From the GA 52–US 411 intersection in Chatsworth, travel US 411 North approximately 4.2 miles to the town of Eton. Turn right at the stoplight in Eton, following the sign for Lake Conasauga. This route is signed as CCC Road farther away from Eton. Once it becomes gravel and enters Forest Service property, it becomes FS 18, also known as Holly Creek Road. Continue straight on CCC Road for approximately 7.3 miles (after 6.0 miles the pavement ends). As you start a sharp curve to the right and uphill away from the creek, look for the trailhead and parking lot on the left.

To the northern trailhead at the Group Camping Area: From the Ellijay square, drive west 9.5 miles on GA 52. At the Lake Conasauga Recreation Area sign, turn right onto FS 18 and continue 3.5 miles. Turn right onto FS 68, continuing uphill and straight ahead. After traveling about 6.0 miles, you will reach the three-way intersection of FS 68 and FS 64 near Potatopatch Mountain. Turn left toward Lake Conasauga, staying on

FS 68. Continue about 3.5 miles to the Group Camping Area on the left. The trailhead is in the back left-hand corner of the open field.

Although the route is straightforward, there is no quick and easy way to set a shuttle between trailheads. You can link the directions given for the southern and northern trailheads. Holly Creek Road heading east from Eton toward the southern trailhead turns into FS 18, the same road mentioned in the directions to the northern trailhead. From the southern trailhead at Holly Creek, you can follow FS 18 2.5 miles farther away from Eton to its three-way intersection with FS 68, mentioned in the northern trailhead directions. The Chattahoochee National Forest Administrative map is indispensible for figuring out shuttles and alternate routes.

Notes

186

Features
Stream, waterfall

Distance
0.5 mile

Difficulty Rating
Easy to moderate

County
Murray

Nearest City
Chatsworth

Map
Tennga
Quadrangle, GA-TN

Blazes
None; none needed

Campsites
Hickey Gap
Primitive
Campground at the
trailhead

Ranger District
Cohutta

Mill Creek Falls Trail

Mill Creek Falls Trail is one of several interesting trails in the Lake Conasauga area outside of the Cohutta Wilderness. It is actually an unblazed, unconstructed, but easily followed footpath created by people walking to the falls from the primitive campground on Mill Creek.

From the camping area, walk downstream betweeen the big rocks and the creek. Continue following this sliding, cascading stream to the falls. At one point, after a large boulder to the right of the path, the trail seems to disappear into the creek. Skirt the moist slabs of rock close to the water's edge; the stream will be on your left and a rock wall will be on your right. The path, recognizable once again, returns to the forest 20 or 30 yards downstream.

Near the end of the trail Mill Creek, quickening its pace over a series of low falls and short slides, takes a running start toward its final long cascade to the falls below. It is much safer to stay away from the slide and the slippery rocks near its edge. To reach the bottom of the falls, follow the path upward to the right, then sharply downhill. About 30 to 35 feet of the wide, sliding waterfall are visible from its base. The roughly circular plunge pool—deep, green, and goose-pimple cold—is 35 to 40 feet across.

During early May, the fringe tree, also known as old-man's beard, blooms on the rock outcrops near the falls. This member of the olive family has fragrant white blossoms that hang in loose, three-flowered clusters, four to eight inches long. The thin petals look like scissor-cut fringe.

Highlights
Mile 0.5: Mill Creek Falls, wide falls with a deep, circular plunge pool.

Directions

From the GA 52–US 411 intersection in Chatsworth, travel approximately 7.3 miles on US 411 North, then turn right onto Grassy Street a short distance past the Crandall Post Office. Continue over the railroad tracks before turning right again. After this second right turn, proceed 0.1 mile, then turn left onto FS 630 (Mill Creek Road) toward Lake Conasauga Recreation Area. Stay on FS 630 (it turns to gravel) for approximately 6.7 miles to FS 630-E, which drops down and to the right (at a 45-degree angle) a short distance to a campground on Mill Creek known as Hickey Gap Primitive Campground.

Notes

FORT MOUNTAIN
STATE PARK

Fort Mountain, situated in the Cohutta Mountains within the Chatta-hoochee National Forest Purchase Corridor, is now the largest state park in Georgia's mountain region. The park preserves 3,268 acres (slightly more than five square miles), enough room for the extensive trail expansion planned for the near future.

The name Fort Mountain stems from the intriguing ancient wall of piled stones that snakes along 885 feet of the mountaintop. The park's name implies one of the explanations for the wall's existence—fortification. But there are other fascinating theories about the origin of this mysterious structure. Read the park signs by the wall and decide for yourself.

Directions

Fort Mountain's approach road is to the north of GA 52 between Ellijay and Chatsworth. From the US 411–GA 52 intersection in Chatsworth, travel GA 52 East for slightly more than 7.0 miles to the Fort Mountain State Park entrance.

From the Ellijay square, follow GA 52 West for approximately 17.5 miles to the park entrance.

Gahuti Backcountry Trail

G ahuti is the Cherokee word for Cohutta Mountain in Murray County. The name comes from the Cherokee words for "a shed roof supported on poles" and refers to a fancied resemblance to the summit of Cohutta Mountain.

Gahuti Backcountry's loop often skirts the isolated border the park shares with the Chattahoochee National Forest. Away from the busy activity areas, the trail winds along the ravines, spur ridges, and slopes of Fort and Cohutta Mountains. It follows the contours of this terrain up and down numerous grades, most easy or moderate. There are a few long, steep descents and a few short, very sharp climbs. But there are no steady, strenuous ascents.

The first 2.6-mile section of the loop follows a tortuous, undulating route. Pay close attention to the frequent orange blazes. If you stop seeing them, you have probably walked past a turn.

The path roller-coasters down through an oak-pine forest to a Mill Creek tributary at mile 1.4. Here it turns left and parallels the branch before crossing Mill Creek below where the streams flow together. The loop continues beside Mill Creek, crossing it again at mile 1.8. After turning away from the stream, the treadway proceeds up and over spur ridges and in and out of ravines until it reaches the park's entrance road at mile 2.6. The trail crosses the pavement at a sharp angle to the left, then climbs a short distance to an old road on top of a ridge.

The wide walkway of the road descends gradually through a maturing forest. After a full mile of this easy hiking, the trail ascends moderately for 0.2 mile. Eighty-five yards before reaching a paved road, the loop turns left off the road onto path. At mile 4.2 it crosses another paved park road. Once across, the trail quickly settles into a pattern of alternating ups and downs similar to its beginning. On this side of the loop, however, the grades are generally longer

WBR
Cohutta Mountains
Fort Mountain State Park

Features
Backpacking trail, cascade, Cool Spring Overlook

Distance
8.2 miles (loop)

Difficulty Rating
Moderate to strenuous

County
Murray

Nearest Cities
Chatsworth (W), Ellijay (E)

Maps
Crandall Quadrangle, GA; park map available at office

Blazes
Orange

Water Sources
Miles 1.4, 1.8, 5.5, and 7.2 (seasonal spring)

Campsites
Three designated sites: mile 1.4: idyllic setting in rhododendron thicket near creek; mile 3.2: heavily wooded site south of trail; mile 5.0: site near scenic overlook and Big Rock Nature Trail

and more strenuous. Here there are many outcrops. After several partial views west, you reach one high outcrop with a clear view.

Following a long, often steep descent, the trail crosses an unnamed stream and turns left onto the Big Rock Nature Trail at mile 5.5. Gahuti Backcountry shares the treadway with the nature trail through this scenic area for 0.2 mile, then parallels Gold Mine Creek as it gently cascades down a run of stair-step ledges.

After crossing the creek, the footpath climbs away from it along a line of bluffs. It then rises to near the top of a ridge before dropping back down to the slopes of Fort Mountain. Here the treadway, a cut path, continues nearly level as it half-circles around ravines. At mile 7.2 it crosses the beginning spring flow of Rock Creek.

Beyond this rivulet, which may be dry in summer, the trail ascends moderately through a dense stand of Virginia pine. This long upgrade ends where Gahuti Backcountry crosses the park road above the turn to Cool Spring Overlook.

The loop's final 0.3 mile dips to an old road, then rises back up to a view of the Cohutta Mountains, a crumpled mass of sharp ridges to the northeast. Up high across the valley, the Cohutta Wilderness preserves the pure wildness of an unbroken mountain forest. The tallest peak in sight, Big Frog, at 4,200 feet, straddles the northern boundary of the wilderness, across the state line in Tennessee.

The Gahuti Backcountry Trail has three designated campsites—one group per site per night. There is a small fee per person per night. Day hikers must stop by the park office and file a trip plan; backpackers must reserve a designated site in advance and obtain a permit from the park office before hiking.

Highlights
Mile 5.5: View west of the Chatsworth Valley.
Mile 5.7: Junction with Big Rock Nature Trail featuring a stair-step cascade on Gold Mine Creek.
Mile 8.2: Overlook of the Cohutta Wilderness to the northeast.

Directions
(See page 188 for directions to the Fort Mountain State Park entrance.) To reach the Gahuti trailhead, travel into the park and past the information office toward the "Old Fort" section of the park. A short distance before the road curls into its turnaround loop, turn right at the sign for Cool Spring Overlook. The trail starts behind its prominent sign in the gravel parking lot.

Old Fort Trails

WBR
Cohutta Mountains
Fort Mountain
State Park

A color-coded system of interconnected pathways leads walkers to the rocky mountaintop's three main attractions: the fascinating stone wall, the lookout tower and the overlook deck. The yellow-blazed trail, which begins and ends at the pavement, makes a 1.3-mile loop around the top of Fort Mountain. This loop leads to the attractions and the other three trails. After less than 100 yards, the yellow-blazed walkway splits into its loop. This description follows the loop to the right, counterclockwise.

As you start your walk through this scenic area, you quickly realize that this is a good place to find building materials for a rock wall. Thousands of rocks, from small stones to room-sized boulders, lie strewn about the mountaintop. After walking slightly less than 0.5 mile along the loop, you reach the spot where the red-blazed trail leads to the left. The red trail, a little more than 0.2 mile long, cuts across the wide top third of the yellow loop, meeting it again at the tower. Leading away from the red trail's midpoint, the blue-blazed trail heads toward the rock wall. Two-tenths of a mile long, the blue trail parallels the serpentine line of piled rocks before it ends at the yellow loop.

Continuing from its junction with the red trail, the loop skirts the mountain's craggy northern rim, then curls back toward its beginning. At 0.8 mile a spur trail to the right sharply descends 140 yards to an observation platform, which provides vistas of valleys and the mountains beyond.

The yellow loop turns left, away from the spur's entrance, and continues 80 yards to the Old Stone Tower built by the Civilian Conservation Corps in the 1930s. Built on the mountain's high point (2,840 feet), the rock and wood tower stands 38 feet high and has always been used for observation purposes only. It has been rebuilt since the late 1970s. You are

Features
Mysterious rock wall, view, lookout tower, boulder field

Distance
1.8 miles of interconnected trails

Difficulty Rating
Easy to moderate

County
Murray

Nearest Cities
Chatsworth (W), Ellijay (E)

Maps
Crandall Quadrangle, GA; park map available at office

Blazes
Yellow for full trail, red for shortcut to tower, and blue for trail to wall

Campsites
Available with reservation in park campground

welcome to walk to its top, which is now slightly below treeline. An imaginative worker placed a heart-shaped stone in one of its sides.

The loop turns to the right at the tower and begins its easy downgrade back to the parking lot. At mile 1.0 the blue trail leads toward the lichen-splotched rocks of the low wall running 855 feet east to west from a cliff to a precipice. Its history is uncertain, but archeologists believe it was constructed as a ceremonial center by the Woodland Indians around 500 A.D. Generally about two to three feet high, the wall has 29 pits spaced at regular intervals. Several theories about the wall are described on interpretive plaques along the trail. Early settlers thought the wall delineated a fort on the mountaintop; that's where the mountain and subsequently the state park got their names.

Highlights

Mile 0.8: Overlook west of Chatsworth and its valley.
Mile 0.8: Stone lookout tower, now below treeline, but still fun to climb.
Mile 1.0: Ancient stone wall built by the Woodland Indians.

Directions

(See page 188 for directions to the Fort Mountain State Park entrance.) To reach the Old Fort trailhead, continue on the park's entrance road straight ahead to its turnaround loop. The trail system begins on the right side of the loop; signs, plaques, and a wooden entryway mark its location. Trail maps are available at the park office.

Notes

Lake Trail

WBR
Cohutta Mountains
Fort Mountain
State Park

This description follows the path to the right (counterclockwise) around the long, narrow lake. Its initial segment closely parallels the forested and relatively undisturbed southern shoreline. After slightly more than 0.3 mile, Gold Mine Creek Trail turns to the right. A small wooden boardwalk and bench are situated at the east end of the lake. Just beyond the boardwalk is a wooden bridge crossing the small stream feeding into the lake. The lake itself is about 40 feet deep and has a surface area of 14 acres. Mountain laurel and ferns line both sides of the trail.

By 0.5 mile the trail has looped to Fort Mountain Lake's northern shoreline and its activity areas for picnicking, swimming, paddle boating, and miniature golfing. The beach is fenced. To continue the trail, walk around the beach house, then work your way back to the lake. The trail finishes its loop by crossing the grassy dam on a pathway below the road. This dam was originally built by the Civilian Conservation Corps in 1938 and was reconstructed in 1981.

Features
Lakeshore

Distance
1.2 miles (loop)

Difficulty Rating
Easy

County
Murray

Nearest Cities
Chatsworth (W),
Ellijay (E)

Maps
Crandall
Quadrangle, GA;
park map available
at park office

Blazes
Blue

Campsites
Available with
reservation at park
campground

Directions

(See page 188 for directions to the Fort Mountain State Park entrance.) To reach the Lake Trail, travel approximately 0.5 mile into the park from its entrance, then turn left at the sign for camping, swimming, and picnicking. Continue approximately 1.3 miles on this road before turning left into a large parking area next to a pavilion. This parking area is past the dam and immediately past the large sign for Big Rock Nature Trail, which is on the right side of the road. The blue-blazed trail is down at the lakeshore.

WBR
Cohutta Mountains
Fort Mountain
State Park

Features
Forest, Gold Mine
Creek

Distance
1.2 miles (loop)

Difficulty Rating
Easy to moderate

County
Murray

Nearest Cities
Chatsworth (W),
Ellijay (E)

Map
Crandall
Quadrangle, GA;
park map available
at office

Blazes
White

Campsites
Available with
reservation at park
campground

Gold Mine Creek Trail

After following the blue-blazed Lake Trail along its forested, southern shoreline for 0.3 mile, you will arrive at Gold Mine Creek's sign and beginning white blazes to the right. The initial segment of Gold Mine Creek also serves as a red-blazed access path to the orange-blazed Gahuti Backcountry Trail.

The trail ascends on easy-to-moderate grades through a predominantly hardwood forest. At 0.2 mile, the footpath, having just passed the loop's return, turns left and follows the loop in a counter-clockwise direction. Here the treadway is an old, somewhat washed out roadbed. There are mountain laurel down the steep bank to the creek, and many eastern white pine saplings are beginning their rise to the canopy amidst the hardwoods.

At 0.5 mile the trail levels off on a ridge top. Here a sign and spur trail lead to Gold Mine Camp, a reservation-only campsite for Gahuti Backcountry Trail users. Beyond the campsite spur, the loop bends to the north and descends, sometimes sharply, to the creek. Many mature 80- to 100-year-old hardwoods (rings counted) are down—deadfalls from 80- to 85-mile-an-hour winds that ripped the park in 1995 during Hurricane Opal.

The loop crosses the rosebay rhododendron-lined brook or its tributaries seven times between 0.6 and 0.7 mile. Although the crossings are easy, the path roller-coasters above the stream between them.

Highlights
Miles 0.6–0.7: Gold Mine Creek.

Directions
(See page 188 for directions to the Fort Mountain State Park entrance.) Gold Mine Creek is an interior trail. You must walk slightly more than 0.3 mile on the blue-blazed Lake Trail to reach its signed junction with the white-blazed Gold Mine Creek Trail. (See page 193 of Lake Trail, also in Fort Mountain State Park, for directions to its trailhead.)

Big Rock Nature Trail

WBR
Cohutta Mountains
Fort Mountain
State Park

The Big Rock Nature Trail traverses an area that is both botanically rich and scenic. The pathside forest includes upland trees—Virginia pine, chestnut oak, sassafras—as well as moisture-requiring species such as sweet birch, witch-hazel, and rosebay rhododendron. Although its "Big Rock" name is singular, there are thousands of rocks along the loop, both large and small. This jumbled boulder field provides pockets of shade and moisture for several species of ferns. The small ones that grow on the boulders are rock cap ferns.

The trail quickly descends to a small unnamed stream. After slightly less than 0.2 mile, the Gahuti Backcountry Trail crosses the stream and joins the Big Rock Nature Trail. The two trails share the same rocky treadway for the next 0.2 mile.

At the loop's midpoint, a cliff-edge outcrop provides a view of the forested valleys and mountains of the Cohuttas. Beyond a wooden walkway, the path curls right then parallels Gold Mine Creek as it gently cascades down a run of stair-step ledges. A bluff line across the creek delineates the stream's beginning gorge. The remainder of the loop leads back uphill, past another flight of stair-step ledges and a wildlife clearing with an observation bench. The path ends at the road downhill from the trailhead.

Features
View, boulder field, cascade

Distance
0.6 mile (loop)

Difficulty Rating
Easy to moderate

County
Murray

Nearest Cities
Chatsworth (W), Ellijay (E)

Maps
Crandall Quadrangle, GA; park map available at office

Blazes
Yellow

Campsites
Available with reservation at park campground

Highlights
Mile 0.4: Cascading waterfall on Gold Mine Creek.

Directions
(See page 188 for directions to the Fort Mountain State Park entrance.) To reach the Big Rock trailhead, travel approximately 0.5 mile into the park from its entrance, then turn left at the sign for camping, swimming, and picnicking. Continue approximately 1.3 miles on this road before turning left into a small parking area across the road from the trail's large sign. This parking area is past the dam.

CARTERS LAKE

Constructed and managed by the US Army Corps of Engineers, Carters Lake is located in the northernmost Piedmont southwest of Ellijay. The Corps has developed public-use areas for camping, picnicking, hiking, and water-related activities at six sites around the 3,220-acre lake.

All the public-use areas have trails; however, much of their mileage serves as short sightseeing trails from the main roads to the lakeshore or as circulation between campsites, comfort stations, and picnic tables. Three of the public-use areas—Damsite, Reregulation Dam, and Ridgeway—have longer, designated trails guided by signs or arrowed posts.

Piedmont
Carters Lake
**Ridgeway Public
Use Area**

Features
Stream, small
waterfall

Distance
1.2 miles (loop)

Difficulty Rating
Easy to moderate

County
Gilmer

Nearest Cities
Chatsworth (W),
Ellijay (E)

Maps
Webb Quadrangle,
GA; Carters Lake
map available at
Damsite Public Use
Area Visitor Center

Tumbling Waters Nature Trail

Tumbling Waters Nature Trail provides an easily accessible introduction to the North Georgia creek valley. Its 1.2 round-trip miles roll from hillside to creekbed, without a single strenuous stretch, through a typical mix of hardwoods, evergreens, abundant rosebay rhododendron, and a rich, diverse forest floor of mosses, ferns, and herbaceous plants.

For 0.2 mile, the trail gradually descends to Carters Lake, where the forest opens up into a small bottom. The trail proceeds across a short woods road in the bottom; you can make a quick detour a few yards to the left to a small, sunny meadow just above the lake. The trail forks at mile 0.4. Take the right fork to an observation deck perched above Tails Creek. Here, below the overlook, a long shoaling run over ledges culminates in a 15-foot-high cascading slide. Back on the main trail, proceed to the right across an impressive foot bridge—75 feet long and 50 feet above the creek. Look north for another full view of the shoals. Behind you is the northernmost tip of the lake.

Across the bridge, follow the signs up and to the right. After about 100 feet, an unmarked 90-degree turn to the right through a narrow path between the trees leads to a second fork. Take the left fork to another observation deck, this one at creek level about midway up the shoals. This platform provides a close view of the creek's ledges, which come to rounded downstream points, forming an overlapping feather pattern of rock. Across the creek, a broad, overhanging clump of rosebay rhododendron will provide striking color in the late spring. The remainder of the trail leads down to a pool, framed by a 20-foot-high bluff at the base of the cascade. Here the path loops back up to the bridge and retraces itself to the trailhead.

Blazes
None; none needed

Campsites
Camping not permitted along this trail; campsites available year-round in the Ridgeway Public Use Area Campground

Highlights

Mile 0.4: Observation deck perched high above Tails Creek. Looking due north, you will see the entire run of noisy shoals culminating in a split cascade before you.

Mile 0.4: Long, high footbridge across Tails Creek. Shoals and cascade lie north; wider water leading to Carters Lake flows south.

Mile 0.6: Twenty-foot-high bluff across the creek pool.

Directions

From the US 411–GA 52 junction in Chatsworth, travel approximately 5.3 miles on US 411 South before turning left onto US 76–GA 282 East. Stay on this highway (it turns several times) for slightly more than 11.0 miles, then turn right onto the dirt road at the "Ridgeway" sign.

From GA 515, the Zell Miller Mountain Parkway, in east Ellijay, travel US 76–GA 282 West a little more than 9.0 miles. Then turn left at the sign between mile markers 4.0 and 5.0. The rough dirt road turns to pavement after about 2.0 miles. After another mile, turn right at the sign pointing to the boat ramp. The trailhead is clearly marked with a sign.

Notes

Piedmont
Carters Lake
Reregulation Dam
Public Use Area

Features
Beaver pond, wildlife habitats

Distance
0.6 mile (loop)

Difficulty Rating
Easy

County
Murray

Nearest Cities
Chatsworth (NW), Ellijay (NE), Oakman (SW)

Maps
Oakman Quadrangle, GA; Carters Lake map available at Damsite Public Use Area Vistor Center

Blazes
None; none needed

Campsites
Camping not permitted in this area; campsites available at nearby Carters Lake campgrounds

Hidden Pond Trail

Constructed as a birders' trail, Hidden Pond's large sign and wide graveled entrance leave no doubt where it begins and ends. And its posts with directional arrows leave no doubt where it goes. After less than 40 yards, the loop turns to the right and crosses a bridge over an unnamed tributary of the nearby Coosawattee River, then slants up and over a low, forested hill. At 0.2 mile the trail crosses a long boardwalk bridge over the marshy end of a beaver pond. This shallow pond is old—the dead snags have almost all fallen—and may soon be abandoned for a site with more food. At the end of the bridge, the graveled walkway to the right leads 160 yards to an overlook. The wooden deck affords a good view of the beaver pond, large by mountain standards.

Farther upstream, an observation platform provides a view of a second pond and an active beaver lodge. Be on the lookout for the belted kingfisher, often sounding its loud ratchet-rattle call on the wing near the pond's edge. In addition to its distinctive call, the belted kingfisher's blue-gray back and breastband, bushy crest, large daggerlike bill, and 13-inch length make it one of the easiest birds to identify. The female's rusty bellyband makes her more brightly colored than the male, a rare exception among birds.

Around 5,000 autumn olive trees and 1,000 bicolor bush clover, or lespedeza, plants have been planted throughout this trail and are now well established. There are also clearings planted with duck wheat and milo, so there is plenty of food for wildlife, which includes waterfowl in winter.

After doubling back to the bridge, the remainder of the loop follows the creek back to the trailhead. This final section of trail also closely parallels the reregulation reservoir, used for overflow releases from Carters Dam.

Highlights

Mile 0.2: Two beaver ponds and one active lodge. Birding is good along the boardwalks and platforms near the ponds.

Directions

From the GA 52–US 411 junction in Chatsworth, travel US 411 South for slightly more than 13.0 miles, then turn left onto GA 136 East. (Or, if traveling north on US 411, continue slightly more than 1.0 mile past Oakman and turn right onto GA 136.) Continue 0.4 mile on GA 136 before turning left onto the first paved road beyond the railroad tracks. Continue less than 0.5 mile and turn right into the first parking area for the reregulation reservoir area. Look right for the trailhead sign and entrance.

Notes

Piedmont
Carters Lake
**Damsite Public
Use Area**

Features
Pond, views, inter-
pretive stations

Distance
2.6 miles (loop)

Difficulty Rating
Moderate

County
Murray

Nearest Cities
Chatsworth (NW),
Ellijay (NE),
Oakman (SW)

Maps
Oakman
Quadrangle, GA;
Carters Lake map
available at visitor
center

Blazes
Blue, also wooden
directional posts

Campsites
Camping not permit-
ted in this area;
campsites available
at nearby Carters
Lake campgrounds

Talking Rock Nature Trail

The trail's starting point is a signed archway. The path descends moderately for 150 yards through an oak-pine forest to a pond with benches and wood duck boxes. Continue to the left with the directional sign at the pond. The footpath quickly passes through an open area labeled as a "food plot," one of several wildlife plots along the trail. Here, and at regular intervals along the first mile, there are interpretive markers describing the various trailside features.

The loop turns right and follows the branch at marker 7. Here the treadway rises sharply to a low ridge. Throughout the area, but especially along this segment, 1995 Hurricane Opal damage is noticeable. The path levels close to the top of the ridge at 0.5 mile. The ridge-crest forest is primarily Virginia pine, struggling to recover from a 1987 pine beetle infestation that killed 60 percent of the pines here.

At 0.7 mile there is a winter view of Carters Lake to the left. A short distance beyond this view, the trail descends from the ridge to a good view of the reregulation reservoir to the right at mile 1.0. The loop continues past a power line right-of-way and descends moderately. After descending to and following a branch for a short distance, the tread-way rises, occasionally sharply, to successive wildlife openings at mile 2.0. Next the trail follows easy then steeper downgrades through a primarily hard-wood forest. The loop ends back at marker 7 at 2.4 miles.

The trail route has changed from the original path shown on the Carters Lake handout. Unblazed spurs or old trails are encountered along the way. Stay on the blue-blazed path and follow the direc-tional arrows on signposts to remain on the desig-nated trail.

Highlights

Throughout: Interpretive posts, food plots, wildlife boxes.
Mile 0.1: Pond with benches and wood duck boxes.
Mile 0.7: Winter view of Carters Lake.
Mile 1.0: View of Reregulation Reservoir.

Directions

From the GA 52–US 411 junction in Chatsworth, travel US 411 South for slightly more than 13.0 miles, then turn left onto GA 136 East. (Or, if traveling north on US 411, continue slightly more than 1.0 mile past Oakman and turn right onto GA 136.) Continue approximately 2.5 miles on GA 136 before turning left at the sign for Carters Lake Dam and visitor center. The road forks after 1.8 miles: 0.4 mile to the right is the visitor center; 0.2 mile to the left is the trailhead.

From the square in Ellijay, travel old Highway 5 southward for 4.3 miles to GA 382. Turn right onto GA 382 and continue 10.0 miles before turning right onto GA 136. Proceed 3.2 miles to the right turn at the Carters Lake Dam and visitor center sign.

Notes

Piedmont
Carters Lake
Damsite Public Use Area

Features
Scenic view, posted nature trail, lake

Distance
0.2 mile

Difficulty Rating
Easy

County
Murray

Nearest Cities
Chatsworth (NW), Ellijay (NE), Oakman (SW)

Maps
Oakman Quadrangle, GA; Carters Lake map available at visitor center

Blazes
None; none needed

Campsites
Camping not permitted in this area; campsites available at nearby Carters Lake campground

Carters Lake Nature Trail

This short nature trail begins outside the back doors of the Carters Lake Visitor Center. A sign marks the exact point. The wide, wood-chip-cushioned path traverses a mixed oak-pine forest near the top of a dry slope above the lake. Along the way, signposts identify and describe many of the tree and shrub species growing beside the trail. Several signposts provide additional information concerning their former uses. The bark of the chestnut oak, for instance, was used by settlers to tan leather and treat burns. Blackgum twigs were used by Native Americans and settlers as toothbrushes. The trail ends at a concrete overlook of Carters Lake.

Highlights
Throughout: Views of the lake and surrounding hills. Natural history information on posts.

Directions
From the GA 52–US 411 junction in Chatsworth, travel US 411 South for slightly more than 13.0 miles, then turn left onto GA 136 East. (Or, if traveling north on US 411, continue slightly more than 1.0 mile past Oakman and turn right onto GA 136.) Continue approximately 2.5 miles on GA 136 before turning left at the sign for Carters Lake Dam and visitor center. Proceed straight ahead for approximately 2.2 miles (take the right fork where the road divides) to the visitor center.

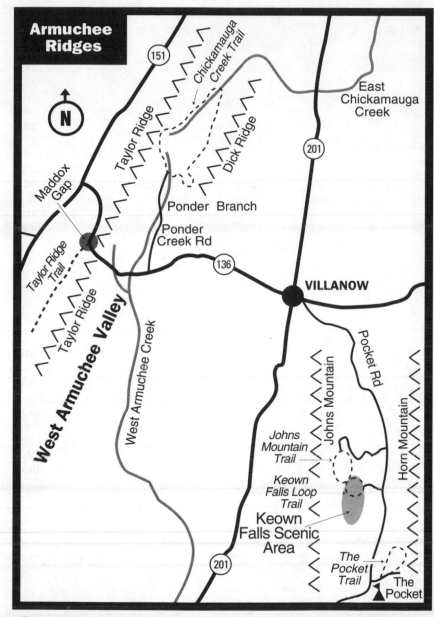

Armuchee Ridges

151

Chickamauga Creek Trail

East Chickamauga Creek

Taylor Ridge

Dick Ridge

201

N

Maddox Gap

Ponder Branch

Taylor Ridge Trail

Ponder Creek Rd

136

VILLANOW

Taylor Ridge

West Armuchee Valley

West Armuchee Creek

Pocket Rd

Johns Mountain

Johns Mountain Trail

Keown Falls Loop Trail

Keown Falls Scenic Area

Horn Mountain

The Pocket Trail

201

The Pocket

78 U S highway	∧ mountain, ridge, or bald	● town
60 Georgia state highway	∿ stream, creek, or river	⚑ campground
FS 654 Forest Service road	⌇ marked trail	● mountain gap

Notes

Taylor Ridge Trail

Ridge and Valley
Armuchee Ridges

A pleasant, fairly easy hike with occasional valley views, Taylor Ridge begins on an overgrown old road. By early fall waist-high herbaceous plants crowd this first section of trail. Some are asters with attractive yellow or lilac flowers.

The treadway follows its namesake ridge to the southwest. At approximately 0.5 mile, after crossing a petroleum pipeline easement, the trail turns right, away from the roadbed, and ascends 0.5 mile to the ridge top. The climb, steep at first, becomes moderate before it gradually descends and levels in a hardwood forest of flowering dogwood, American chestnut saplings, and several species of oak and hickory. Just before reaching the ridge top, the path passes beside an old rock-pile wall, probably built by early farmers.

You are rewarded on top of Taylor Ridge with the first view of the valley to the west. During the summer it is hard to see through the trees and bushes, but during fall and winter the views are good. At about mile 1.5, there is a view of West Armuchee Valley to the east. A little farther along, there's another view to the west.

After approximately 2.0 miles, a dirt road appears parallel and below the trail on the left. This is FS 635-A. Here the path turns sharply to the left, then quickly drops to its end at FS 635-A.

Features
Views from ridge top

Distance
2.4 miles

Difficulty Rating
Easy to moderate

County
Walker

Nearest City
La Fayette

Map
Catlett
Quadrangle, GA

Blazes
White

Ranger District
Armuchee

Highlights
Mile 1.0: View of valley below.
Mile 1.5: Views of valleys below.

Directions
From La Fayette travel east on GA 136 for approximately 7.0 miles, almost to the top of Taylor Ridge. Turn right (south) at the small brown Taylor Ridge Trail sign. This is FS 217. There are two gated roads; the one to the left is the trailhead.

Ridge and Valley
Armuchee Ridges

Chickamauga Creek Trail

Features
Streams, hardwood
coves, spring
wildflowers

Distance
6.3 miles (loop)

Difficulty Rating
Easy to moderate

Counties
Walker and Whitfield

Nearest Cities
La Fayette (W),
Dalton (E)

Map
Catlett
Quadrangle, GA

Blazes
White

Water Sources
Miles 0.0–0.5:
Ponder Branch and
tributaries; mile 2.0:
rivulet; miles
4.2–5.0: East
Chickamauga Creek
and tributaries; miles
5.6–6.3: Ponder
Branch and tribu-
taries

Ranger District
Armuchee

Chickamauga Creek's loop provides an excellent example of Ridge and Valley topography and drainage patterns. The loop is bounded east and west by two parallel, north-south running ridges—Taylor to the west, Dick to the east. The ridge tops are gen-erally less than 1.5 miles apart. A lower cross-ridge, which divides the loop north and south, connects the two parallel ridges, forming a crooked H of high ridge land.

This cross-ridge, the middle of the H, is a major hydrologic boundary—the Tennessee Valley Divide. To the north and south small streams flow out from the cross-ridge, through the valleys between the par-allel ridges. The water flowing north, East Chicka-mauga Creek, eventually joins the Mississippi south of Illinois, then heads south to enter the Gulf of Mexico in Louisiana. The water flowing south, Ponder Branch, makes a much shorter journey. It enters the gulf near Mobile, Alabama, which is more than 100 miles from the Mississippi Delta to the west.

Starting at 1,020 feet, the trail quickly crosses a footbridge over Ponder Branch before reaching the loop's beginning at a power line right-of-way at mile 0.1. This description follows the easier way to walk the loop, to the right, counterclockwise. The path rises easily, winding through the hardwood hollows on Rocky Ridge, a Dick Ridge spur. Continuing to ascend, the route crosses an old woods road 0.1 mile before crossing the power line right-of-way at mile 1.5. Here the walkway levels to mile 2.1, where it turns left onto a woods road.

The trail ascends with the old road to the oak-pine top of Dick Ridge and the trail's high point (1,560 feet) at mile 2.6. Here, at the "Foot Travel Only" sign, the treadway turns left off the old road and makes switchbacks down the western slope of

Dick Ridge. By mile 3.5 the route is a woods road, which quickly joins a wider road. Turn left onto the wider road, take the right fork, then descend on a series of switchbacks.

After leaving the road in a switchback at mile 4.2, the path swings parallel to East Chickamauga Creek (950 feet). The route then rises on easy grades as it follows the creek upstream, crossing the brook or its tributaries (dry-shod crossing at normal water levels) numerous times. At mile 5.3 the treadway crosses the Tennessee Valley Divide and FS 250 at a gap (1,250 feet) in the cross-ridge.

South of the divide, the remainder of the loop quickly drops into the upper Ponder Branch Valley—Baker Hollow. Continuing steadily down the hollow, the trail often crosses the meandering Ponder Branch or its feeder streams. This final segment passes through a rapidly maturing hardwood forest with American beech, white oak, tuliptree, and hickory common in the canopy. The power line right-of-way marks the loop's end.

Highlights

Miles 3.2–3.4: Winter views west to Taylor Ridge.
Miles 4.2–5.0: Trail parallels East Chickamauga Creek.
Miles 5.6–6.3: Trail parallels Ponder Branch.

Directions

Trail access is to the north of GA 136 along the segment of that highway from Villanow to the east and La Fayette to the west.

From La Fayette travel GA 136 East. From the GA 151–GA 136 junction closest to La Fayette continue 3.2 miles on GA 136 East before turning left onto Ponder Creek Road.

From the GA 136–GA 201 junction in Villanow, travel GA 136 West 3.4 miles and turn right onto Ponder Creek Road. Proceed 0.6 mile on Ponder Creek Road, take the right fork onto FS 219 and follow that road for 1.8 miles to its end at the trailhead parking area.

Notes

Ridge and Valley
Armuchee Ridges
**Keown Falls
Scenic Area**

Features
Bluffs, wet-weather
waterfalls, scenic
view

Distance
1.7 miles (loop)

Difficulty Rating
Easy to moderate

County
Walker

Nearest Cities
La Fayette (NW),
Dalton (NE),
Summerville (SW)

Map
Sugar Valley
Quadrangle, GA

Blazes
None; none needed

Campsites
Camping not permit-
ted in the picnic or
parking area; this
area is day use only

Ranger District
Armuchee

Keown Falls Loop Trail

Located in the Ridge and Valley physiographic
province of northwestern Georgia, 218-acre
Keown Falls is the only scenic area in the separate,
western section (Armuchee Ranger District) of the
Chattahoochee National Forest. It is named for land
surveyor Gordon Keown.

The graveled, rock-lined trail enters the forest at
the Keown Falls Recreation Area. From there, at an elevation of 980 feet, the treadway immediately passes
under an A-frame shelter and continues into the
Keown Falls Scenic Area, where it forks into a loop at
0.1 mile. Along the way, you will soon notice two
things: the abundance of ground-covering rocks,
which get larger as the trail progresses toward the
cliffs, and the trees that appear to be shedding their
bark in long, curving strips. This distinctive tree,
uncommon throughout much of its range in Georgia,
is the shagbark hickory.

The trail, following the loop to the right, counterclockwise, quickly approaches a small stream that
gives an indication of how much water—if any—is
spilling over the falls. Both of the waterfalls in
Keown Falls Scenic Area come from tiny spring-fed
branches; together they form this unnamed tributary
of Johns Creek. During a drought the falls may dwin-
dle to a trickle or, worse yet, dry out completely.
Winter, spring, and early summer after a substantial
rain are good times to visit the falls. A trailhead sign
indicates whether they are dry or not.

After the loop trail turns away from the stream,
it winds up a series of switchbacks designed to keep
the grade easy or moderate. At 0.7 mile a short, steep
climb up rock steps leads to an observation deck
perched atop a bluff (1,420 feet). To the right, picturesque Keown Falls, usually divided in two, sails
over a ledge and showers the rocks 60 feet below. To
the left, beyond Furnace Valley, is the long ridge of
Horn Mountain.

Johns Mountain Trail, another loop trail that
shares the observation deck view with Keown Falls

Trail, is 25 yards to the right.

The Keown Falls Trail leads through the hollowed-out area behind the waterfall, then continues below a line of overhanging bluffs, sometimes 40 feet high, for 0.2 mile to the second waterfall. With roughly half the flow and half the height of the first, this fall is most often a mossy slide. Fern gardens grow on the ledges to the left of the dropping water. From the second fall, the path steadily descends a rock-strewn hillside to the end of the loop.

Highlights

Mile 0.7: Observation deck atop a bluff with views of Keown Falls, Furnace Valley, and Horn Mountain.

Directions

From the US 27–GA 136 junction in La Fayette, travel GA 136 East approximately 13.0 miles, then turn right onto paved Pocket Road. This turn is just up the hill from the Forest Service Work Center in Villanow and is marked with a large, green "Keown and Pocket Recreation Area" sign.

Pocket Road also can be reached from Calhoun by traveling northwest on GA 136 Conn., then GA 136 West from Calhoun toward La Fayette. When traveling GA 136 West to Pocket Road, look for the recreation area sign and left-hand turn approximately 19.0 miles past Calhoun.

After turning off GA 136 onto Pocket Road, travel approximately 5.0 miles, then turn right onto the Keown Falls entrance road at its sign. This gravel road ends at the Keown Falls Recreation Area parking lot after approximately 0.6 mile. Keown Falls Scenic Area is located on Pocket Road next to Keown Falls Recreation Area.

The Johns Mountain entrance road and the Keown Falls entrance road are closed during the off-season, usually on the same dates.

Note: When the recreation area is closed during the off-season, the entrance sign is removed and the entrance road is gated. If you want to hike the Keown Falls Trail when the recreation area is closed, you will have to park near the gate and walk the 0.6-mile access road to and from the trailhead. The US Forest Service (Armuchee District) has given hikers permission to walk its trails when the recreation areas are closed. They ask that you carry all your trash back out to your car and that you park so that emergency access through the gate is not blocked.

Ridge and Valley
Armuchee Ridges
Keown Falls
Scenic Area

Features
Scenic views, bluffs,
wet-weather waterfall

Distance
3.1 miles (loop)

Difficulty Rating
Hiked counterclock-
wise: moderate;
hiked clockwise:
easy to moderate

County
Walker

Nearest Cities
La Fayette (NW),
Dalton (NE),
Summerville (SW)

Map
Sugar Valley
Quadrangle, GA

Blazes
White

Ranger District
Armuchee

Johns Mountain Trail

This trail begins next to an observation deck on a high point (1,883 feet) along the ridge of Johns Mountain. Looking straight out, you can see Dick Ridge, Taylor Ridge, and several more ridges beyond.

Following the loop to the right, counterclockwise, the trail heads southward along the ridge top. The old roadbed quickly passes a communications building, then returns to the forest, which is mostly chestnut oak, hickory, and Virginia pine. This section of trail remains level or gently undulating, with an overall slight elevation loss, until it turns left at mile 1.3.

The loop continues level or downhill until it crosses a short wooden walkway at mile 2.3. This descending section of trail parallels a line of bluffs that rim the plateau-like top of Johns Mountain. Near the end of the descent, these bluffs, which are characteristic of the ridges in northwestern Georgia, become higher and more defined. A warning sign stands guard near a 50-foot drop-off.

Immediately beyond the walkway, a side trail leads 25 yards to the Keown Falls observation deck, elevation 1,420 feet.

While you can easily switch from Johns Mountain Trail to Keown Falls Trail, the two loops do not intersect nor are they contiguous at any point. They do, however, have short side trails that lead to the same observation deck. The deck is the lowest point on the Johns Mountain Trail, the highest on the Keown Falls Trail. Approximately 2.0 miles of the Johns Mountain Trail are within the Keown Falls Scenic Area.

As you might have guessed, to complete the loop, continue uphill and to the left. Most of this final segment gains elevation. The last 0.4 mile climbs moderate grades on an old roadbed.

Highlights

Mile 0.0: Johns Mountain Overlook provides a panoramic view of the valley and of Taylor Ridge to the west.

Miles 1.6–2.2: Views of valley and bluffs to the east.

Mile 2.4: Observation deck atop a bluff with views of Keown Falls, Furnace Valley, and Horn Mountain.

Directions

(See page 209 of Keown Falls Loop Trail for directions to Pocket Road.) After turning off GA 136, travel approximately 4.0 miles on Pocket Road before turning right onto the Johns Mountain entrance road (FS 208) at its large sign. Continue approximately 2.2 miles on this gravel road to the trailhead parking area. Johns Mountain Trail is a loop with two trailheads; if you start at one sign you will end at the other.

Notes

Ridge and Valley
Armuchee Ridges
Pocket Recreation Area

Features
Springs, small streams, interpretive nature trail, wildlife viewing deck

Distance
2.6 miles (main loop)

Difficulty Rating
Easy

Counties
Walker and Floyd

Nearest Cities
Dalton (NE), Summerville (SW), La Fayette (NW)

Map
Sugar Valley Quadrangle, GA

Blazes
White

Campsites
Available seasonally in recreation area campground

Ranger District
Armuchee

The Pocket Trail

The Pocket is a large, horseshoe-shaped piece of nearly level land enclosed on three sides by the steep ridges of Horn and Mill Mountains. It was formed when the white limestone subsurface here eroded more quickly than the surrounding rock of the ridges. Most of the low-lying ground inside the loop of the trail has an elevation of less than 1,000 feet, while the ridges are often 400 to 500 feet higher. The area's many spring-fed streams comprise the headwaters of Johns Creek, which flows out of the top of the pocket. The Pocket Recreation Area, now a popular campground, was the site of a Civilian Conservation Corps camp from 1938–1942.

The first section of this trail passes an area of seeps and small streams, and the forest's diversity quickly becomes apparent. To the left, you'll see moisture-loving trees such as sycamore, American beech, sugar maple, and witch-hazel; on the hill to your right, trees preferring drier soil dominate— blackgum, sassafras, shortleaf pine, as well as black-jack and several other oak species.

At 0.4 mile the trail crosses a short wooden bridge and turns left. Twenty or thirty yards to the right of the bridge, the two largest trees along the loop, an impressive loblolly pine and an equally thick white oak, stand side by side. Although much more abundant in Georgia's Piedmont, the loblolly is also common in the southernmost reaches of the Chattahoochee National Forest, particularly on south-facing slopes. Easy to identify, loblollies are large pines, often over 100 feet tall with straight trunks. Needles six to nine inches long, arranged in bundles of three, spray up from branch ends. Wide, light-reddish-brown cones grow four to six inches in length. The loblolly's bark changes as it matures. Young trees have dark, furrowed bark, but mature ones have a bright orange-brown bark divided into broad, flat plates by shallow fissures.

Beyond the two big trees, the loop begins its pattern of rising slightly to drier ground, dipping to the next stream or seepage area, then rising again. At 0.7 mile, the loop crosses a road and continues gently uphill along several low ridges before slanting down toward water. Periodically, you can glimpse the walls that form the pocket. At mile 1.5, the trail features a 65-yard-long boardwalk that takes you across a large seep full of lush vegetation. Beyond this first boardwalk, the path rises through a predominantly pine forest, then dips to a second one at mile 2.0. The loop ends at the one-way road in the camping area, directly across from the picnic area parking lot where it started.

Walked counterclockwise, the first segment of the Pocket Trail now shares its treadway with the Pocket Nature Trail. At 0.6 mile the nature trail turns away from the main trail, then loops back to its beginning on a woods road. Just before the nature trail splits away, an 80-yard spur to the right leads to an aquatic viewing platform.

Highlights
Throughout: Springs, small streams, and diverse forest.
Miles 0.3–1.0: Flowering dogwoods and azaleas bloom in mid-April throughout this stretch.

Directions
(See page 209 of Keown Falls Loop Trail for directions to Pocket Road.) After turning off GA 136, travel approximately 7.0 miles on Pocket Road before turning left into the Pocket Recreation Area at its large sign. Shortly after entering the one-way camping loop, turn right into the large picnic area parking lot opposite the rest room on the left side of the road. This parking lot is approximately 0.3 mile from the entrance gate on Pocket Road.

Notes

CROCKFORD-PIGEON MOUNTAIN WILDLIFE MANAGEMENT AREA

Located in the Cumberland Plateau in northwestern Georgia, this 15,824-acre Wildlife Management Area was named, in part, for its mountain, which was named for the now extinct passenger pigeon. Although you won't see the pigeon, chances are good that you will see one of the mountain's larger animals: deer, coyote, bobcat, turkey, gray fox, and red fox.

This WMA now has a network of trails totaling nearly 50 miles. All the trails except Rocktown, however, are designated for horse, bike, and hike usage. Triple-designation trails have not been included in this hiking guide.

Cumberland Plateau
Pigeon Mountain
Crockford-Pigeon Mountain WMA

Features
Rocktown, hoodoos

Distance
1.0 mile

Difficulty Rating
Easy

County
Walker

Nearest City
La Fayette

Maps
Cedar Grove Quadrangle, GA; pamphlet and map available from the WMA

Rocktown Trail

Rocktown, which covers 140 acres and ranges from 1,740 to 1,800 feet in elevation, is a maze of oddly shaped, sandstone-conglomerate boulders scattered throughout a plateau-like area atop Pigeon Mountain. The mountain, separated from Lookout Mountain to the northwest by McLemore Cove, is a gentle syncline (trough of stratified rock) that preserves sandstones and conglomerates of Lower Pennsylvanian age belonging to the Pennington Formation. Portions of these boulders are often striated, pitted, pocked, or honeycombed. Many are eroding faster on their shale sides than on their sandstone tops, leaving overhanging caps with no support. The narrow passageways between broken boulders, the weathering patterns, and the unusual profiles they produce—mushroom, parapet, fish fin, upside-down bowling pin—look like the hoodoos in the national parks of southern Utah.

This easily walked trail immediately crosses a headwater branch of Allen Creek, then quickly passes the remains of a stone foundation, perhaps from an old mine building. The footpath continues on nearly level grades through a predominantly hardwood forest dominated by oaks. A short distance after the route makes a left turn at 0.5 mile, it reaches the first group of boulders, a small-scale version of what lies ahead.

The reddish rocks along the trail or imbedded in the sandstone formations are iron ore deposits. At one time there were ten iron mines on the mountain. Look for scattered samples of botryoidal iron ore in the first 0.2 mile of the trail; they resemble bunches of grapes.

Toward its center, Rocktown's boulders become progressively larger and more fascinating. Near its end the treadway winds through rock formations 20 to 35 feet high, occasionally passing beside upward-jutting overhangs. The trail ends in a small clearing in the heart of Rocktown, where the tallest of these strangely eroded hoodoos has grown to 65 feet.

Blazes
Pink

Campsites
Camping not permitted along the trail; this area is day use only; no fires; there are designated camping areas in the WMA

Highlights
Miles 0.5–1.0: A maze of large, oddly shaped sandstone-conglomerate boulders scattered throughout a 140-acre, plateau-like area atop Pigeon Mountain, known as Rocktown.

Directions
From the US 27–GA 193 junction in La Fayette, travel GA 193 North for 2.8 miles before turning left onto Chamberlain Road. This turn is marked with a Crockford-Pigeon Mountain WMA sign. Proceed 3.4 miles on Chamberlain Road, then turn right onto a wide gravel road at a large WMA sign.

Continue on the gravel road (pass a DNR check station, stay right at the fork at mile 3.5) for 4.7 miles to the top of Pigeon Mountain. Turn left onto a one-lane dirt-gravel road with a dead-end sign. Follow the road 0.7 mile to the trailhead parking area.

Notes

CLOUDLAND CANYON
STATE PARK

Located in the extreme northwestern corner of the state, 2,350-acre Cloudland Canyon is, to the eyes of many, the most scenic state park in the North Georgia region. Nature has combined the best features of many parks into one; waterfalls and sparkling streams, overlooks and picturesque vistas, as well as boulders and canyon cliffs make the park a photographer's paradise.

The canyons are shaped like a "Y" tilted 90 degrees to the right. Situated in the narrow point of the wedge, the main overlook provides magnificent views of the gulches and their long horizontal bands of exposed sandstone. To the left, Daniel Creek has sculpted the West Canyon and its waterfalls. To the right, the East Canyon is Bear Creek's masterpiece; together the canyons merge to form the long part of the "Y"—Sitton Gulch. Far below, Sitton Gulch Creek flows 900 feet beneath the highest point on the canyon rim.

Here at this Cumberland Plateau canyon, geologic history and processes have been laid bare by vast time and the steady chiseling of ice and water.

West Rim Loop Trail

T he yellow-blazed loop starts at the trailhead sign beside the railing near the overlook parking lot. From this point the trail gently descends along the rim, past where the Waterfall Trail turns to the right, into the upper reaches of the canyon, where it crosses Daniel Creek at near water level. Across the creek the path curves to the right and climbs steadily for the first and only time.

The trail gains the opposite rim from where it started at 0.6 mile. From here, it closely follows the top of the chasm, often across bare rock only a step or two away from cliff's edge. Looking across the canyon you can see, below the timbered cap of the plateau, the alternating layers of cliff face and forest that stretch the length of Sitton Gulch. Looking down into the gorge in winter, you can see the gray-boulder talus—debris from section after section of fallen cliff—wedged on the slopes below. Almost at your feet, you can see where the most recent section of cliff top has split apart and has slumped a few feet toward its eventual fall. For now, the sandstone boulders still lie there like crooked lines of puzzle pieces separated by fissurelike clefts on three and sometimes four sides.

After 1.1 miles the trail begins to curl around a hanging side canyon carved by a small, unnamed stream. This branch soon becomes the thin waterfall visible from the opposite rim. At mile 1.3 the loop portion of the trail begins and ends where it crosses the spring-fed stream. A loop, of course, can be traveled in either direction; the quicker way to the succession of railed overlooks, however, is straight ahead across the creek and back out to the main canyon.

These overlooks provide views into all three of the park's gorges. Down and to the right, Daniel and Bear Creeks have cut a double-sided cliff at the wedge point where their canyons meet. Below and to the

Cumberland Plateau
Lookout Mountain
Cloudland Canyon State Park

Features
Canyon rim, canyon views, unusual rock formations

Distance
4.9 miles (loop)

Difficulty Rating
Easy to moderate

County
Dade

Nearest Cities
La Fayette (SE), Trenton (W)

Maps
Durham Quadrangle, GA; park map available at visitor center

Blazes
Yellow

Campsites
Available with reservation in park campground

left, Sitton Gulch Creek deepens its trough to nearly 900 feet before it flows into Lookout Valley. Cloudland looks like a region strayed eastward from across the Mississippi. Adding to this somewhere-out-west image of rock-wall chasm and talus slope, photogenic Virginia pines grow stunted and wind-twisted where nothing else can exist on the cliff-edge rock.

The loop continues to parallel the west rim, past blazed side trails leading to the cabins, to a second set of lookouts at mile 2.1. These two overlooks afford vistas of Sitton Gulch as it widens toward its mouth and, in the valley beyond its entrance, the city of Trenton with its surrounding patchwork of fields and woodlots. The trail reaches its last railed overlook a half-mile farther along the canyon. A short distance from this final view of Sitton Gulch and Lookout Valley, it turns away from the cliffs and enters the forest of the plateau. At mile 2.9 the trail crosses a road, then completes its loop portion at the creek where it began.

The canyon rim is potentially dangerous. Children should not hike this trail unsupervised.

Highlights
Miles 1.6–2.6: The west rim provides overlook views of the canyon's three gorges.

Directions
From La Fayette travel US 27 North approximately 4.0 miles, then turn left onto GA 136 and follow signs to Cloudland Canyon State Park.

The West Rim Loop and Waterfall trails begin at the same sign near the picnic area parking lot adjacent to Campground 1 and cottages 1–5. The trail sign is along the railed canyon rim to the left of the parking lot and below the line of cottages.

Notes

Waterfall Trail

Cumberland Plateau
Lookout Mountain
Cloudland Canyon
State Park

Features
Two waterfalls, cliffs,
huge boulders

Distance
0.7 mile

Difficulty Rating
Moderate to
strenuous

County
Dade

Nearest Cities
La Fayette (SE),
Trenton (W)

Maps
Durham
Quadrangle, GA;
park map available
at visitor center

Blazes
Yellow

Campsites
Available with
reservation in park
campground

The two waterfalls on Daniel Creek are about 0.4 mile upstream from the junction of Daniel and Bear Creeks on the canyon floor. This trail takes you to both of them in succession. But before you descend into the canyon, you can view it from several overlooks along its rim. As you look at the wall opposite, notice the shale layers amid the sandstone. They are often covered with vegetation, since they are more easily eroded than sandstone and provide a better hold for plant roots. When you descend to the canyon floor, you will see shale outcrops that are composed of thin, dark layers of stone that may be easily chipped. They are the result of mud deposits.

The parking lot is located on the high ground between the two branches of the canyon. The trail begins on the west side of this bluff and skirts the canyon's east rim, the Daniel Creek branch of the canyon. Walk southwest along this rim several hundred feet until you find the trailhead marker behind the cabins. At the first fork, as the sign indicates, the Waterfall Trail continues to the right, the West Rim Loop Trail to the left.

After slightly more than 0.3 mile the trail forks again. To the left it is 0.1 mile further to the upper falls; to the right it is 0.3 mile to the lower falls. Near the end of the trail to the upper waterfall, huge boulders, packed one behind the other, are slowly slipping toward the opposite bank of Daniel Creek. Eastern hemlock and rosebay rhododendron—vegetation associated with Southern Appalachian trout streams—flourish in the cool, moist soil of the canyon floor. At trail's end, Daniel Creek dives over its amphitheater wall, plunging into a dark-green catch pool 50 feet below.

The stairway trail to the lower falls is the more strenuous of the two. The walkway skirts a cliff face, then descends sharply to the bottom of the canyon, which has deepened to nearly 400 feet. The entrenched area at the end of the steps is one of the most beautiful spots in Georgia. Gracefully tapering eastern hemlocks and large tuliptrees grow between streamside rocks. Spring-blooming hepaticas, also known as liverleaf, are abundant. Their distinctively patterned three-lobed leaves, supported by underground stems, make these plants easy to identify even when not in bloom. When they do blossom, usually in late March or early April, their flowers range from white to shades of pastel purple and blue.

With the exception of the 20-foot-high, spray-catching rock that sits in its plunge pool, the lower waterfall is a double-scale replica of the one above. At trail's end, Daniel Creek again leaps over an amphitheater wall, this time plummeting to a dark-green catch basin 100 feet below.

Note: The area downstream from the upper falls is potentially dangerous. Immediately downstream from the large boulders, Daniel Creek begins its shallow slide to the top of the lower falls.

Highlights
Mile 0.3: An impressive rock overhang.
Mile 0.4 along the left fork of the trail: The upper waterfall plunges 50 feet into its large catch pool.
Mile 0.6 along the right fork of the trail: The lower waterfall drops 100 feet from a sandstone ledge. A bus-sized boulder sits at the edge of the splash pool.

Directions
See page 218 of West Rim Loop Trail for directions to the Waterfall trailhead.

Notes

Backcountry Trail

Cumberland Plateau
Lookout Mountain
Cloudland Canyon
State Park

Features
Primitive camping,
canyon views

Distance
5.4 miles (loop)

Difficulty Rating
Moderate

County
Dade

Nearest Cities
La Fayette (SE),
Trenton (W)

Maps
Durham
Quadrangle, GA;
park map available
at visitor center

Blazes
Red

Water Sources
Mile 0.7: Bear
Creek; mile 1.0:
seasonal rivulet

Campsites
Designated camping
areas at miles 2.0,
3.0; reservations
only

The Backcountry Trail was constructed to provide primitive camping opportunities in a remote section of the park. The trail is a loop on the plateau to the east of Bear Creek Canyon and Sitton Gulch. Although it does not remain level for long, most of its grades are easy or moderate. You will encounter only one strenuous upgrade longer than 0.1 mile. That will be at the end of your hike, after you cross Bear Creek for the second time.

The trail begins by descending through a mixed deciduous-evergreen forest to Bear Creek, which it crosses by bridge at 0.7 mile. The last 0.2 mile is a steep, rocky series of switchbacks through rhododendron to an undercut bluff at stream's edge. The backcountry trail rises from the creek until its loop begins beside a rivulet at 0.9 mile. The loop was built to be walked to the right, counterclockwise. The path continues to follow the small watercourse upstream, crossing it seven times in 0.2 mile. This rivulet, which may be dry during periods of little rain, is the last water source before the two campsites.

At mile 1.3 the treadway ascends for 0.2 mile to the plateau above the gorges. Once on top, the loop undulates up and over a series of low hardwood ridges for the next 1.5 miles. It then descends through a cove and swings parallel to Bear Creek Canyon. Here the path follows an old road through Virginia pine, occasionally approaching close to the cliffs. There are several good lookouts and lunch spots with views of the upper and lower falls and the canyon rock formations.

At mile 3.9 the path curls down and away from the rim. A long, easy downslope leads you back to the loop junction.

Note: The Cloudland Backcountry Trail has two designated campsites, one at approximately mile 2.0 and the other at mile 3.0. In order to camp at one of these sites, you must make a reservation, obtain a permit from the park office, and pay a small fee per person per night. You may camp at either of the sites, both of which are group areas that accommodate more than one party per night.

Park rangers request that you camp within the blazed area at the designated sites. They also request that day hikers stop by the park office before walking the Backcountry Trail.

Highlights

Mile 0.7: A bluff with trees growing from improbable places perched over Bear Creek.

Miles 3.5, 3.9: The trail follows the canyon rim with views of the canyon walls and the upper and lower falls.

Directions

From La Fayette travel US 27 North approximately 4.0 miles from town, then turn left onto GA 136 and follow signs to the park. Check in at the park office before backpacking or day hiking this trail.

Notes

LONG TRAILS

Four long footpaths—the Appalachian, Bartram, Benton MacKaye, and Duncan Ridge—offer hikers over 224 miles of trail in the mountains of North Georgia. With the exception of several Benton MacKaye sections, these trails traverse the public land within the Chattahoochee National Forest.

Whenever possible, these long trails have been divided into sections between paved and easily traveled dirt access roads. These sections, ranging from 4.5 to 20.4 miles, make excellent day hikes as well as two- or three-day backpacking trips.

APPALACHIAN NATIONAL SCENIC TRAIL

The Appalachian Trail—with its southern terminus at Springer Mountain, Georgia, and its northern terminus at Mount Katahdin, Maine—winds its way along the Appalachian Mountains for more than 2,150 miles through 14 states. Georgia's segment of the trail, from Springer Mountain to Bly Gap on the North Carolina border, is 76 miles in length.

Wide and easily followed, the trail is marked with white blazes; double white blazes, one above the other, warn hikers of potentially confusing turns or sudden changes in direction. Water sources, shelters off the main trail, and major side trails are marked with blue blazes. Blue W's with arrows indicate water.

Because of its national reputation, the Appalachian Trail is the most heavily used long footpath in Georgia. Those who want a high degree of solitude may want to consider other trails in this guide.

Georgia's segment of the Appalachian Trail passes through one national recreation area and five congressionally designated wildernesses. Within wilderness there will be fewer blazes and a lower trail maintenance standard.

The Georgia Appalachian Trail Club (GATC), a volunteer organization, maintains Georgia's portion of the trail. Changes resulting from maintenance work and relocations occur every year.

224

Amicalola Falls State Park to Springer Mountain

Features
Waterfall, national recreation area, southern terminus of AT, views

Distance
8.1 miles

Difficulty Rating
Moderate to strenuous

Counties
Dawson, Gilmer, and Lumpkin

Nearest Cities
Dahlonega (E), Ellijay (W), Dawsonville (S)

Maps
Nimblewill and Noontootla Quadrangles, GA; AT map

Blazes
Blue

Water Sources
Mile 1.4: Little Amicalola Creek crossing; mile 4.6: wet-weather spring 0.1 mile to right from top of Frosty Mountain; mile 7.1: near Black Gap Shelter

Campsites
Mile 7.1: Black Gap Shelter to the left of the trail

Ranger District
Toccoa

Southern Terminus Approach Trail

Because of the Appalachian Trail's popularity and allure, people with little or no backpacking experience often pick it for their first long hiking trip. Many of the people—with boots that are too new and packs that are too heavy—start on the Approach Trail at Amicalola Falls State Park, eager to reach Springer Mountain and the AT. Slowed by blisters and aching muscles, some of these inexperienced hikers fail to make the climb to the top of Springer Mountain the first day.

The visitor center in the state park has a scale to weigh your pack. If you are uncertain about how much weight you can comfortably carry, ask the park ranger for advice. You may want to lighten your load before starting out.

The AT is a well-marked, highly scenic trail, but if you plan to enjoy walking long distances of it carrying a pack, you need to be in good physical condition and have suitable gear. The Approach Trail will give you a good idea of what lies ahead. If the alternating ascents and descents to Springer Mountain prove to be too strenuous, you will not enjoy the rest of the AT.

This trail traverses a ridge line string of knobs and named peaks collectively known as Amicalola Mountain. Beyond the state park, the trailside forest is predominantly hardwood. Oaks, hickories, American holly, flowering dogwood, black locust, tuliptree, sourwood, and sweet birch are common. On many of the low, flat-topped knobs, the forest is undergoing quick and obvious successional change. The Virginia pine, a pioneer species that formed dense stands 30 years ago, is being rapidly replaced by taller hardwoods. The fallen pine trunks keep trail crews busy. By the year 2010, most will have fallen and rotted.

The Approach Trail has a trailhead you can't miss. Its beginning is the log-lined walkway that leads away from the back of Amicalola's visitor information center (1,790 feet). The initiation starts immediately: the trail's first 0.5 mile makes an easy-to-moderate climb to East Ridge Spring, then switchbacks up sharper grades to a left turn onto an old road at 0.7 mile. The road's open left side affords good views of valleys and ridges.

One-tenth mile before the trail crosses the paved road to the lodge, you can head to the left and down to view Amicalola Falls. The Approach continues straight ahead and becomes path again where it skirts what used to be the shoreline of Amicalola Lake. At mile 1.4 the footpath crosses Little Amicalola Creek and the dirt road that turns into FS 46. Across the road the trail ascends moderately for 0.3 mile to the ridge. On the way up, at the red-blazed trees, it leaves the park and enters the Chattahoochee National Forest. Once the treadway reaches the ridge, it does what the ridge top does: it runs level, then easy, up to a low crest (2,940 feet) at mile 1.9; it runs level along the crest and then gently down to a gap at mile 2.4; it then travels up, over, and down the next knob on the ridge.

After leaving the ridge at mile 2.8, the Approach makes a moderate-to-strenuous climb to mile 3.1, where it crosses High Shoals Road. Once across, the path continues upward, quickly gaining the next ridge and rising to near the top of a flat-headed knob at mile 3.3. The trail slides off the ridge again at the next gap. Instead of proceeding straight ahead, the trail gains elevation gradually along the western flank of Frosty Mountain to mile 4.0, where it curls onto an eastward-running ridge that leads to the mountaintop. Here the treadway ascends moderately to the mountain's western peak at mile 4.4. Two-tenths of a mile farther, across a saddle, it enters the clearing at Frosty Mountain's high point (3,382 feet). The wide walkway to the right of the clearing, a former fire tower site, heads to water.

Continuing toward Springer Mountain, the path descends steadily until it crosses FS 46 at mile 5.0. After a short level stretch, the trail starts an easy-to-moderate upgrade over the double humps of Woody Knob (3,390 feet) before making the steep, rocky, downridge run to Nimblewill Gap (3,049 feet) at mile 5.9. The Approach crosses the gap at a Forest Service junction—FS 46 ends at the gap, FS 28 passes through it.

The final 2.2-mile segment, from Nimblewill Gap to the top of Springer Mountain, is easier walking than it has been in the past. Instead of making a straight upridge ascent over Black Mountain, the trail now gradually rises around the west side of the mountain before descending to Black Gap (3,190 feet) at mile 7.1. The Black Gap Shelter is located to the left in the gap. And instead of a straight-up-the-ridge climb to the top of Springer, the path now switchbacks up to the west side of the summit.

The Approach ends where the AT begins—on a rock outcrop overlook atop Springer Mountain (3,782 feet), where the two forks of the Blue Ridge that separate south of Roanoke, Virginia, rejoin. Here, where the wind always seems to be blowing through the short, weather-bent oaks, two plaques commemorate the Appalachian Trail. This is one of those special places where toasts are made and adventures begin.

The entire trail corridor is publicly owned, first by state park, then by national forest. While in the park this trail is also known as the East Ridge Spring Trail. After it leaves the park, the Approach Trail remains within the 23,330-acre Ed Jenkins National Recreation Area.

Highlights

Mile 1.1: View of Amicalola Falls. Walk left and down to view the falls from above.

Mile 8.1: Southern terminus of the Appalachian Trail atop Springer Mountain. Exact terminus, marked with two plaques, is a rock outcrop overlook open to the west.

Directions

To the southern trailhead at Amicalola Falls State Park: Amicalola Falls State Park is located on the north side of GA 52 between Dahlonega and Ellijay. The park can be accessed from many different directions; the three easiest routes are from Dahlonega, Dawsonville, and Ellijay. There are numerous park signs to direct you.

From the Ellijay square travel GA 52 East approximately 21.0 miles.

From the Dahlonega square travel GA 52 West approximately 18.0 miles.

From the Dawsonville square travel GA 53 West and GA 183 North before turning right onto GA 52 East. The distance to the park entrance is approximately 15.0 miles.

The Approach Trail starts at the back of the Amicalola visitor information center, which is to the right on the lower park road. All vehicles left overnight must be registered at the visitor center and parked in the AT lot across the road. A Georgia Park Pass costing a small fee is required for the day of arrival.

To the northern junction with the AT atop Springer Mountain: (See the next trail description—AT, Section 1—for directions to the beginning of the AT.)

Appalachian National Scenic Trail, Section 1

WBR
Springer Mountain
Springer Mountain
to Woody Gap

Section 1 of the Appalachian Trail makes an excellent two- or three-day backpacking trip. The beginning 8.1-mile portion, from Springer Mountain to Hightower Gap, is the least strenuous (easy-to-moderate) long segment of the Appalachian Trail in Georgia. It is after Hightower Gap that Section 1 earns its overall rating of moderate to strenuous. By setting up a shuttle, day hikers can walk to or away from Hightower Gap.

From its beginning at Springer Mountain, the trail heads generally north to Three Forks, east from Three Forks to Gooch Gap, then northeast to Woody Gap. The first 11.6 miles of Section 1, from Springer to Cooper Gap, wind through the Blue Ridge Wildlife Management Area. Overall, the trailside forest is varied. Tall eastern hemlock and eastern white pine are common from the first crossing of FS 42 through the Three Forks area. Beyond Hawk Mountain hardwoods predominate.

The Appalachian Trail begins amid the gnarled oaks atop Springer Mountain's rock outcrop overlook (3,782 feet). The exact spot is marked by a plaque with this inscription: "Georgia to Maine—a footpath for those who seek fellowship with the wilderness."

The trail heads north. At 0.2 mile a spur leads to the deluxe Springer Mountain Shelter (picnic table in front, spring nearby). Twenty yards beyond the path to the shelter, Section 1 reaches its first junction. The AT follows the directions of the sign and takes the left fork. The diamond-blazed Benton MacKaye Trail veers right.

The treadway descends steadily from the fork to mile 0.9, where it crosses FS 42 (3,380 feet) and continues through a clearing. At mile 1.2 the Benton MacKaye turns onto the Appalachian Trail. For the next 0.6 mile, both trails share the same path along

Features
Southern Terminus of AT, scenic views, waterfall, national recreation area

Distance
20.0 miles

Difficulty Rating
Moderate to strenuous

Counties
Gilmer, Fannin, Union, and Lumpkin

Nearest Cities
Dahlonega (SE), Ellijay (W), Dawsonville (S)

Maps
Noontootla and Suches Quadrangles, GA; AT map

Blazes
White rectangles; all approach trails and side trails to shelters, vistas, water, and campsites are blazed in blue; sharp turns and confusing junctions are marked with two vertical white blazes

Water Sources

Mile 0.2: spring at Springer Mountain Shelter; mile 2.1: stream; mile 2.5: Stover Creek; mile 3.6: Stover Creek; mile 4.0: Chester Creek; mile 5.0: blue-blazed side trail to Long Creek Falls; mile 5.5: small stream; mile 7.5: stream 0.1 mile before side trail to Hawk Mountain Shelter; mile 13.6: Justus Creek; mile 14.0: small stream; mile 14.3: Blackwell Creek; mile 14.6: small stream; mile 16.1: spring near Gooch Gap Shelter

Campsites

Mile 0.2: Springer Mountain Shelter; mile 2.5: Stover Creek Shelter; mile 7.6: Hawk Mountain Shelter; mile 16.1: Gooch Gap Shelter

Ranger Districts

Springer Mountain to Cooper Gap: Toccoa; Cooper Gap to Woody Gap: Brasstown

the broad ridge of Rich Mountain, through a forest dominated by tall eastern white pine and tuliptrees. After the trails split apart, the AT heads downslope, turns left onto an old road at mile 2.2, continues downhill through a rosebay rhododendron thicket, then turns left onto another old road.

At mile 2.5 a sign points to the Stover Creek Shelter, about 60 yards to the left. Here the walkway turns right at the sign, quickly crosses a split log bridge over Stover Creek and turns right again. For the next 1.0 mile, the trail follows the slightly descending grade of an old road that parallels Stover Creek downstream. Even though the cascading creek is nearby, it is usually blocked from view by the dense evergreen of rosebay rhododendron. Groves of virgin eastern hemlock—many of the individual trees at least 200 to 300 years old—line the stream's opposite corridor.

At mile 3.6 Section 1 crosses a bridge over Stover Creek and continues to lose elevation on the wide walkway of the old road. The Benton MacKaye joins in again at mile 3.9. Together they dip 0.1 mile to Three Forks (2,540 feet), where Stover, Chester, and Long Creeks flow together at right angles to create Noontootla Creek. At Three Forks the trails cross a footbridge over Chester Creek, cross FS 58, and proceed on the gravel road as it parallels Long Creek upstream. A sign at mile 5.0 marks the blue-blazed spur that leads 100 yards to Long Creek Falls—a ledge-sliding drop of 20 to 25 feet. The trails split apart: Benton MacKaye left, Appalachian straight at another sign 0.1 mile past the waterfall.

On its own again, the AT continues on the road, crossing rivulets at miles 5.2 and 5.5. Immediately after this second crossing, Section 1 leaves the road and turns right onto a path. It then rises through heath thickets to a ridge, ascends easily across FS 251 at mile 5.8, and climbs 0.5 mile to the top of a knob (3,360 feet).

After losing elevation gradually to a slight gap

(3,220 feet) at mile 6.9, the footpath skirts the northern slopes of Hawk Mountain far below its peak. The headwater stream in the cove to the left is Long Creek. Section 1 passes the side path to the Hawk Mountain Shelter at mile 7.6 before working its way down 0.5 mile to Hightower Gap (2,847 feet).

The AT crosses Hightower Gap at the FS 42–FS 69 junction. The trail continues straight across this junction, reentering the tall hardwood forest to the right of FS 42. Here the footpath climbs, steeply at first, then more moderately, 0.3 mile to the top of an unnamed knob (2,980 feet). It then dips 0.4 mile to a low gap (2,980 feet) beside FS 42. From that gap the treadway roller-coasters with the ridge on easy-to-moderate grades to mile 9.7, where it drops sharply 0.3 mile to Horse Gap (2,673 feet) next to FS 42.

Continuing to the east, Section 1 makes a steady, switchbacking, moderate ascent along the southern side of the ridge. On the way up, it passes beside a rim-like line of rock outcrop. At mile 10.6 an overlook opens to the south. According to the Suches Quadrangle, the view should be of Conner Mountain, the headwater valley of the Etowah River and low ridges beyond. The white-blazed walkway reaches the crest of Sassafras Mountain (3,336 feet) at mile 11.0.

The AT crosses FS 42 through a stand of tall tuliptrees in Cooper Gap (2,820 feet) at mile 11.6. Traversing rugged terrain similar to that on Sassafras Mountain, the path rises moderately by switchback for 0.6 mile to the crown of Justus Mountain (3,222 feet). It then loses elevation for 0.3 mile to the saddle of Brookshire Gap (2,940 feet), follows the ridge over Phyllis Spur (3,081 feet) and descends. At mile 13.5 the trail crosses an old road, turns right onto another, and quickly crosses a bridge over Justus Creek. Still on old road, Section 1 gradually rises over a low ridge before crossing another stream, Blackwell Creek, by bridge at mile 14.3. The area between Justice and Blackwell Creeks is an especially rich botanical area for both wildflowers and ferns.

Beyond Blackwell Creek, the wide walkway continues level or slightly uphill through rosebay rhododendron thickets to mile 14.8, where it curls to the right and climbs sharply for 0.2 mile to a high point (3,004 feet) on Horseshoe Ridge. After an easy downgrade to a gap at mile 15.4, the treadway skirts the northern slopes of Gooch Mountain, rising gently for 0.5 mile before heading down. At mile 16.1, where the AT crosses a bridge over a rivulet, there is a blue-blazed spur to the Gooch Gap Shelter. At mile 16.4, just before the trail crosses FS 42 in Gooch Gap, another blue-blazed spur leads to the same shelter.

From Gooch Gap (2,820 feet), the AT proceeds on easy grades around two low knobs to the stand of tall, straight-boled tuliptrees in Liss Gap (3,020 feet) at mile 17.9. A private land holding has just been acquired, so watch for a trail relocation in this area in the next couple of years. It then rises, moderately at first, 0.4 mile to Page Knob (3,252 feet), runs down the ridge to Jacks Gap (3,020 feet) at mile 18.5, ascends 0.2 mile to Ramrock Mountain (3,200 feet) and drops to Tritt Gap (3,060 feet) at mile 19.0. There is a view to the right (south) atop Ramrock Mountain. The predominantly level remainder of Section 1 swings around the southern flank of Black Mountain to Woody Gap (3,160 feet).

From its beginning atop Springer Mountain to where it crosses FS 251 at mile 5.8, Section 1 remains within the 23,330-acre Ed Jenkins National Recreation Area.

The GATC is planning to reroute much of Section 1 from Springer Mountain to Long Creek Falls.

Highlights

Mile 0.0: Top of Springer Mountain. The southern terminus of the premier hiking trail in the world, the Appalachian Trail. Look for the bronze commemorative plaque embedded in the rock outcrop overlook.

Miles 2.6–3.6: Virgin groves of eastern hemlock line Stover Creek's opposite bank.

Mile 4.0: Three Forks. Three mountain streams—Chester, Long, and Stover Creeks—converge to create Noontootla Creek.

Mile 5.0: Side trail leads a short distance to Long Creek Falls—a 20- to 25-foot drop.

Mile 18.7: View from Ramrock Mountain. An excellent view from a rock outcrop open to the south.

Directions

To the AT trailhead at Springer Mountain: From the Ellijay square travel approximately 7.6 miles on GA 52 East, then turn left onto paved "16 Roy Road" immediately past Stanley's Grocery and Service Station. You can see a large power apparatus to the right of GA 52 just beyond the turn onto Roy Road. If you wish to approach Roy Road from the east, or set up a shuttle between Amicalola Falls State Park and Springer Mountain, continue driving on GA 52 West approximately 12.0 miles beyond the GA 52–GA 183 junction, then turn right onto Roy Road.

After proceeding approximately 9.5 miles on Roy Road, turn right onto another paved road at the stop sign. Travel approximately 2.1 miles on this road before turning right onto gravel FS 42 opposite Mount Pleasant Baptist Church. Continue approximately 6.7 miles on FS 42 (usually a good road) to the "Hiker Trail" sign that marks the spot where the Appalachian Trail crosses the road. Park in the clearing to the left.

The Appalachian trail crosses FS 42 and enters the parking-camping area clearing 0.9 mile from its southern terminus atop Springer Mountain. If you are in the right spot, you should find the wide stair-step gap, the double white blaze and the sign with a hiker symbol to the right of the road 15 or 20 yards beyond the left turn into the clearing.

Shorter segments of Section 1 can be day hiked by setting up a shuttle at the intersection of FS 69 and FS 42 in Hightower Gap. Consult your maps for other possibilities to plan shuttles or alternate routes to Hightower Gap.

Notes

EBR
*Blood Mountain
Wilderness*
Woody Gap to
Neels Gap

Features
Scenic views, Blood
Mountain, wilderness

Distance
10.7 miles

Difficulty Rating
Moderate

Counties
Lumpkin and Union

Nearest Cities
Dahlonega (S),
Cleveland (SE),
Helen (E),
Blairsville (N)

Maps
Neels Gap
Quadrangle, GA;
AT map

Blazes
White rectangles; all
approach trails and
side trails to shel-
ters, vistas, water,
and campsites are
blazed in blue; sharp
turns and confusing
junctions are
marked with two ver-
tical white blazes

Appalachian National Scenic Trail, Section 2

This section, with only one long, steady uphill grade, makes an excellent day hike or a leisurely weekend backpacking trip. Starting at the picnic area and large gravel parking lot at Woody Gap (3,160 feet), the trail gradually gains elevation along the western hardwood slopes of Steel Trap and Jacobs Knobs for the first 0.5 mile. Following a short, 100-yard dip to the stand of tuliptrees at Lunsford Gap (3,330 feet), the footpath makes a moderate-to-strenuous, switchbacking climb to Preaching Rock, an outcrop overlook at mile 1.0. The trail continues to rise on the eastern side of the ridge to near the crest of Big Cedar Mountain (3,721 feet). It then descends, alternating between moderate and easy downgrades for most of the distance, to Dan Gap at mile 2.0.

Beyond Dan Gap, the path slants down off the ridge onto the western flank of Granny Top, where it remains slightly downhill or level to Miller Gap (3,005 feet) at mile 2.6. Dockery Lake Trail ends at its sign in Miller Gap. The AT continues north from the gap, gently undulating through a predominantly deciduous forest on the eastern slopes of Baker Mountain. Here it ascends moderately to ridge top, then drops to Henry Gap (3,100 feet) at mile 3.7. For the next 1.6 miles, the treadway follows the ridge up, over, and down the two low knobs of Burnett Field Mountain. Both of the switchbacking upgrades are moderate.

The trail enters Jarrard Gap (3,300 feet) at mile 5.3. Jarrard Gap Trail ends at its sign to the left of the gap. Across the road that bisects the gap, the AT rises moderately by switchback to near the crest of Gaddis Mountain (approximately 3,520 feet) before descending 0.2 mile to the next gap—Horsebone (3,460 feet). The gap-mountain-gap pattern continues as the footpath ascends moderately, then easily, to the level top of Turkey Stamp (approximately 3,780 feet). Beyond the short, downridge grade off the mountaintop, the path remains predominantly level or easy up to Bird Gap, where the western end of the Freeman Trail comes in from the right. At mile 7.1 it crosses Slaughter Creek (often dry in late summer and early fall) near its source. This point marks the beginning of the no-campfire zone that extends to Neels Gap. The mountain that fills your view to the left—the one you're hoping you don't have to climb—is Slaughter. The trail enters the small clearing of Slaughter Gap (3,860 feet) at mile 7.5. Slaughter Gap (marked with a sign) is a major trail junction. The old road to the left is the end of the Slaughter Creek Trail. The gap is also the eastern end of the blue-blazed Duncan Ridge Trail, which quickly leads to the Coosa Backcountry Trail. Duncan Ridge Trail is to the left of the large campsite that is straight through the gap.

After the AT turns 90 degrees to the right in Slaughter Gap, it begins the 0.9-mile upgrade to the short, twisted oaks and Catawba rhododendron thickets atop Blood Mountain. The remaining 600-foot elevation gain to the top of Blood (4,461 feet), the highest point along the AT in Georgia, is surprisingly easy. The gradient starts out mild, then becomes moderate as the treadway switchbacks steadily up the slope. At mile 8.4 the trail reaches "Picnic Rock," and the cabin-sized, two-room stone shelter on Blood's crest. Built in the 1930s by the Civilian Conservation Corps, the shelter was refurbished in 1981 by the GATC. A few yards past the shelter the trail enters Blood's sunny crown, stripped down to its backbone. The bare rock affords dramatic views of ridges and peaks and valleys to the south.

The final 2.3 miles of Section 2 loses 1,350 feet to Neels Gap. The first 1.0 mile of the descent works its way quickly down the mountain on short, steep switchbacks through rocky terrain. At mile 9.9, on

Water Sources
Mile 0.0: spring 200 yards to left; mile 1.5: spring on left; mile 2.9: cross rivulet; mile 5.2: intermittent spring to right; mile 5.3: blue-blazed Jarrard Gap Trail leads 0.3 mile to stream; mile 7.0: cross Slaughter Creek headwater streams; mile 9.7: blue-blazed Byron Herbert Reece Trail on left leads 0.2 mile to stream

Campsites
Mile 8.3: Blood Mountain Shelter

Ranger District
Brasstown

the mountain side of Flatrock Gap (3,420 feet), the AT reaches its junctions with the Freeman Trail on the right and the Byron Herbert Reece Trail on the left. The last 1.0 mile is easily walked.

Section 2 has a good spring wildflower display. In late April and May about 2.0 miles before Jarrard Gap, look for hundreds of large-flowered trillium carpeting a steep slope to the left of the trail, their three-petaled blooms held high by 10- to 15-inch stems.

All of Section 2 of the Appalachian Trail is in the 7,800-acre Blood Mountain Wilderness, with the exception of approximately 0.4 mile between Jarrard Gap and Horsebone Gap. Campfires are not allowed along the AT in the Blood Mountain Wilderness from Slaughter Creek to Neels Gap. (See page 294 for campfire regulations for the Blood Mountain Wilderness.)

Highlights
Mile 1.0: Preaching Rock, a large granite overlook with a great view south.
Mile 8.4: Blood Mountain Shelter and summit. At 4,461 feet, Blood Mountain is the highest point on the Georgia AT. It offers panoramic views. The stone shelter is listed on the National Register of Historic Places.

Directions
From Stonepile Gap, where US 19 splits away from GA 60, continue northward on GA 60 for 5.5 miles to Woody Gap, which is marked with a sign and parking lot on the northeastern side (right if you are heading north) of the road. The trailhead to Neels Gap is to the back of the parking area.

Notes

Appalachian National Scenic Trail, Section 3

EBR
Raven Cliffs
Wilderness
Neels Gap to
Hogpen Gap

This section is the shortest segment of the Appalachian Trail between paved road crossings in Georgia. Section 3, with only one long, strenuous climb, makes an ideal introductory trip for fit day hikers and backpackers.

Starting at Neels Gap (3,109 feet), the trail tunnels through the Walasi-Yi Center's breezeway before ascending the lower slopes of Levelland Mountain. Here heath thickets are common beneath the open, predominantly oak forest. Mountain laurel and pinxter-flower (*Rhododendron nudiflorum*) bloom during late April and much of May. Also blossoming at this time, the lousewort—an unusual wildflower with fern-like leaves and whorled, yellow-reddish-brown blooms—is common beside this initial segment of trail below 3,500 feet.

The trail makes a steady, easy-to-moderate climb from Neels Gap to Levelland Mountain's western high point at mile 1.5. Across the saddle between the mountain's twin crests (3,920 feet), the trail reaches the rock-slab overlook atop Levelland's eastern knob at mile 1.7. The prominent mountain to the south is Hogpen.

The treadway switchbacks downridge from Section 3's first vista to Swaim Gap (3,420 feet) at mile 2.1. Here it rises up and over a low, unnamed knob (3,540 feet), then gently undulates with the ridge crest to a campsite at mile 2.9. Less than 100 yards past this area, look for a climbing vine called Dutchman's pipe to the right of the trail. Its strongly curved, pipe-like flowers bloom in late April and early May.

Continuing eastward, the path passes below a top and over a stamp—Rock Spring Top and Corbin Horse Stamp—before it dips to a shallow gap. From this gap the treadway makes a short, moderate

Features
Scenic views,
wilderness

Distance
6.4 miles

Difficulty Rating
Moderate to
strenuous

Counties
Union, Lumpkin,
and White

Nearest Cities
Cleveland (SE),
Helen (E),
Blairsville (N),
Dahlonega (S)

Maps
Neels Gap and
Cowrock
Quadrangles, GA;
AT map

Blazes
White rectangles; all
approach trails and
side trails to shel-
ters, vistas, water,
and campsites are
blazed in blue; sharp
turns and confusing
junctions are
marked with two ver-
tical white blazes

Water Sources
Mile 1.1: spring 200 yards to left at Bull Gap; mile 2.8: spring to left of trail; mile 4.2: spring down side trail to left at Baggs Creek Gap; mile 6.4: spring down side trail to right just before AT crosses highway at Hogpen Gap

Campsites
Mile 6.2: Whitney Gap Shelter is 1.1 miles south on its blue-blazed side trail

Ranger District
Chattooga

upridge run to Wolf Laurel Top (3,766 feet), where a spur leads to an open spot with a view. The trail descends a short distance to a second overlook from Wolf Laurel Top, then continues to lose elevation to Baggs Creek Gap (3,540 feet) at mile 4.2. For the next 0.6 mile the path heads up—easily at first, then moderately, then easily again—to the crown of Cowrock Mountain (3,852 feet). The treadway passes two outcrop overlooks on the way to the top.

The sharp, switchbacking downgrade through rocky terrain to Tesnatee Gap at mile 5.5 is Section 3's steepest and longest descent. At Tesnatee Gap (3,138 feet), the AT angles to the right toward Richard B. Russell Scenic Highway, parallels the pavement for a few yards, then bears off to the right, up and away from the road. Before it enters the forest again, the trail passes the entrance to an old road. That old road is the end of the historical Logan Turnpike Trail. The spur trail leading to water from Tesnatee Gap is much longer and more difficult than the one from Hogpen.

From Tesnatee Gap, the footpath climbs 0.6 mile to an elevation of 3,680 feet on Wildcat Mountain. Here Section 3 gets on the elevator, earning the "strenuous" part of its rating. The first 0.4 mile of ascent rises sharply through a scenic area of large lichen-spotted outcrops. To the right at mile 6.0, there is a view of Town Creek Cove and the rock face of Cowrock Mountain. Two-tenths of a mile farther, on top of Wildcat, the trail comes to the sign for Whitley Gap Shelter, which is 1.1 miles to the south.

Even if you do not intend to stay at the shelter, you may want to walk the blue-blazed side trail out toward Whitley Gap. Within the first 0.5 mile the ridge crest affords several open, rock outcrop views of the cliff faces of Cowrock Mountain and the upper Town Creek Valley, both in the Raven Cliffs Wilderness. There are winter views of Brasstown Bald to the north. Catawba rhododendron blooms on top of Wildcat Mountain during late May and early June.

Immediately beyond the spur to the shelter, the AT turns left and heads down toward Hogpen Gap on long, easy switchbacks. Near the highway, where the trail turns left again, a blue-blazed spur drops a short distance to the Dodd Creek headwaters. The end of Section 3 angles to the left across the highway and follows the white blazes to Hogpen Gap parking area (3,460 feet).

Except for the 250 yards after Neels Gap, Section 3 remains within the 9,115-acre Raven Cliffs Wilderness.

Highlights

Throughout: During September and early October much of this section's ridge top is an aster garden.
Mile 1.7: Scenic view from Levelland Mountain.
Mile 3.4: Scenic view from Wolf Laurel Top toward Wildcat Ridge.
Miles 4.4, 4.6: Scenic views southeast from Cowrock Mountain.
Mile 6.0: Scenic view from Wildcat Mountain.

Directions

From Turners Corner, where US 19 joins US 129, continue north on US 19–US 129 for approximately 7.7 miles to the Walasi-Yi Center at Neels Gap. The trailhead is to the east of the highway, behind the Walasi-Yi Center.

From the Blairsville square, travel south on US 19–129 for approximately 13.0 miles to Neels Gap.

Do not park at the Walasi-Yi Center and hike the AT from Neels Gap; parking in front of the store is for customers only. You can park off to the right side (heading north) of the highway just past the Walasi-Yi Center, or you can drive 0.5 mile farther north past Neels Gap to the Byron Herbert Reece Memorial Picnic Area, where there is usually plenty of parking.

Notes

238

Features
Winter views,
wilderness

Distance
13.6 miles

Difficulty Rating
Moderate

Counties
Towns, White, and
Union

Nearest Cities
Helen (SE),
Hiawassee (N)

Map
Cowrock, Jacks
Gap, and Tray
Mountain
Quadrangles, GA;
AT map

Blazes
White rectangles; all
approach trails and
side trails to shel-
ters, vistas, water,
and campsites are
blazed in blue; sharp
turns and confusing
junctions are
marked with two ver-
tical white blazes

Appalachian National Scenic Trail, Section 4

Of the three long sections of the Appalachian Trail in Georgia—Sections 1,4, and 5—Section 4 is the shortest and least strenuous. This section, with miles of gentle grades mixed with the usual alternating ascents and descents, makes an excellent long day hike or two-day backpacking trip.

The first 4.2 miles of Section 4 follow the typical pattern of the Appalachian Trail: the gap-mountain-gap-mountain sine wave of the ridge crest. Starting at Hogpen Gap (3,460 feet), the trail gradually gains elevation around the eastern side of Strawberry Top before it dips slightly with the ridge to Sapling Gap (3,480 feet) at mile 1.6. The path rises easily to moderately from Sapling Gap to the top of Poor Mountain (3,640 feet) at mile 1.9, descends steadily to Wide Gap (3,180 feet) at mile 2.5, ascends moderately to the crown of Sheep Rock Top (3,550 feet) at mile 3.6, then drops to Low Gap (3,020 feet) at mile 4.2. The Low Gap Shelter is 0.1 mile to the right of the trail.

Continuing northeastward, the trail follows the unexpectedly mild grades of an old road until mile 8.0, where it returns to its usual up-and-down pattern. This 3.8-mile segment—the easiest long stretch on the Appalachian Trail in Georgia—winds through a mature oak-hickory forest on the eastern flank of Horsetrough Mountain for most of its length.

Near Cold Springs Gap (3,460 feet) at mile 8.0, the path leaves the roadbed and makes a moderate 0.2-mile ascent to the top of an unnamed knob. Following the sharp downgrade from the first knob, the treadway climbs 0.6 mile (the first 0.4 mile is moderate to strenuous, the rest easy to moderate) to near the high point of another unnamed knob before dipping slightly to Chattahoochee Gap (3,500 feet) at mile 9.2. Chattahoochee Spring, the official source of the Chattahoochee River, is about 200 yards to the right of the gap. To the left, blue-blazed Jacks Knob Trail leads 4.5 miles to the parking lot near the summit of Brasstown Bald.

In Chattahoochee Gap the AT angles to the right, slants down off the ridge, then skirts the southern slopes of Jacks Knob to Red Clay Gap (3,440 feet) at mile 9.8. Here the trail switches to the other side of the ridge and enters a moist, north slope forest on the flank of Spaniards Knob. To either side of the rock-jumbled footpath, scores of dead American chestnuts have fallen into tangled windrows. Striped maples, common in cool, moist locations throughout the Blue Ridge Mountains of North Georgia, are abundant beside this richly vegetated portion of the trail. A small tree, the striped maple is easily identified by the whitish, vertical stripes that line the smooth green bark of its thinner branches and by its three-lobed leaves, which have rounded or heart-shaped bases, notched margins, and long slender tips on the end of each lobe.

The treadway descends to Henson Gap (3,580 feet) at mile 11.0. Four-tenths mile farther Section 4 passes the blue-blazed side trail to Blue Mountain Shelter. With the exception of two short, downhill grades, the next 1.2 miles (from Henson Gap) ascend to the crest of Blue Mountain (4,030 feet). This long grade, which angles steadily upward on mountainside before climbing hard along the ridge, is moderate in overall difficulty. The remainder of Section 4 drops steadily, occasionally sharply, down the rocky northeastern slopes of Blue Mountain to Unicoi Gap (2,949 feet).

Section 4 is entirely within the 16,400-acre Mark Trail Wilderness.

Highlights

Throughout: Winter views.
Mile 9.2: Chattahoochee Spring. The source of the Chattahoochee River—the main water supply for

Water Sources
Mile 4.2: spring at Low Gap Shelter to right; mile 4.6: rivulet crosses under trail; mile 6.1: several rivulets cross trail; mile 9.2: blue-blazed side trail to right at Chattahoochee Gap leads 200 yards to Chattahoochee Spring; mile 10.7: spring several yards to left of trail; mile 11.3: spring to left of trail 0.1 mile before side trail to Blue Mountain Shelter

Campsites
Mile 4.2: Low Gap Shelter; mile 11.4: Blue Mountain Shelter

Ranger District
Chattooga

Atlanta—is 200 yards downslope to the right of Chattahoochee Gap. The river flows all the way to the Gulf of Mexico.

Directions

From Helen take GA 75 North 1.4 miles beyond the Chattahoochee River bridge and turn left onto GA Alt. 75 South, crossing the Robertstown bridge over the Chattahoochee River. Continue on GA Alt. 75 South for 2.3 miles, then turn right onto Richard B. Russell Scenic Highway (also GA 348 North). Proceed slightly more than 7.0 miles to the large parking area to the right. Hogpen Gap, marked with a sign to the left of the road, is the highest point on the highway. The trailhead is at the back of the parking area.

Notes

Appalachian National Scenic Trail, Section 5

This section, offering scenic views and isolated forest, makes an ideal two- or three-day backpacking trip. The second half of this segment, from Young Lick to Dicks Creek Gap, follows the ridge that serves as the boundary between two wildlife management areas. Lake Burton WMA, 12,600 acres, is to the east; Swallow Creek WMA, 19,000 acres, is to the west.

Starting to the right of the commemorative plaque at the parking area in Unicoi Gap (2,949 feet), Section 5 climbs moderately, through rocky terrain and a predominantly oak forest, to the crown of Rocky Mountain (4,020 feet) at mile 1.3. Along the way at mile 1.0, the blue-blazed Rocky Mountain Trail junction is to the left. The rivulet it crosses on the way up is the Hiwassee River. Atop the mountain, a splendid view to the right extends beyond the unmistakable profile of Yonah Mountain all the way to the Piedmont.

The trail descends, with occasional short, steep, rocky pitches, to FS 283 in Indian Grave Gap (3,100 feet) at mile 2.7. Outcrops on Rocky Mountain's open southern shoulder afford two more year-round views on the way down. The upper elevation end of Andrews Cove Trail and the lower elevation end of Rocky Mountain Trail meet the AT at Indian Grave Gap.

Across the road, the AT enters the evergreen tunnel of a heath thicket. Here the path slants gently upward to its crossing of FS 79 (Tray Mountain Road) at mile 3.3, continues 0.2 mile to the ridge top, then quickly crosses a jeep road in an unnamed gap, the site of the "old cheese factory," a nineteenth-century farm. Through the gap, the treadway rises moderately as it winds to the northeast onto York Ridge. After the initial upgrade, the trail remains nearly level through an open forest of old, gnarled oaks to Tray

Features
Scenic views, wilderness, Tray Mountain

Distance
16.1 miles

Difficulty Rating
Moderate to strenuous

Counties
Towns, White, Habersham, and Rabun

Nearest Cities
Helen (SW), Hiawassee (NW), Clayton (NE)

Maps
Tray Mountain Quadrangle, GA, Macedonia and Hightower Bald Quadrangles, GA-NC; AT map

Blazes
White rectangles; all approach trails and side trails to shelters, vistas, water, and campsites are blazed in blue; sharp turns and confusing junctions are marked with two vertical white blazes

Water Sources

Mile 0.6: small stream; mile 3.6: springs 75 yards to left by Tray Mountain Road; mile 5.5: spring near Tray Mountain Shelter; mile 7.2: spring downhill to right at Steeltrap Gap; mile 10.0: spring downhill to right at Sassafras Gap; mile 10.8: small stream down old road from Addis Gap 0.3 mile to the right; mile 12.6: spring near Deep Gap Shelter; miles 15.0–16.1: springs and small streams

Campsites

Mile 5.5: Tray Mountain Shelter, 0.2 mile to the right; mile 12.6: Deep Gap Shelter, 0.3 mile to the right

Ranger District

Unicoi Gap to Addis Gap: Brasstown; Addis Gap to Dicks Creek Gap: Tallulah

Gap (3,841 feet), where it crosses FS 79 again at mile 4.3. Two-tenths mile before Tray Gap there is a good view, especially when the leaves have fallen, of Hickorynut Ridge.

Proceeding east from Tray Gap, Section 5 ascends moderately on wide loops that switchback through rocky terrain. At mile 5.0, where the treadway turns sharply to the right, there is an excellent outcrop overlook to the left. Two-tenths mile farther, the twisting footpath reaches the protruding topknot at Tray's summit (4,430 feet). Here, atop the second highest point on the Appalachian Trail in Georgia, the bare rock affords one of the most scenic 360-degree vistas in the Chattahoochee National Forest. Yonah's half dome is to the south; Brasstown Bald's tower lies northwest; the Nantahala's sharp peaks are almost due north. On clear days, usually after a front has passed through, you can even see Atlanta's sky-line—with binoculars.

The AT traverses the saddle between Tray's high points, then descends steadily to an unnamed gap (3,780 feet) at mile 5.9. On the way down, at mile 5.5, a blue-blazed spur trail leads to the Tray Moun-tain Shelter and to water. Beyond this first gap, the trail gently undulates on or just below the ridge line, losing elevation through two more gaps—Wolfpen (3,580 feet) at mile 6.7 and Steeltrap (3,500 feet) at mile 7.2.

The downgrade from Tray Mountain is through an open, oak-hickory forest. Two of North Georgia's most brightly colored birds—the rose-breasted gros-beak and the scarlet tanager—are common during the summer along this descending segment of Section 5, as well as on other portions of the Appala-chian Trail with similar habitat and elevations.

Continuing from Steeltrap Gap, the path slabs around the west side of Young Lick Knob. It then skirts the upper slopes of a knob and dips to a low gap—the Blue Ridge Swag (3,460 feet) at mile 9.0. From the swag the footpath gains elevation moderately along the eastern side of Round Top before dropping to Sassafras Gap (3,540 feet) at mile 10.1. Here the AT follows a north-running ridge over a low knob and down to Addis Gap (3,340 feet) at mile 10.9.

The long green tunnel, as the AT is fondly called, makes a long, steady ascent on the western slope of Kelly Knob to about 4,140 feet before switching sides and descending to the stand of tuliptrees in Deep Gap (3,560 feet) at mile 12.6. The Deep Gap Shelter is down the blue-blazed path to the right. The treadway rises on the west side of Whiteoak Stomp before passing the east side of Wolfstake Knob. After proceeding through McClure Gap (3,740 feet) at mile 13.7, the trail gains about 100 feet of elevation toward the top of Powell Mountain before veering off the ridge.

Here the AT drops steadily along Powell's southeastern flank to Moreland Gap (3,060 feet) at mile 14.9. In this gap the trail turns 90 degrees to the right onto an old road. The remainder of the section is predominantly downhill or level to Dicks Creek Gap (2,675 feet). The last mile, most of it on the wide walkway of an old road, passes through a scenic area of steep-sided coves and small streams.

A 6.6-mile segment of Section 5, from Tray Gap to Addis Gap, passes through the 9,702-acre Tray Mountain Wilderness.

Highlights
Throughout: Mature, open hardwood stands. Some of the trees on the ridges are gnarled and wind-blasted.
Mile 1.3: View from Rocky Mountain.
Mile 5.2: 360-degree view from the summit of Tray Mountain.
Mile 13.5: Blue-blazed side trail leads to scenic view south.

Directions
From the Chattahoochee River bridge in Helen, travel approximately 9.5 miles on GA 75 North to Unicoi Gap. The gap's large gravel parking area to the right of the highway has a boulder-embedded plaque commemorating the Appalachian Trail. Section 5 begins to the right of the road as you face north.

EBR
Hightower Bald
Dicks Creek Gap to Bly Gap

Features
Wilderness, winter views

Distance
8.8 miles

Difficulty Rating
Moderate to strenuous

Counties
Rabun and Towns

Nearest Cities
Clayton (E), Hiawassee (W)

Maps
Hightower Bald Quadrangle, GA-NC; AT map

Blazes
White rectangles; all approach trails and side trails to shelters, vistas, water, and campsites are blazed in blue; sharp turns and confusing junctions are marked with two vertical white blazes

Appalachian National Scenic Trail, Section 6

There are no long, steep upgrades along Section 6. There are, however, a few short, strenuous grades and numerous moderate grades, both up and down, that take their toll on those carrying heavy packs. Notice the constant change and wide range of the elevations for the gaps.

Starting straight back from the picnic tables at Dicks Creek Gap (2,675 feet), the white-blazed footpath rises moderately through a mixed deciduous-evergreen forest to the top of a sharp ridge at 0.4 mile. Here it crosses over the ridge, dips to a saddle on a spur ridge, then continues gradually upward along the southern slopes of Little Bald Mountain. At mile 1.1 the treadway angles up to the ridge and follows it easily uphill for 0.3 mile before slanting down to its western side. After crossing the ridge, the path makes a steady, predominantly moderate descent to Tom Cowart Gap (2,900 feet) at mile 1.8. On the way down, it passes through a rich forest of basswood, buckeye, and ash along the headwaters of Little Hightower Creek.

Across the old road that once bisected the gap, the trail climbs moderately for 0.4 mile back to the ridge top, where it drops to the slopes again and skirts below the high point of an unnamed knob. The trail then leads through a gap at mile 2.4, and rises on the easy-to-moderate grades of a north-running ridge for 0.5 mile. After this elevation gain, it slips off the ridge onto the upper flank of Buzzard Knob, remaining nearly level until it dips to Bull Gap (3,540 feet) at mile 3.2.

Beyond Bull Gap, the footpath ascends for 0.1 mile before crossing over the ridge and dropping to its eastern side. The next 1.0 mile, a gradual downgrade through a cove forest to Plumorchard Gap (3,100 feet), is the easiest walking on Section 6. The triple-decker Plumorchard Gap Shelter (mile 4.3) is located approximately 0.2 mile to the right. There is a spring a short distance down the old road to the left of the gap as well as at the shelter.

Continuing northward to Bly Gap, the trail climbs easy-to-moderate grades for 0.5 mile, then gently undulates with the ridge to the southern highpoint of As Knob (approximately 3,440 feet). Here, instead of following the knob's crest, the treadway slides onto the mountain's western slopes and descends easily to FS 72 in Blue Ridge Gap (3,020 feet).

Water Sources
Mile 0.0: rivulet; mile 1.6: permanent branch to left; mile 4.3: stream at Plumorchard Gap shelter to right; mile 8.6: spring to the right near trail; mile 8.8: springs at Bly Gap

Ranger District
Tallulah

The path holds its course on moderate, then easy, upgrades to mile 6.2, where it bears to the left onto the western pitch of Wheeler Knob. Once off the ridge, the treadway is predominantly level or slightly downhill to Rich Cove Gap (3,420 feet). From this gap at mile 6.8, the trail heads upridge for less than 0.2 mile before making a half circle below the crest of Rocky Knob. After it regains the ridge at mile 7.1, the AT alternates level, then ascending, easy or moderate grades as it climbs toward Rich Knob.

At mile 8.4 the footpath leaves the ridge and undulates easily on the eastern side of Rich Knob to Bly Gap (3,840 feet), just over the state line in North Carolina. One-tenth mile before entering the gap, the trail turns 90 degrees to the left, travels 60 yards uphill, then turns 90 degrees to the right. One hundred yards beyond the second sharp turn, the AT reaches the old road in the small clearing of Bly Gap. Continuing into North Carolina, the next vehicular access is at Deep Gap, 6.8 miles beyond Bly Gap.

Along the higher elevations of the last half of Section 6, from Plumorchard Gap to Bly Gap, you may notice small clusters of squaw-root—a common parasitic wildflower. Usually 3 to 8 inches tall, squaw-root closely resembles a slender, elongated pine cone. These unusual plants range from yellow to brown and become darker as they grow older.

The pitch pine, which ranges only as far south as the mountains in northeastern Georgia, is fairly common along this section of the trail. The pitch—usually 50 to 60 feet tall, rarely 100—is a medium-sized pine. It is shorter than the white and shortleaf, generally taller and thicker than the Virginia or tablemountain. Its stiff, often twisted, dark yellow-green needles—3 to 5 inches long and three to the sheath—stand at right angles to the branch. The tree's numerous horizontal branches give it a short-trunked appearance, especially when compared to the shortleaf pine.

The trail enters the 23,714-acre Southern Nantahala Wilderness across Blue Ridge Gap at mile 5.6. The rest of Section 6 remains in the wilderness.

Highlights
Throughout: Good winter views from ridge tops. Hightower Bald is northwest (west as the trail approaches Bly Gap). North Carolina's Standing Indian Mountain (5,498 feet), which the AT crosses, is to the northeast. *Mile 8.8:* View at Bly Gap. Trees are reclaiming the former opening to the left; the view will soon disappear.

Directions
From the GA 75–US 76 intersection near Hiawassee, travel approximately 7.6 miles on US 76 East to the picnic area and parking lot to the left of the highway at Dicks Creek Gap.

Dicks Creek Gap can also be reached by traveling approximately 16.5 miles on US 76 West from Clayton. A prominent stick-figure hiker sign marks the AT crossing at US 76.

Notes

BENTON MᴀᴄKAYE TRAIL

Benton MacKaye, a forester, was the first to envision a continuous trail along the crest of the entire Appalachian Mountain chain. His completed dream, the Appalachian Trail, is now 60 years old. MacKaye also foresaw the need to create major loop trails that would join the Appalachian. In 1980, a trail association was established to make the idea of a major loop in the South—the Benton MacKaye Trail—a reality.

If it is completed as proposed, the 250-mile footpath will have its southern terminus at Springer Mountain and its northern terminus at Davenport Gap, on the northeastern edge of Great Smoky Mountains National Park. Completed in 1989, Georgia's 80-mile segment of the Benton MacKaye begins atop Springer Mountain and ends at Double Spring Gap on the Tennessee border. Double Spring Gap is located on the northern boundary of the Cohutta Wilderness near Big Frog Mountain. After being thwarted at the border of the Cherokee National Forest for several years, the Benton MacKaye is again making progress. The trail is now complete to US 64 in Tennessee.

The Benton MacKaye Trail Association, a volunteer organization, is constructing and maintaining the trail.

WBR
Springer Mountain

**Springer Mountain
to Three Forks**

Features
Springer Mountain,
southern terminus of
AT, Three Forks,
view, national
recreation area

Distance
6.0 miles

Difficulty Rating
Easy to moderate

County
Fannin

Nearest Cities
Ellijay (W),
Dawsonville (S),
Dahlonega (SE)

Map
Noontootla
Quadrangle, GA

Blazes
White diamonds

Water Sources
Mile 0.2: spring near
shelter on Springer
Mountain; miles 2.0-
2.2: Chester Creek
on left; miles 2.6,
2.7: two forks of
Davis Creek; mile
6.0: Chester Creek
at Three Forks

Ranger District
Toccoa

Benton MacKaye Trail, Section 1

The summit of Springer Mountain serves as the southern terminus for the two longest trails in Georgia—the Appalachian Trail and the Benton MacKaye. Slightly more than 0.2 mile from its start, the Appalachian Trail arrives at a sign-posted junction. The Appalachian Trail, blazed with white rectangles, follows the left fork. The Benton MacKaye Trail (BMT), blazed with white diamonds, follows the right fork at an elevation of approximately 3,750 feet. From Springer Mountain to Three Forks, Benton MacKaye travels northward, intersecting the Appalachian Trail twice to form a figure 8 and permitting a 10-mile loop hike.

Curling to the east with the ridge, Section 1 starts with an easy-to-moderate descent to a shallow gap at 0.5 mile. Beyond this unnamed gap, the trail rises through a heath thicket, skirts the southeastern side of Ball Mountain, then continues the steady downgrade from Springer. At mile 1.4 a sign signals "view" to the right. A short spur leads to an outcrop overlook, open to the southeast, that most definitely affords a view—the completely forested Jones Creek Cove and its surrounding ridges.

After crossing FS 42 in Big Stamp Gap (3,146 feet) at mile 1.7, the treadway undulates on easy grades until it swings beside a rhododendron-lined tributary of Chester Creek. Section 1 parallels this stream on the wide walkway of an old road before crossing it at mile 2.2. Continuing to the northwest, the trail crosses the two forks of Davis Creek (another Chester Creek tributary)—the first at mile 2.6, the second at mile 2.7—heads uphill for 0.3 mile, then turns left. At mile 3.2 it turns right at the sign and joins the AT. For 0.6 mile both trails share the same treadway along a Rich Mountain ridge dominated by tall eastern white pines and tuliptrees.

After the trails split, the Benton MacKaye ascends easily with the ridge through an understory of Carolina silverbell for 0.3 mile before dropping to an old road at mile 5.0. It follows this road gently downhill through eastern hemlock and rosebay rhododendron on the lower slopes of Rich Mountain. Chester Creek is deeply entrenched to the right. At mile 5.9, Section 1 turns right and shares the gravel road walkway with the Appalachian Trail. Together they dip 0.1 mile to Three Forks (2,540 feet), where Stover, Chester, and Long Creeks flow together at right angles to create Noontootla Creek.

At Three Forks the trails cross a footbridge over Chester Creek, then cross FS 58.

All of Section 1 of the BMT is within the 23,330-acre Ed Jenkins National Recreation Area.

Note: The Georgia Appalachian Trail Club (GATC) plans to move the AT to the east side of Rich Mountain. The AT will cross the BMT at about mile 3.0 and again at mile 3.9.

Highlights

Mile 0.2 to the south from the southern trailhead: View from Springer Mountain and the southern terminus of the AT.

Mile 1.4: Spur trail leading right to an overlook with a view of Jones Creek Cove.

Mile 6.0: Chester Creek at Three Forks.

Directions

The directions to Benton MacKaye's southern terminus atop Springer Mountain are exactly the same as those for Section 1 of the Appalachian Trail. (See page 230 for these directions.) After reaching the place where the Appalachian Trail crosses FS 42, you have two options. You can walk 0.7 mile on the Appalachian Trail to the beginning of the Benton MacKaye, or you can drive approximately 1.9 miles farther on FS 42 and walk 1.7 miles on the Benton MacKaye to its beginning. Springer Mountain is to the south (to the right and uphill) of FS 42. A trail sign marks where the Benton MacKaye crosses FS 42.

Notes

WBR
Ed Jenkins
National Recreation
Area
Three Forks to
GA 60

Features
Long Creek Falls,
view, Toccoa River,
national recreation
area

Distance
11.5 miles

Difficulty Rating
Moderate

County
Fannin

Nearest Cities
Ellijay (W),
Blue Ridge (NW),
Blairsville (NE),
Dahlonega (SE)

Maps
Noontootla and
Wilscot
Quadrangles, GA

Blazes
White diamonds

Benton MacKaye Trail, Section 2

From Three Forks (2,540 feet), Section 2 follows the old road that parallels Long Creek to the east. A sign at mile 1.0 marks the blue-blazed spur that leads 100 yards to Long Creek Falls—a ledge-sliding drop of 20 to 25 feet. One-tenth of a mile farther the Benton MacKaye and AT split apart at another sign. Here Section 1 of the blue-blazed Duncan Ridge Trail begins. It shares the treadway with the BMT for the remaining 10.4 miles to GA 60.

The Benton MacKaye turns left onto path at the split and quickly crosses Long Creek. It then winds through heath thickets beside a small tributary stream for 0.8 mile, swings to the west, and makes a moderate, diagonal climb to a ridge-top clearing (3,260 feet). This wildlife opening at mile 2.1 affords an excellent view of Springer Mountain to the south.

For the next 2.3 miles Section 2 roller-coasters, rising to knobs and dipping to the gaps between them, on or near the crest of an unnamed ridge. The downgrades are often steep and slope off the ridge. Most of the upgrades are easy or moderate and stay on the ridge. The forest is open and predominantly oak.

After an easy, 0.4-mile descent from Wildcat Ridge, the trail enters a shallow gap at mile 4.7. Beyond this gap, the Benton MacKaye makes a 1.7-mile "S," walked south to north, around the two peaks collectively known as John Dick Mountain. Here the footpath climbs for 0.4 mile toward the southern peak (Big John Dick Mountain), slants down off the ridge onto its eastern side, then swings to the west on its northern slopes. At mile 5.4 it turns to the right (north) and drops sharply for 0.2 mile to the middle of the "S," at Bryson Gap (2,900 feet). The trail continues to the northwest, rising over a low spur before completing the half loop around Little John Dick Mountain on the easy grades of an old road.

Continuing toward the Toccoa River, the BMT turns left onto another old road and heads downhill through a heath thicket on a north-running spur. The route passes through Sapling Gap (2,780 feet) at mile 6.5. With the exception of a few short, upridge grades, the path steadily works its way down, losing approximately 1,000 feet in elevation to the Toccoa River (1,900 feet) at mile 8.4. Here the path crosses the shoaling, usually green river on a deluxe, 265-foot-long suspension bridge.

The remainder of Section 2 is a long upgrade followed by a downgrade of nearly equal length. Across the river, the footpath makes a moderate, occasionally strenuous ascent to the twin high points (both 2,720 feet) of Toonowee Mountain. It then descends for 1.1 miles, winding steadily and sometimes steeply down the slopes of Toonowee to GA 60 (2,028 feet).

Section 2 of the Benton MacKaye remains within the 23,330-acre Ed Jenkins National Recreation Area from Three Forks to the southern foot of Toonowee Mountain.

Water Sources
Mile 0.0: Chester Creek at Three Forks; miles 0.0–1.0: Long Creek; mile 5.6: spring to right at Bryson Gap; mile 8.4: spring run into south bank of Toccoa River; mile 11.5: Little Skeenah Creek and its tributaries are not recommended for drinking water even with a water filter

Ranger District
Toccoa

Highlights
Mile 1.0: Spur trail to Long Creek Falls, a 25-foot waterfall.
Mile 2.1: Wildlife opening with a view of Springer Mountain to the south.
Mile 8.4: The trail crosses the Toccoa River on a 265-foot-long suspension bridge.

Directions
From the square in Ellijay travel about 7.6 miles east on GA 52. Turn left onto paved Roy Road immediately past Stanley's Grocery. There is a large power apparatus to the right of GA 52 just past the turn onto Roy Road. If you are approaching from the east, Roy Road is approximately 12.0 miles beyond the GA 52–GA 183 junction. After about 9.5 miles on Roy Road, turn right onto another paved road at the stop sign. Continue 4.9 miles and turn right onto FS 58. A short distance beyond a church, the main road (now dirt) forks. Veer right with FS 58 and continue 5.5 miles to a trail post on the right side of the road just after you cross Long Creek. The trail is the blocked road to the left.

252

Features
Forest, views

Distance
5.6 miles

Difficulty Rating
Moderate to
strenuous

Counties
Fannin and Union

Nearest Cities
Blue Ridge (NW),
Blairsville (NE),

Maps
Wilscot and Mulky
Gap Quadrangles,
GA

Blazes
White diamonds

Water Sources
Mile 0.0: Little
Skeenah Creek is not
recommended as a
source for drinking
water even with a fil-
ter; mile 3.6: spring
about 25 feet to right
of trail

Ranger District
Toccoa

Benton MacKaye Trail, Section 3

With elevation gains of 1,070 feet and 730 feet for Wallalah and Licklog Mountains, this is the most strenuous short section of the Benton MacKaye Trail.

Starting near a bench mark with a recorded elevation of 2,028 feet, Section 3 immediately crosses Little
Skeenah Creek, then climbs moderately toward the
ridge. At mile 1.0 the path turns right onto an old
woods road atop Duncan Ridge and ascends sharply
by switchback. Before reaching the rocky crown of
Wallalah Mountain (3,100 feet) at mile 1.7, the treadway passes beside an outcrop overlook open to the
south. Toonowee Mountain is south and the Toccoa
River watershed is southeast.

After descending 0.4 mile to an unnamed gap
(2,730 feet), the footpath heads steadily upridge to
the crest of Licklog Mountain (3,472 feet) at mile 3.2.
(The name Licklog, which is common in the mountains, comes from the old days when farmers would
fit a salt block for cattle into a downed tree.) It then
loses elevation to another unnamed gap (3,140 feet)
and starts to rise to the next high point on the
ridge—Rhodes Mountain.

Section 3 has been relocated at Rhodes Mountain. Rather than climbing to the top of the mountain, where it once split away from the Duncan Ridge
Trail, it now leaves the DRT at mile 4.2 (3,260 feet)
0.1 mile south of the summit.

After splitting away from the DRT, the treadway
slabs around the upper western slope of Rhodes
Mountain to a northwest-running ridge. The remainder of this section heads downhill on or near this
ridge crest through an oak-pine forest with mountain
laurel. Section 3 of the BMT ends at Skeenah Gap
Road at Skeenah Gap (2,380 feet).

Highlights
Mile 1.4: Rock outcrop view of mountains and Toccoa River Valley to the south.
Mile 2.3: Good winter views to the south.
Mile 3.2: Winter views from the summit of Licklog Mountain.

Directions
From Stonepile Gap, where US 19 and GA 60 split apart, continue northward on GA 60. Section 3 of the Benton MacKaye Trail crosses GA 60 approximately 22.0 miles beyond Stonepile Gap and approximately 3.0 miles beyond Deep Hole Recreation Area. When you pass the trout farm ponds to the right of the highway, continue approximately 0.2 mile to the trailhead.

The Benton MacKaye Trail shares the same treadway with the Duncan Ridge Trail across GA 60. Look for the blue blazes, white diamond blazes, and a small trail sign. Both trails cross GA 60 at the entrance to FS 816 to the left of the highway. Section 2 of the Benton MacKaye Trail ends at GA 60.

Notes

254

Features
Winter views

Distance
5.3 miles

Difficulty Rating
Moderate

Counties
Union and Fannin

Nearest City
Blue Ridge

Map
Wilscot Quadrangle,
GA

Blazes
White diamonds

Water Sources
Mile 2.1: spring 150
yards to the right
(north) of the trail at
Payne Gap

Ranger District
Toccoa

Benton MacKaye Trail, Section 4

Section 4 follows the ridge crests in a half circle that arcs east to west and is convex to the north. While there are no long, steady ascents or descents like those encountered on Sections 3 and 5, this section constantly changes elevation, heading up and down 30 to 270 feet at a time. Many of these short grades are over 10 percent.

Beginning at Skeenah Gap (2,380 feet), the trail rises 200 feet to the first knob, then continues to roller-coaster with the ridge, dipping to shallow gaps and rising to the high points. The route ascends to two knobs slightly over 2,800 feet at miles 1.6 and 1.9 before descending to Payne Gap (2,620 feet) at mile 2.1.

Heading west from Payne Gap, Section 4 rises over the high point of a knob (2,860 feet) at mile 2.7 and downgrades to a narrow gap (2,700 feet) where it crosses FS 640-A at mile 3.0. Next the path climbs steadily through an oak-hickory forest to the highest point of Section 4 (3,020 feet) just south of Dead-ennen Mountain's peak (3,041 feet). The treadway follows switchbacks down through several regenerating cuts to the intersection of old roads at Lula Head Gap (2,580 feet) at mile 4.4.

The remaining 0.9 mile slabs the upper southern slope of Wilscot Mountain to 2,740 feet before descending below the ridge line to Wilscot Gap (2,420 feet) at GA 60. The trail passes through a stand of eastern white pine near the top of the mountain.

Highlights
Throughout: Good winter views of surrounding mountains.

Directions
From Blue Ridge travel US 76 East 4.0 miles from the US 76–GA 5 junction before turning right onto GA 60. Continue on GA 60 South approximately

13.0 miles (pass through Morganton and watch for turns on GA 60), then turn left onto Skeenah Gap Road (not signed) just before the bridge over Skeenah Creek. Proceed 3.1 miles to Friendship Baptist Church #1. The trail crosses the road 0.2 mile past the church, just before the Union County line. Look for a set of steps on the left.

From Stonepile Gap, where US 19 and GA 60 split apart, travel GA 60 North approximately 31.0 miles and take the first right after the bridge over Skeenah Creek onto Skeenah Gap Road. Then follow the directions given above to Skeenah Gap.

Notes

256

Features
Winter views,
Toccoa River

Distance
7.5 miles

Difficulty Rating
Moderate

County
Fannin

Nearest City
Blue Ridge

Maps
Wilscot and Blue
Ridge Quadrangles,
GA

Blazes
White diamonds

Water Sources
Miles 2.0, 2.3, 2.8:
seasonal springs;
mile 4.1: spring to
right of trail at
Garland Gap

Ranger District
Toccoa

Benton MacKaye Trail, Section 5

Westward-heading Section 5 makes its toughest climb right at the beginning, at Wilscot Gap (2,420 feet). The treadway gains 730 feet in 1.3 miles to the top of Tipton Mountain. A long, looping switchback on the northern slope keeps the climb from being a short, steep, straight-up-the-ridge pull. From the top there are good winter views of Blue Ridge Lake to the northwest and the Brawley Mountain fire tower to the southwest.

The trail gradually descends by switchback to Owen Gap (2,780 feet) at mile 2.0, then slabs around the northwest slope of Bald Top. After passing through Ledford Gap (2,620 feet, FS 45 in gap) at mile 2.3, the path follows switchbacks to the crown of Brawley Mountain (3,207 feet) at mile 3.2. Beyond Brawley's fire tower bear right onto an old road and turn right onto path after 35 yards. Section 5 descends with the ridge crest to Garland Gap (2,420 feet) at mile 4.1.

Continuing to the west, the route rises to 2,640 feet on the north slope of Garland Mountain before descending with the ridge to a gap (1,880 feet, mile 5.6) at Dial Road. Here Section 5 crosses the road, rises to 2,140 feet on the east lead of Free Knob and descends with a woods road to Shallowford Bridge Road at mile 6.9. Turn right and follow the dirt-gravel Forest Service road as it closely parallels the shoaling Toccoa River through private property. Section 5 ends across the bridge over the Toccoa River at paved Aska Road (1,774 feet).

Highlights
Miles 0.0–5.2: Occasional good winter views of Blue Ridge Lake and surrounding mountains.
Mile 1.3: Winter views of Blue Ridge Lake from the top of Tipton Mountain.
Mile 3.2: Fire tower on top of Brawley Mountain.
Miles 6.9–7.5: Toccoa River.

Directions

From Blue Ridge travel US 76 East 4.0 miles from the US 76–GA 5 junction before turning right onto GA 60. Continue on GA 60 South (pass through Morganton and watch for turns on GA 60) for 9.5 miles to Wilscot Gap. The gap is not marked, but it is obvious you are at the high point on the highway. Section 5 begins on the right side of the highway at an old, gated road. White diamond blazes cross the pavement from a gravel pull-off on the left side of the highway.

From Stonepile Gap, where US 19 and GA 60 split apart, travel GA 60 North approximately 34.5 miles to Wilscot Gap.

Notes

WBR
Rich Mountains
**Shallowford Bridge
to Weaver Creek
Road**

Features
Toccoa River,
streams, Fall Branch
Falls, views

Distance
9.5 miles

Difficulty Rating
Moderate

Counties
Fannin and Gilmer

Nearest City
Blue Ridge

Map
Blue Ridge
Quadrangle, GA

Blazes
White diamonds

Water Sources
Miles 0.4–3.6:
Stanley Creek and its
tributaries; mile 7.8:
rivulet 250 yards to
right of the trail at
shallow gap; mile 9.4:
trail crosses Laurel
Creek

Ranger District
Toccoa

Benton MacKaye Trail, Section 6

The first 3.4-mile segment of Section 6 is a road-walk. Starting at the Shallowford Bridge over the Toccoa River (1,774 feet), the trail follows paved Aska Road and the Toccoa River for 0.3 mile to the west (downstream) before turning left onto Stanley Creek Road. A road sign and a large Rich Mountain WMA sign mark the turn.

The route follows unpaved Stanley Creek Road, which frequently parallels or crosses its namesake stream and its tributaries, as it winds west for 3.1 miles. Before the trail leaves the road, it passes through an old farm with outbuildings right next to the road. Immediately after the road crosses Fall Branch (2,000 feet), the Benton MacKaye turns right from the road at the parking area (cabin to right). This parking area allows you to skip the road walk and start your hike at this point. The land to the right of the branch is private property.

The walkway follows Fall Branch upstream on moderate grades 0.2 mile to the short side trail (2,200 feet) that leads down and to the right. There is an observation deck in front of the 70-foot Fall Branch Falls. Past the top of the falls, the trail follows switchbacks left then right through an oak-pine forest as it gently rises to a Rich Mountain ridge. The path heads west and uphill on the ridge line to mile 4.5 (2,640 feet), where it joins the Stanley Gap Trail.

The trails share the same treadway through a mature hardwood forest for the next 2.1 miles. Instead of following the ridge top up and over each crest, the route works its way up gradually, alternating between ridge top and slope. After turning to the north onto the Tennessee Valley Divide, the trail skirts around Rocky Mountain's eastern slopes well below its high point. The treadway crosses over Bellcamp Ridge (3,120 feet), a Rocky Mountain lead, at mile 5.8, then continues on an easy upgrade along the ridge. At mile 6.6 the trails split apart: Stanley

Gap turns right; Benton MacKaye continues straight ahead, uphill with the ridge.

Continuing along the Tennessee Valley Divide to the northwest, the path quickly reaches the section's highest elevation (3,260 feet) before the long descent to Weaver Creek Road begins. The treadway passes through a gap (2,620 feet) at mile 7.8, then rises over Scroggin Knob (2,730 feet) at mile 8.2. The remainder of Section 6 leaves the Tennessee Valley Divide—the Blue Ridge—and steadily descends in a half loop to the southwest to Weaver Creek Road (1,920 feet).

Highlights

Miles 0.0–0.3: Toccoa River.

Mile 3.6: Short side trail leads to observation deck at 70-foot-high Fall Branch Falls.

Mile 5.8: View south to the 4,000-foot peaks in or near the Rich Mountain Wilderness.

Mile 6.7: Winter views of Blue Ridge Lake to the northeast from the high point of Section 6.

Mile 8.2: Winter views of Blue Ridge Lake from the top of Scroggin Knob.

Directions

From the GA 5–US 76 junction in Blue Ridge (where GA 5 heads north to McCaysville at the McDonald's) travel US 76 East 0.7 mile to Windy Ridge Road (the first right past the Wendy's). Turn right onto Windy Ridge Road and continue a short distance to a three-way intersection. Turn left at this intersection and continue 0.1 mile before turning right onto signed Aska Road across from Harmony Baptist Church.

Continue approximately 8.3 miles on Aska Road to Shallowford Bridge. After approximately 8.0 miles you will pass the wide, signed entrance to dirt-gravel Stanley Creek Road on the right. This section of the Benton MacKaye turns onto Stanley Creek Road (further marked with a large Rich Mountain WMA sign) after the first 0.3 mile on Aska Road. Continue 0.3 mile past the entrance to Stanley Creek Road to Shallowford Bridge over the Toccoa River on the left.

Piedmont
Boardtown Creek
Weaver Creek
Road to Bushy
Head Gap

Features
Streams, lakes,
Indian Rock

Distance
8.7 miles

Difficulty Rating
Easy to moderate

Counties
Fannin and Gilmer

Nearest City
Blue Ridge

Maps
Blue Ridge and
Cashes Valley
Quadrangles, GA

Blazes
White diamonds

Water Sources
Private property
streams at frequent
intervals

Campsites
Mile 4.3: shelter on
Sisson property

Benton Mackaye Trail, Section 7

Section 7 of the Benton MacKaye is unlike any other long trail section in North Georgia. Section 7 traverses a narrow band of Piedmont—the Hightower-Jasper Ridges District—that fingers into North Carolina. With the exception of a very short distance at the Weaver Creek Road end, the entire section winds through private property. Section 7 is primarily a road walk rather than a forest path. While other long trail sections are harder to walk and easier to follow, this section, with its many turns and easy grades, is harder to follow but easier to walk. There are no climbs until the route gains 350 feet in the final mile. One final difference: this section passes beside four lakes.

This section of the Benton MacKaye was rerouted when two private landowners—David Higdon and Joe Sisson—allowed the trail to cross through their land, taking some of the trail off the roadsides and moving it into the forest.

From the trailhead (1,920 feet), Section 7 follows unpaved Weaver Creek Road to the west 2.5 miles to US 76. The southwestern end of Long Mountain is to the right. The road crosses Laurel Creek and its tributaries frequently.

Cross US 76 at its intersection with county road 158. Once across, turn left, continue along the shoulder for 0.1 mile, then turn right at the drive and follow the path on the outside of the fence. Next, turn right through the opening in the fence and ascend over a low ridge. On the other side of the ridge, the route descends to a covered bridge over Cherry Log Creek (1,540 feet) at mile 2.9, the lowest point on the BMT in Georgia.

Across Cherry Log Creek, the trail turns left along an old railroad, turns right from the railroad at mile 3.0, crosses a stream, passes a small waterfall, and recrosses the stream before reaching a road at mile 3.3. After turning sharply left at mile 3.4 (staying on the road), turn right onto a narrow woods road at mile 3.6. Here the BMT rises to Cherry Lake and follows a boardwalk back to the road again at 3.9 miles. It then turns left and leaves the road at a gap at mile 4.1. The trail descends through a cove to the north, crosses a stream, and passes Indian Rock Shelter at 4.3 miles.

Beyond the shelter and the dam on Indian Rock Lake, turn right onto a road and take the left fork beyond the covered bridge. Next, turn left and cross a stream at mile 4.7 before ascending to Cohutta Mountain Road at mile 4.9. Turn right onto Cherry Lake Road (level, not uphill), then turn right onto the trail at mile 5.0. The route descends through a cove to the next lake at mile 5.4. Beyond the lake, cross a road and follow a woods road that descends sharply along the property line to another road at mile 5.7. Turn left and follow this road to paved Lucius Road at mile 6.0.

After turning right onto Lucius Road, Section 7 turns right onto Boardtown Road at mile 6.6. It then follows paved Boardtown Road to its three-way intersection with paved Bushy Head Gap Road at mile 7.0. Turn left onto Bushy Head Gap Road. The remainder of this section follows Bushy Head Gap Road to the north to the parking area at Bushy Head Gap (2,090 feet).

Highlights
Miles 2.6–6.0: Four small lakes—Moon, Indian Rock Creek, Cherry, and Bear.
Mile 4.5: Indian Rock, a huge rock turned on end at the headwaters of Indian Rock Creek Lake.

Directions
From the GA 5–US 76 junction in Blue Ridge (where GA 5 heads north to McCaysville at the McDonald's) travel US 76 East for 0.7 mile to Windy Ridge Road (the first right past the Wendy's). Turn right onto Windy Ridge Road and continue a short distance to a three-way intersection. Turn left at this intersection and continue 0.1 mile before turning right onto signed Aska Road across from Harmony Baptist Church. Proceed for 1.0 mile on Aska Road, then turn right onto Weaver Creek Road. Travel 3.7 miles to the intersection where Weaver Creek Road ends. To the left is Griffith Parkway. The trail begins straight ahead at the Benton MacKaye Trail sign.

From Blairsville travel US 76 West just over 19.0 miles toward Blue Ridge. Turn left (south) onto Windy Ridge Road.

262

Features
Winter views,
streams

Distance
12.8 miles

Difficulty Rating
Moderate to
strenuous

Counties
Fannin and Gilmer

Nearest Cities
Blue Ridge (E),
Ellijay (S)

Maps
Cashes Valley and
Dyer Gap
Quadrangles, GA

Blazes
White diamonds

Water Sources
Mile 2.6: Spring 200
yards north of
Hudson Gap; mile
5.4: trail crosses
stream in cove; mile
8.6: spring 200 yards
north of Halloway
Gap; mile 9.7: spring
30 yards west of trail;
mile 10.3: trail cross-
es stream; mile 10.7:
trail crosses stream

Ranger District
Cohutta

Benton MacKaye Trail, Section 8

Section 8 makes a half loop southwest then north-west, following the Blue Ridge and the Tennessee Valley Divide throughout. Not only is this stretch the longest BMT section in Georgia, it is also one of the most remote. In marked contrast to Section 7, this section remains on national forest land its entire length and does not cross or follow a single paved road.

Section 8's first half passes through multiple-use forest lands, where there are signs of active timber management. The second half—winding along the boundary of the large Cohutta Wildlife Management Area—is higher, wilder, and more pristine. From mile 6.0 to mile 12.0 the trail stays above 3,000 feet in elevation.

Starting from Bushy Head Gap (2,090 feet), Section 8 climbs over a series of knobs on Bear Den Mountain. The upgrade's high point, on the south side of Bear Den, is 2,860 feet at mile 1.7. Along this stretch of the path, Indian pink (*Spigelia marilandica*) blooms abundantly in spring. This wildflower, which belongs to the logania family, the source of strych-nine, has a trumpet-shaped blossom that is red on the outside and yellow-green on the inside. No other member of this family is indigenous to the Southern Appalachians.

After descending to Hudson Gap (2,620 feet), where the path crosses FS 793 at mile 2.6, the route ascends to near the high point of an unnamed knob (2,940 feet) before skirting around its uppermost southern slope. The BMT then descends with the oak-pine ridge to an unnamed gap (2,680 feet) at mile 3.8. The knob-gap-knob pattern continues: the trail rises over the next knob (2,860 feet) and dips to McKenny Gap (2,780 feet) at mile 4.2, where it crosses FS 793 again.

For the next 1.1 miles, the footpath undulates on the section's easiest grades as it slabs around a knob and descends to Hatley Gap (2,660 feet). Here Section 8 makes the second climb worth mentioning as it rises to the top of Fowler Mountain (3,392 feet) at mile 6.6. From the crown of Fowler the treadway roller-coasters with the ridge crest for 2.0 miles to Halloway Gap (3,260 feet). The largest upgrade is 150 feet; the largest downgrade is 260 feet to the gap. This segment's high point is the top of a knob (3,540 feet) on Horse Ridge.

Turning north at Halloway Gap, the route follows switchbacks up to and over the next high point (3,620 feet) on the ridge, dips to a shallow gap at mile 9.5, crosses an old woods road near a wildlife opening, then crosses a road that leads to Double Hogpen at mile 9.9. The trail next descends to and crosses two headwater streams of the South Fork Jacks River. After crossing the second stream (3,510 feet) at mile 10.7, Section 8 makes its final climb—to Flat Top Mountain (3,732 feet) at mile 11.4. A former fire tower site, the opening on Flat Top's crown affords good winter views of the surrounding ridges.

From Flat Top, this section's high point, the remainder of Section 8 drops 862 feet along the ridge to Dyer Gap (2,870 feet).

Highlights
Throughout: Flame azalea, mountain laurel, and abundant wildflowers in spring.
Throughout: Winter views from the high ridge lines.

Directions
From East Ellijay travel northeast on US 76–GA 5 toward Blue Ridge. Approximately 9.5 miles beyond where US 76 and GA 5 converge in East Ellijay, turn left onto County Road 187 (also known as Lucius Road) at the community of Lucius. Proceed 2.5 miles on Lucius Road to its three-way intersection with Boardtown Road. Turn right and continue 0.4 mile, then turn left onto Bushy Head Road. Continue up this road to the gap—about 1.5 miles. Just after the big intersection at the top, look for the trailhead on the left.

264

Features
South Fork Jacks
River, wildlife
openings, views

Distance
4.5 miles

Difficulty Rating
Easy to moderate

County
Fannin

Nearest Cities
Ellijay (S),
Blue Ridge (E)

Maps
Dyer Gap
Quadrangle, GA,
Hemp Top
Quadrangle, GA-TN

Blazes
White diamonds

Water Sources
Miles 0.0-2.1:
numerous sources

Ranger District
Cohutta

Benton MacKaye Trail, Section 9

Section 9 of the Benton MacKaye Trail is a 4.5-mile stretch offering a variety of plant communities and elevations in the Cohutta Wildlife Management Area. From Dyer Gap (2,870 feet), this section briefly follows FS 64, then turns right into the woods. From this sharp turn the route descends to the South Fork Jacks River. The Benton MacKaye shares the treadway with the older South Fork Trail for 1.6 miles.

The trail follows the river through cool, moist forests of rosebay rhododendron and eastern hemlock. Water is plentiful for the next 1.5 miles.

Here Section 9 passes clearings—wildlife openings—that provide open and edge-effect habitat important to many birds and mammals.

At mile 2.2, where the Benton MacKaye and South Fork Trails split apart, Section 9 turns right (northeast) on an old logging road. The treadway rises 120 feet to the top of an unnamed ridge at mile 2.4.

Most of the remainder of this section undulates on easy-to-moderate grades along a low ridge—part of the Blue Ridge—west of Dyer Mountain. From mile 2.7 to mile 3.1 there are views to the left (northwest) of the forested ridges of the Cohutta Wilderness. The final 0.3 mile drops 260 feet to Watson Gap (2,720 feet).

Highlights
Mile 0.6: Wildlife openings along the South Fork Jacks River.
Miles 2.7–3.1: Winter views of the Cohutta Wilderness to the northwest.

Directions
From the US 76–GA 5 intersection just north of Blue Ridge, travel north on GA 5 toward McCaysville for 3.7 miles. Turn left onto Old GA 2 at the "Old State Route 2" sign and small Watson Gap sign. Continue on this road for approximately 10.5 miles (the pavement ends at mile 9.0) to the major Forest Service intersection at Watson Gap.

At Watson Gap turn south (left) on FS 64 and continue 3.2 miles to Dyer Gap. The trailhead is located 0.1 mile west of the cemetery on FS 64.

Benton MacKaye Trail, Section 10

WBR
Cohutta Mountains
Watson Gap to
Double Spring Gap

Heading north toward Tennessee, Georgia's last BMT section is its first to traverse wilderness. From mile 1.4 to Double Spring Gap, Section 10 remains within the 36,977-acre Cohutta Wilderness.

Although this section passes through some low elevation streamside and cove habitat, beyond the first 3.0 miles it is primarily a ridge and upper slope trail. But unlike other ridge-running sections, this section's grades remain, for the most part, easy or easy to moderate.

Starting at Watson Gap (2,720 feet), Section 10 follows FS 22 for 0.3 mile before angling sharply to the left onto path. Once the trail leaves the road, it rises to a ridge crest through the small timber of an oak-pine forest. The route passes through an old homestead at 0.8 mile, then quickly crosses Mill Branch. Here the walking is easy through a forest where tall eastern white pines are common.

The treadway crosses a fork of Bear Branch in Peter Cove at mile 2.0. Before crossing Bear Branch at mile 2.3, the route parallels a string of beaver ponds downslope to the left. Three-tenths mile after crossing the branch, the BMT turns right onto the orange-blazed Jacks River Trail, shares the treadway for 85 yards, then turns left on its own again. These turns are signed and blazed.

Immediately before Section 10 turns left from the Jacks River Trail, there are two magnificent old eastern hemlocks to the right of the trail. The larger of the two is the state record eastern hemlock.

Continuing to the north, the trail ascends a hardwood cove back to ridge top at mile 2.9. Here the route remains on or near the ridge crest as it follows predominantly easy grades over a string of flat-topped knobs, most of them nearly the same height. After gradually rising over the highest knob (3,040 feet) at mile 3.8, the path descends to mile 4.1 (2,940

Features
Streams, winter views, wilderness

Distance
8.5 miles

Difficulty Rating
Easy to moderate

County
Fannin

Nearest Cities
Ellijay (S),
Blue Ridge (E)

Maps
Hemp Top Quadrangle, GA-TN; Cohutta Wilderness map

Blazes
White diamonds

Water Sources
Mile 0.8: Mill Branch crossing; mile 1.0: small stream crossing; mile 2.0: cross fork of Bear Branch; mile 2.3: Bear Branch crossing; mile 8.5: Double Spring Gap: seasonal, sometimes boar-wallowed seepage spring to either side of the gap

Ranger District
Cohutta

feet), where it turns left (north) onto the white-blazed (rectangular and infrequent) Hemp Top Trail. Section 10 shares the treadway with Hemp Top Trail all the way to its end at Double Spring Gap (3,220 feet) at the Tennessee line. (See page 142 of Hemp Top Trail for a description of the remainder of Section 10.)

The Benton MacKaye now continues from Double Spring Gap through the Big Frog Wilderness into Tennessee. Write the Benton MacKaye Trail Association (address provided on page 296) for the current location of the trail as it moves toward its completion.

Highlights
Miles 2.1, 2.2: Trail passes above a string of beaver ponds.
Mile 2.6: State record eastern hemlock to right of trail.
Miles 3.2–8.5: Winter views. Big Frog Mountain is to the north.

Directions
From the US 76–GA 5 intersection just north of Blue Ridge, travel north on GA 5 toward McCaysville for 3.7 miles. Turn left onto Old GA 2 at the "Old State Route 2" sign and small Watson Gap sign. Continue on this road for approximately 10.5 miles (the pavement ends at mile 9.0) to the major Forest Service intersection at Watson Gap.

Approximately 50 yards before it reaches the middle of the four-way, dirt-road intersection in Watson Gap, the Benton MacKaye (usually marked with a prominent sign and always blazed with white diamonds) comes out of the woods onto FS 64. The trail follows FS 64 to the gap, where it switches roads but continues straight ahead, uphill, on FS 22. The first 0.3 mile of this trail section is FS 22, usually signed at its narrow uphill entrance. If you take the paved road route (Old Highway 2) from near Blue Ridge, FS 22 will be the hard right turn at the Watson Gap intersection.

Duncan Ridge National Recreation Trail, Section 1

WBR
Springer Mountain
Near Three Forks
to GA 60

The Duncan Ridge Trail was originally constructed so that it would form a loop with the AT, a loop that would begin and end atop Springer Mountain. Even though it no longer begins at Springer Mountain, Duncan Ridge still forms a somewhat shorter loop with the AT.

To reach Section 1 of the Duncan Ridge Trail, walk 1.1 miles east on the Benton MacKaye Trail to the point where it turns north away from the AT 0.1 mile past Long Creek Falls. All of Section 1 shares the same treadway with the Benton MacKaye Trail (See Section 2 of the Benton MacKaye Trail, page 250, for a description of Section 1 of the Duncan Ridge Trail).

Directions

The nearest vehicular access to Section 1's junction with the AT near Long Creek Falls is from FS 58 at Three Forks. The Benton MacKaye and Appalachian Trails share the same treadway (an old road) across FS 58 to the beginning of the Duncan Ridge Trail. When the old road reaches the beginning of the blue-blazed Duncan Ridge Trail, Benton MacKaye turns left and shares the same treadway with Duncan Ridge. The Appalachian Trail continues straight ahead—by itself. It is 1.1 miles from FS 58 to the beginning of the Duncan Ridge Trail. Look for the Benton MacKaye sign and the first blue blaze of Duncan Ridge 0.1 mile beyond the side path to Long Creek Falls.

To reach Three Forks by way of FS 58, follow the directions for Section 1 of the Appalachian Trail to the point where you turn right onto FS 42 opposite the church. Instead of turning onto FS 42, however, continue straight ahead on the paved road. After traveling approximately 2.8 miles beyond the entrance to FS 42, turn right onto FS 58. A short dis-

Features
Long Creek Falls,
Toccoa River,
Benton MacKaye
Trail, national
recreation area

Distance
10.4 miles

Difficulty Rating
Moderate

County
Fannin

Nearest Cities
Ellijay (W),
Blue Ridge (NW),
Dahlonega (SE),
Blairsville (NE)

Maps
Noontootla and
Wilscot
Quadrangles, GA;
one-page Forest
Service map

Blazes
Blue

Water Sources
Obvious or marked
sources occur at
regular intervals
along this section

Ranger District
Toccoa

tance beyond a church with a cemetery across the road, the main dirt road forks. The right fork is FS 58.

After driving approximately 5.5 miles on FS 58, you should come to a trail post on the right side of the road immediately after crossing Long Creek. This post has an Appalachian Trail sign, a Benton MacKaye sign and a stick-figure hiker sign. If you are in the right place, there should be an intersecting gravel road next to the sign. A triangle of large logs blocks this road to the right. To reach the Duncan Ridge Trail, walk the AT to the left.

Note: The Georgia Appalachian Trail Club has plans to reroute the AT in the Three Forks area. The mileage should not change significantly, and the AT will still pass by Long Creek Falls and the Duncan Ridge junction.

Notes

Duncan Ridge National Recreation Trail, Section 2

EBR
Duncan Ridge
GA 60 to Slaughter Gap

Beyond its first climb, Section 2 follows a well-defined line of named mountains, knobs, and gaps—Duncan Ridge—all the way to trail's end at Slaughter Gap. From GA 60 this section arcs northeast to southeast to its terminus, which is almost due east from its beginning. The trail follows the northern boundary of Coopers Creek Wildlife Management Area from Rhodes Mountain to Wolfpen Gap.

Section 2 of Duncan Ridge is the most strenuous long segment of trail in Georgia. This section roller-coasters along the crest of the ridge up, over, and down nearly every peak. Many of the gap-to-mountain ascents are moderate or strenuous, and many of the mountain-to-gap descents are steep. Do not plan to backpack this entire section unless you have mountain experience, are in good shape, and are seeking rugged terrain.

At Mulky Gap, FS 4 divides Section 2 of the Duncan Ridge Trail into segments of nearly equal lengths. If you want to day hike or backpack one of these two segments, you can set up a shuttle and use Mulky Gap as a beginning or ending point. The trail is less strenuous hiked as it is described, from west to east.

The blue-blazed Duncan Ridge Trail shares its treadway with the Benton MacKaye Trail, blazed with white diamonds, to near the top of Rhodes Mountain. Starting near a bench mark with a recorded elevation of 2,028 feet, Section 2 immediately crosses Little Skeenah Creek, then climbs moderately toward the ridge. At mile 1.0 the trail turns right onto an old road atop Duncan Ridge and ascends sharply by switch-back. Before reaching the rocky crown of Wallalah Mountain (3,100 feet) at mile 1.7, the treadway passes beside an outcrop open to the south. The nearest mountain is Toonowee.

Features
Scenic view, Coosa Bald Scenic Area, Blood Mountain Wilderness, Georgia's most challenging trail

Distance
20.4 miles

Difficulty Rating
Strenuous

Counties
Fannin and Union

Nearest Cities
Blue Ridge (W), Blairsville (N), Dahlonega (S)

Maps
Wilscot, Mulky Gap, Coosa Bald, and Neels Gap Quadrangles, GA; one-page Forest Service map

Blazes
Blue

Water Sources
Marked sources occur at regular intervals, usually in the gaps

Ranger Districts
GA 60 to Mulky Gap Road: Toccoa; Mulky Gap Road to Slaughter Gap: Brasstown

After descending 0.4 mile to an unnamed gap (2,730 feet), Section 2 heads steadily upridge to the crest of Licklog Mountain (3,472 feet) at mile 3.2. It then loses elevation to another unnamed gap (3,140 feet) and rises to the next high point on the ridge—Rhodes Mountain (3,380 feet)—at mile 4.3. Here the footpath drops sharply again to Rhodes Mountain Gap (2,980 feet) at mile 4.7. From Rhodes Mountain Gap the trail undulates 0.8 mile on easy-to-moderate grades to Gregory Gap (3,060 feet).

Continuing eastward on Duncan Ridge, Section 2 roller-coasters up, over, and down two knobs—Gregory (3,360 feet) at mile 5.8 and Payne (3,420 feet) at mile 6.3—in quick succession. From Gregory Gap to Sarvis Gap (3,020 feet) at mile 6.8, the treadway gains and loses 1,200 feet of elevation in 1.3 miles. The ascents are strenuous; the descents are steep.

The path angles up the northern flank of Parke Knob to approximately 3,320 feet before it dips to the clearing in Fish Gap (3,100 feet) at mile 7.9. FS 88 ends at the clearing. Beyond Akin Gap (3,020 feet) at mile 8.6, Section 2 climbs over Clements Mountain (3,500 feet), then Akin Mountain (3,531 feet at the bench mark) in similar fashion. Both times the trail steadily gains elevation along the southern slope of the mountain. It appears that the trail would continue below the crest, but instead it turns sharply to the left and ascends straight up to the summit.

The trail passes beside the bench mark atop Akin Mountain at mile 10.0. The long, occasionally steep downgrade to Mulky Gap has several sharp turns. The first and easiest to miss is at mile 10.4, where the footpath turns to the right off the ridge at a double blaze.

Section 2 crosses FS 4 in Mulky Gap (2,780 feet) at mile 10.9. Beyond this intersecting dirt road, the treadway climbs strenuous switchbacks to Wildcat Knob (3,500 feet) at mile 11.8, descends 0.3 mile to Wildcat Gap (3,380 feet), rises over Buck Knob (3,540 feet), then loses elevation easily to Bryant Gap (3,200 feet) at mile 12.9. The trail approaches Duncan Ridge Road, FS 39, for the first of several times at Bryant Gap. Section 2 does not cross Duncan Ridge Road; blazed side paths that cross the road lead to water.

After swinging beside the road again in Buckeye Gap (3,280 feet) at mile 13.5, the trail works its way up, gradually at first, to the high point of Buckeye Knob (3,820 feet) at mile 14.5. It then heads steadily downridge for 1.0 mile to a slight gap, proceeds over a low knob, then dips to Whiteoak Stomp (3,460 feet) at mile 16.2. Here, beside the road again, the long upgrade to Coosa Bald begins. The middle part of this climb is a straight-up-the-ridge grunt. Near the top, above the steep portion of the ascent, the treadway passes through a grove of yellow birch. At the southern limit of its range in northernmost Georgia, this tree is easily identified by its yellowish bark, which curls into papery strips. To the right of the path at mile 17.1, a bench mark embedded in a low knot of protruding rock designates Coosa Bald's official high point—4,271 feet.

At mile 17.3 the yellow-blazed Coosa Backcountry Trail joins the Duncan Ridge Trail. These two trails share the same treadway for the next 3.0 miles.

Section 2 follows an old road down a steep grade to another Wildcat Gap (3,780 feet), where it turns left onto Duncan Ridge Road, skirts its edge for 30 yards, then returns to the forest on the left side of the road. Beyond this second Wildcat Gap, the trail ascends a second Wildcat Knob before following sharp switchbacks down to Wolfpen Gap (3,260 feet) at mile 18.7. At Wolfpen Gap it crosses GA 180 onto a dirt road, and immediately turns left onto blazed path. The next 0.9 mile rises to the upper slopes (approximately 4,140 feet) of Slaughter Mountain. The first 0.5 mile of this climb is strenuous. Beyond mile 19.7, the remainder of Section 2 is nearly level until it drops to its end at Slaughter Gap (3,860 feet). A short distance beyond the sign in Slaughter Gap, Duncan Ridge Trail rejoins the white-blazed Appalachian Trail.

After crossing Little Skeenah Creek (contaminated from homes and livestock upstream) next to GA 60, Section 2 does not cross or closely parallel a stream for the remainder of its 20.4-mile length. Marked water sources, however, do occur at regular intervals, usually in the gaps. Designated by blue W's, side paths lead downhill to the nearest spring.

The final 6.0 miles of Section 2 passes through a scenic area and a wilderness. From Buckeye Knob to Wolfpen Gap, Duncan Ridge runs through the 7,100-acre Coosa Bald Scenic Area. From Wolfpen Gap to its eastern end at Slaughter Gap, the trail traverses the 7,800-acre Blood Mountain Wilderness.

The Blood Mountain Wilderness fire regulations apply to Slaughter Gap and along the AT in either direction from the gap. Please note these regulations, which are provided on page 294.

The final segment of Duncan Ridge, from Wolfpen Gap to Slaughter Gap in the Blood Mountain Wilderness, is no longer designated as a "National Recreation Trail."

Highlights

Throughout: Georgia's most challenging long trail and winter views.
Mile 1.5: Rock outcrop view open to the south.
Mile 17.1: Coosa Bald's official high point—4,271 feet.
Mile 20.4: The AT at Slaughter Gap.

Directions

From Stonepile Gap, where US 19 and GA 60 split apart, continue northward on GA 60. The Duncan Ridge Trail crosses GA 60 approximately 22.0 miles beyond Stonepile Gap and approximately 3.0 miles beyond Deep Hole Recreation Area. When you pass the trout farm ponds to the right of the highway, continue approximately 0.2 mile to the trailhead.

The Benton MacKaye Trail shares the same treadway with the Duncan Ridge Trail across GA 60. Look for the blue blazes, white diamond blazes, and a small trail sign. Both trails cross GA 60 at the entrance to FS 816 to the left of the highway. Section 2 of the Benton MacKaye Trail ends at GA 60. Section 2 of the Duncan Ridge Trail begins to the right of GA 60.

To reach Wolfpen Gap, where the Duncan Ridge Trail crosses GA 180 near its ending point, travel GA 60 approximately 16.0 miles from Dahlonega, then turn right onto GA 180 East. (This turn is 2.0 miles beyond Woody Gap Recreation Area.) Continue 7.8 miles on GA 180 to a pull-off parking area on the left side of the highway. The parking area is marked with signs for Coopers Creek WMA, FS 39 (Duncan Ridge Road), and Wolfpen Gap.

FS 4, which runs through Mulky Gap, divides Section 2 of the Duncan Ridge Trail into two segments of nearly equal length. Depending on which segment you want to hike and where you are driving from, there are numerous combinations of routes that will lead you to Mulky Gap. The Forest Service Administration map, available from the Forest Supervisor's Office for a small fee, features the system roads of the Chattahoochee National Forest.

Notes

BARTRAM NATIONAL HERITAGE TRAIL

The 36.8-mile segment of the Bartram Trail in Rabun County is but a small link of a once-envisioned 2,550-mile trail winding through eight southeastern states. The goal of this trail is to trace, wherever possible, the exact route of eighteenth century naturalist William Bartram. From 1773 to 1776, Bartram traveled an estimated 920 miles in Georgia. He explored portions of what is now Rabun County in 1776, when "bears, tygers, wolves, and wildcats were numerous."

The Bartram Trail is described from north to south—from Hale Ridge Road to GA 28—because it is considerably less difficult when hiked in this direction. Of the four long trails described in this section, the Bartram is by far the least strenuous.

274

Features
Georgia's second
highest mountain,
views, streams,
waterfalls

Distance
17.6 miles

Difficulty Rating
Moderate to
strenuous

County
Rabun

Nearest Cities
Clayton (W),
Dillard (W)

Maps
Rabun Bald
Quadrangle, GA-NC;
one-page Bartram
Trail map available
from ranger distict

Blazes
Yellow

Water Sources
From Beegum Gap
at mile 2.7 all the
way to Courthouse
Gap at mile 14.0:
water is scarce,
coming only from a
few seasonal
springs; you may
have to leave the
trail at gaps to get
water

Ranger District
Tallulah

Bartram National Heritage Trail, Section 1

Beginning 0.1 or 0.2 mile from the North Carolina line, Section 1 of the Bartram Trail maintains a meandering, southwestward course for most of its length. This isolated footpath winds through a predominantly hardwood forest, much of it dominated by stands of mature oak. There are no signs of recent logging. From Rabun Bald to Courthouse Gap, the Bartram follows the northwestern boundary of the 14,000 acre Warwoman Wildlife Management Area.

Starting at an elevation of approximately 3,280 feet, this wide, well-constructed trail gently undulates—dipping slightly to a stream, rising, then dipping to the next stream—through a diverse, mature forest to Beegum Gap. At 0.4 mile a rivulet slides over rock to the right of the path. This small waterfall comes from one of Holcomb Creek's many headwater streams that cross this initial segment of Section 1. Slightly more than 0.1 mile beyond the waterslide, a look over your left shoulder will give you a good view (when the leaves are gone) of rockfaced mountains in North Carolina. A large outcrop at mile 1.2 makes for a scenic picnic spot. In spring, you can enjoy many native wildflowers in the outcrops and seeps: purple fringed orchid, pink lady's slipper, wild ginger, and violets.

As the trail approaches the foot of Rabun Bald, there are several houses as close as 50 yards from the trail. A short distance after crossing a narrow dirt road, the Bartram reaches Beegum Gap (3,640 feet), where it turns left onto an old fire tower road at mile 2.7. Here the trail climbs steadily for the next 1.5 miles to Rabun Bald (4,696 feet), the second highest mountain in Georgia. This is the longest, most difficult upgrade on the Bartram; however, because the rocky road loops up the steeper slopes, the ascent is not as difficult as you might expect. This is a tourist route, a heavily trod road with several decades of erosion problems.

Following his discovery of "a new and beautiful species of that celebrated family of flowering trees," William Bartram named a nearby "exhalted peak" Mount Magnolia. Authorities believe that Bartram's Mount Magnolia is our Rabun Bald. The beautiful species that he first identified on Martin Creek—the Fraser magnolia, a deciduous magnolia native only to the Southern Appalachians—is common along the lower elevations of the trail.

The observation tower atop the bald provides views of the Blue Ridge Mountains to all points of the compass. To the northeast, east, and south, you can see many square miles of heavily forested mountains that remain largely wild. The narrow path that enters the clearing opposite the tower's steps is Rabun Bald Trail.

If you spend some time on the summit, you will probably see or hear one of North Georgia's rarest birds: the common raven. Noticeably larger than the American crow, the raven's thick bill and wedge-shaped tail make it easy to identify, as does its loud "crunk" call. The common raven, which is increasing its range in the Southern Appalachians, flies alternately flapping and gliding like a hawk.

For the next ten miles, the trail generally follows the Tennessee Valley Divide and the boundary of the 14,000-acre Warwoman Wildlife Management Area. The small yellow signs marking this boundary are good trail markers when the blazes become infrequent. Water sources are scarce. Though the trail avoids going directly over any mountaintops, there are good climbs on Flat Top, Wilson Knob, Rock Mountain, and Pinnacle Knob.

Guided by the first of its nearly vandal-proof trail signs—an engraved rock—the Bartram descends easily through Catawba and rosebay rhododendron, then drops off the ridge and follows switchbacks steadily down hardwood slopes to Saltrock Gap (3,740 feet) at mile 5.9. Continuing to the southwest, the trail ascends the eastern side of Flat Top to near its crest (4,100 feet) at mile 6.5. Look for the slowly decaying trunks of American chestnut trees and for saplings springing up nearby. From this open hardwood ridge, there are many good views of Warwoman Wildlife Management Area.

At mile 7.1, on the western flank of Wilson Knob, a 20-foot side path leads to a rock outcrop open to the west. The rock faces a high valley, wild and completely forested, hemmed in by higher ridges all around. Double Knob and Wilson's Gap are in clear view. This valley, Ramey Field, was once cleared and farmed.

Following a sharp 0.3 mile downgrade, the treadway turns west, gradually rises along the northwestern slopes of Double Knob, then dips to Tuckaluge Road in Wilson Gap (3,220 feet) at mile 8.5. The Bartram follows this road (FS 153) to the right and downhill to mile 9.1, where it angles right and away from the road. Look for this turn where the main road curves sharply left at a junction.

Back in the forest again, the path climbs moderately on the eastern side of Rattlesnake and Blacks Creek Knobs before descending easily to Windy Gap (3,180 feet) at mile 10.5. During the next mile, the trail winds in and out of a rich, open hardwood forest of tuliptree, sweet birch, basswood, flowering dogwood, red maple, and several species of oak and hickory. The trail continues gently up and down to Rock Mountain Gap (3,260 feet) at mile 10.9, then ascends 0.5 mile to the crest of Rock Mountain (3,680 feet). After a sharp descent to an unnamed gap (2,900 feet) at mile 12.3, the treadway descends easily along the southern flank of Raven Knob to mile 13.9, where it drops 0.1 mile to Courthouse Gap (2,540 feet).

Beyond Courthouse Gap to the end of Section 1, the Bartram forms a 3.6 mile semicircle, open to the west. After rising sharply from the gap (a wide bare spot) on an old road, the path angles suddenly to the left into a hole in the rhododendron, then quickly reaches Martin Creek Falls at mile 15.6. The 45-foot waterfall, narrow and framed by eastern hemlock, free-falls twice over ledges.

Section 1 continues downhill beside the clear, cascading creek for 0.3 mile before turning away from the stream. After the path swings parallel to Warwoman Road, it dips to a junction above Becky Branch. The Bartram Trail turns right and heads upstream to the bridge in front of a 20- to 25-foot sliding falls. The last 0.1 mile of Section 1 descends above the branch to Warwoman Road (approximately 1,920 feet).

Highlights

Mile 4.2: Top of Rabun Bald, Georgia's second highest peak. Old stone tower provides a year-round vista.

Mile 7.1: A view of Ramey Field is reached by a spur trail on the right from Wilson Knob. A sunny outcrop opens to the west and faces a high valley, much of it hemmed in by higher ridges all around.

Mile 15.6: Martin Creek and the falls are isolated and beautiful.

Mile 17.5: Becky Branch Falls.

Directions

To the northern trailhead on Hale Ridge Road: From Clayton, travel US 441 North past Mountain City and Dillard. Slightly more than 1.0 mile north of Dillard, turn right onto GA 246 toward Highlands, NC. Continue on GA 246, which becomes NC 106 as it crosses the state line, for about 7.0 miles. Turn right onto paved Hale Ridge Road just before the green "Scaly Mountain" community sign. This turn is just past the ski lifts (uphill to the right) and before the Scaly Mountain Post Office.

After traveling 2.1 miles on Hale Ridge Road, you will reach a Y-shaped fork—dirt-gravel to the left, paved to the right. Continue on Hale Ridge Road (FS 7) to the left and proceed 1.1 miles to the Bartram Trail sign on the right side of the road.

To the southern trailhead at Warwoman Dell Recreation Area: In Clayton, where US 76 turns west, turn east onto Rickman Street (locally known as Warwoman Road). If you are traveling north on US 441, this turn will be to your right at the Hardee's, which is the second building to the right on Rickman Street. Continue a short distance on Rickman Street, then turn right onto Warwoman Road at its sign.

After traveling about 3.0 miles from the turn off US 441, you will come to the Warwoman Dell sign and entrance on the right side of the road. The Bartram Trail crosses Warwoman Road just before a pull-off parking area to the left a few hundred yards before the entrance of Warwoman Dell Recreation Area. Please do not block the entrance of the recreation area. It is barred and locked during the off-season and at night during the summer.

Notes

278

Features
Chattooga River,
large streams,
waterfall

Distance
19.2 miles

Difficulty Rating
Moderate

County
Rabun

Nearest City
Clayton

Maps
Rabun Bald
Quadrangle, GA-NC,
Rainy Mountain
Quadrangle, GA-SC,
Whetstone
Quadrangle, SC-GA,
Satolah Quadrangle,
GA-SC-NC;
Chattooga National
Wild and Scenic
River map; one-
page Bartram Trail
map available from
ranger distict

Blazes
White diamonds to
Warwoman Creek
bridge

Bartram National Heritage Trail, Section 2

Section 2 of the Bartram Trail is a good two- or three-day backpacking trip. Sandy Ford Road, which divides this section into nearly equal segments, provides opportunities for day hikers.

From Warwoman Road to Sandy Ford Road, the Bartram travels to the east, winding its way up, along, and over a series of low, unnamed, oak-pine ridges as it heads toward the Chattooga. This 9.4-mile segment is constantly undulating. All the long upgrades are easy or moderate. The downgrades are occasionally steep.

From Sandy Ford Road to GA 28, Section 2 parallels the Chattooga River to the northeast on generally easy grades. This segment remains, for the most part, within the protected corridor of the Chattooga National Wild and Scenic River. The trailside forest is diverse—eastern hemlock and riparian hardwoods are mixed in with the usual slope and ridge species.

This portion of the Bartram is the least strenuous long section of trail (over 15.0 miles) in North Georgia, especially in comparison to sections of the Duncan Ridge and Appalachian Trails of similar length. Beginning at Warwoman Road (1,920 feet), the most demanding part of Section 2 occurs within the first mile as it climbs through Green Gap, then nears the high point of an unnamed knob (2,560 feet) before descending. Because the highest point on this section is less than 2,800 feet, and because there are not substantial or frequent changes, elevations have not been included beyond the first ascent from Warwoman Road.

Section 2 begins beside the Bartram historical marker to the right of Warwoman Road a few hundred yards before the entrance to Warwoman Dell Picnic Area. The trail descends from Warwoman Road into the picnic area, turns right onto the road and follows it to the pavilion parking lot. The tread-way continues up and to the left of the parking lot, behind the Bartram and Blue Ridge Railroad signs.

Beyond the dell, the path makes an easy-to-moderate climb, winding through coves to a ridge top at mile 1.1 and then descending to a dirt road by mile 1.5. Here the trail turns right onto Green Gap Road and follows it for 65 yards before reentering the forest to the right. At mile 1.9 the Bartram crosses the road again and ascends to the next ridge at mile 2.7. It then roller-coasters on easy-to-moderate grades up to and over another ridge at mile 4.0.

Water Sources
Water is scarce for the first 9.4 miles to Dicks Creek Road; water is abundant beyond Dicks Creek Road

Ranger District
Tallulah

After dropping sharply for 0.2 mile, the trail rises back onto the ridge, undulates along its spine to mile 5.4, and then steadily descends to Pool Creek Road at mile 5.9. Across the road, the path climbs moderately for 0.4 mile through a forest dominated by Virginia pine and blackjack oak. In winter, gaps through these trees afford views of Rabun Bald to the north. At mile 7.2 the treadway angles left across an old road, then remains predominantly level or downhill until it crosses Sandy Ford Road at mile 9.4.

About 100 yards past the road, the Chattooga River Trail ties into the Bartram Trail at a Y-shaped junction marked with a stone trail sign. Beyond this junction, Section 2 descends through a stand of tall eastern white pine, crosses a bridge over Dicks Creek at mile 9.8, and almost immediately enters a small clearing. To the right of this clearing, across a small bridge, an old road leads 200 yards to one of North Georgia's most beautiful scenes—Dicks Creek Falls. Here the creek's final run splashes 60 feet down a solid slide of rock to the Chattooga. In front of the waterfall, the wide river booms over a bank-to-bank ledge, a Class IV rapid known as Dicks Creek Ledge. A steep path drops to the boulders at the base of the falls.

Continuing straight ahead from the clearing, the path gradually rises over a low ridge before winding down through coves to the river at mile 10.5. For the next 0.6 mile, the Bartram closely parallels the Chattooga, an enticing dark green where it deepens, on an old road through eastern hemlock. The trail continues along the easy grades of the road as it swings away from the river and heads to Earls Ford Road at mile 12.2. In the past hikers forded the creek here, but now the trail crosses Earls Ford Road and parallels Warwoman Creek for approximately 200 yards to the steel bridge where you can easily cross.

Beyond the bridge the treadway works its way up to a ridge. From this ridge, the trail's next 1.8 miles wind along the Chattooga's protective boundary, well away from the river. Easily walked, this segment alternates between old road and constructed footpath on the lower ridges and slopes of Willis Knob. A horse trail ties into the Bartram twice along this stretch.

At mile 14.7 you cross Laurel Branch on a bridge. Then the trail heads up another ridge-running road, quickly turning right onto a path and dropping to the bridge over Bynum Branch at mile 15.6. The Bartram crosses a bridge over Adline Branch at mile 16.2, then turns right onto an old road. Section 2's remaining 3.0 miles mostly follow old roads through a flood plain, close to but usually out of sight of the river. This area, Long Bottom, was fenced and farmed until perhaps the 1960s. The size of the trees in the pine plantation gives you an idea of when the open land returned to forest.

At mile 16.5 the trail approaches close enough for a view before bending away from the river. Four-tenths of a mile beyond that point, the walkway turns left onto another old road. The entrance to this road may look like a path. If you continue straight ahead and miss this turn, you will have overshot it by 130 yards when you reach the Chattooga River.

The treadway crosses a bridge over Holden Branch at mile 17.8, then closely parallels the Chattooga one more time before curling beside the West Fork. At mile 18.8 the Bartram fords the West Fork of the Chattooga River below a Class II rapid called Big Slide. This ford is very wide and can be mid-thigh deep or deeper. It is potentially dangerous during cold weather or after heavy rains.

After this ford, Section 2 follows the West Fork downstream, turns to parallel the main branch of the Chattooga, and soon ends at Russell Bridge on GA 28.

The Bartram Trail continues upstream along the Chattooga across Russell Bridge on the South Carolina side of the river.

Highlights

Mile 9.9: Dicks Creek Falls and a Class IV rapid—Dicks Creek Ledge on the Chattooga River.

Miles 10.5–11.1: Trail closely parallels the Chattooga.

Mile 12.2: Parallels then crosses Warwoman Creek, a scenic Chattooga River tributary.

Mile 18.8: West Fork ford. A little excitement before the end of the hike during warm weather and low water levels. Potentially dangerous during high water or cold weather; definitely dangerous during high water and cold weather.

Directions

To the GA 28, Russell Bridge trailhead: From the Warwoman Dell Recreation Area, travel 11.2 miles northeast and farther away from Clayton on Warwoman Road. Turn right onto GA 28 toward Walhalla, South Carolina. Continue 2.2 miles on GA 28 to the Russell Bridge that crosses the Chattooga River. You will see a Bartram Trail emblem and sign to the right of the highway just before Russell Bridge. There is a parking area on the opposite (left) side of the highway. (See Section 1 of the Bartram Trail for directions to the Warwoman Dell Recreation Area trailhead.)

To Sandy Ford Road: This road intersects Section 2 at its midpoint. From Warwoman Dell Recreation Area, continue traveling on Warwoman Road farther away from Clayton (northeastward) for approximately 2.9 miles. Immediately past the house with the A-shaped roof over its door, turn right onto unpaved Sandy Ford Road (still locally known as Dicks Creek Road). Sandy Ford Road is rough, but four-wheel-drive vehicles or pickups will have no problem fording its two streams. Bear right with the main road and continue 0.7 mile before turning left over a small bridge. Another 3.7 miles brings you to a Bartram Trail sign, an engraved rock on the right.

Note: The Bartram National Heritage Trail needs volunteers to help remove blowdowns and to perform regular trail maintenance. Contact the Tallulah Ranger District if you are willing to help.

Notes

General Hiking Information

This section of the book offers tips to help you plan a safe and enjoyable hike that will leave little impact on our state's trails.

Environmental Guidelines and Backcountry Courtesy

Before You Leave Home

Limit group size—six or fewer for backpacking and eight or fewer for day hiking is optimum.

If you are the leader of a large organized horde, seriously consider splitting your group into two or three smaller parties. That way the smaller groups can go to different destinations, travel opposite directions on the same loop, stagger their starts, or try another tactic to avoid overwhelming everyone and everything in their paths.

Remember that large creeks with waterfalls and swimming holes, open areas with views, and major trail junctions with level ground and water will be heavily used during warm-weather holidays and weekends.

Take a backpacking stove so you won't have to build fires for cooking.

Repackage food supplies into sealable bags or plastic bottles so there won't be so many boxes and tinfoil pouches to burn or carry.

Take a litter bag to carry out refuse—yours and any you might see along the way.

On the Trail

Walk single file in the middle of the path.

Stay on the main trail and do not shortcut switchbacks.

Travel quietly.

Step to the uphill side of the trail to let horses, bikes, and other hikers pass.

Backcountry Rules

Don't litter. Even the smallest candy wrappers or cigarette butts are litter. If you pack it in, pack it out—all of it.

Don't be a hider. The undersides of rocks should be salamander sanctuaries and tree hollows should be wildlife dens—not beer can repositories.

Organic scraps are definitely litter. No one wants to see your orange peels or peanut hulls. And no one enjoys a campsite compost pile crowned with eggshells. Either burn it or carry it out. No backsliding.

Deposit human waste in catholes dug 6 to 8 inches deep at least 150 feet from campsites, water sources, and trails. Cover and disguise the cathole when finished.

Wash yourself and your dishes by carrying water 150 feet from campsites, trails, and streams, and use small amounts of biodegradable soap.

Treat our natural heritage with respect. Leave plants, rocks, and historical artifacts as you find them.

Fires

Use a backpacking stove for cooking to avoid the need for fires.

If you must build a fire, keep it small and use only dead and down wood that can be broken by hand. Leave the saws and axes at home. Standing dead trees are valuable for wildlife; do not use them for firewood.

Never build a fire on a dry, windy day.

Don't build fire rings—tear them down.

Completely extinguish all fires.

Erase all evidence of a campfire built where there is no fire ring. Scatter the ashes, replace the duff, and camouflage the burned area.

No-Trace Camping

Don't use worn-out, naked-ground campsites. Let them heal. Use lightly worn existing campsites or, better yet, move well away (150 feet) from trail and stream and make a no-trace campsite that will rarely, if ever, be used again.

Don't cut standing trees or pull up or beat down vegetation to make room for your tent or tents. Fit in and tuck in, don't hack in.

Don't enlarge an existing campsite. There is no need for large groups to circle the wagons against the night. Again, fit in and tuck in here and there.

Leave the blueprints and hard hats at home—there should be absolutely no campsite construction. No boot bulldozing, trenching, building rock or log furniture or shelves; no hammering nails in trees, digging latrines, piling rocks to dam or bridge streams, etc.

Before you move on, make your campsite look at least as natural as when you found it. Replace branches, twigs, and leaves cleared for the sleeping area.

Limit length of stay to one or two nights.

Wear soft-soled shoes in camp.

Backcountry Courtesy

Take consideration with you—do nothing that will interfere with someone else's enjoyment. It is considered insensitive to enter a wilderness with a very large group (a small busload, for example) that will completely overrun and overwhelm other hikers.

Keep as quiet as possible. Drunken parties and war whoops are frowned upon and are downright rude.

Leave radios and tape players at home.

Leave the dogs at home.

Campsites are first come, first served. If someone already has the camp you really wanted, don't whine, argue, or try to crowd in. Move on down the trail.

Help preserve the illusion of solitude for yourself and for others. Make yourself as unobtrusive and invisible as possible. Use earth-tone tents and tarps, and if possible, camp far enough off the trail so that other hikers can't see you and vice versa. When choosing the color of your daypack or backpack, however, temper the ideal of unobtrusiveness with the necessity of being visible to hunters.

Tips for Beginning Hikers

This is a where-to and why-to book, not a how-to book. There are already plenty of those, and much of what they have to tell you is common sense. Who needs to be told to avoid a high, exposed ridge during a lightning storm?

After all the finger-wagging do's and don'ts in the environmental guidelines section, we are ambivalent about including still more. The wilderness and the wild areas of our mountains are places of freedom (after you obey the environmental guidelines), where you make your own decisions and fill out your own report card.

However, since wild areas are also places where discomforts and the consequences of mistakes are magnified, we want to mention a few practical points for the benefit of beginning hikers.

Foot Care

Blisters are frequently the beginning hiker's most persistent problem. To help prevent this discomfort, wear two pairs of socks—a heavy outer pair and a lighter inner pair. Wool is generally considered to be the best material; however, wool-nylon and wool-acrylic blends are also quite good.

Although it is sometimes impossible to do so, try to keep your feet dry. Carry extra socks and use foot powder to absorb some dampness. If excess moisture makes your feet uncomfortable, you may want to use a pair of very thin "dry-wick" socks; they draw perspiration through to the heavier socks, thereby keeping your skin drier.

Moleskin, cushioning shoe pads, arch supports, and Second Skin should prevent or alleviate most foot problems. As soon as you feel chafing, stick some moleskin on your feet. It will protect you from blisters for days and days. If you already have a blister, try Second Skin to ease the pain and cushion the area.

Water

The water in the mountains—even the water in the clear, cold, high springs and rivulets—is no longer safe to drink. Over the last twenty years the Mini Watu (what Sioux Indians call water imps) have moved into our mountains. The worst of these imps is *Giardia*. Without going into all of the nauseous, gaseous details, it must be unequivocally stated that you do not want these protozoan parasites to set up shop in your stomach. They make you sick, some of the prescribed pills make you sick, and even after the protozoan imps are dead and you are cured, they can leave your gut ravaged for months.

There are three general ways to purify water: boiling, filtering, or treating chemically. Boiling, because of the time and fuel required, is usually considered impractical. Water filters continue to become lighter and more effective. Before buying one, however, make sure it will at least remove all particles larger than 0.4 micron. You can also use water purification tablets, available at most backpacking shops. How-to books and outdoor recreation magazines recommend tablets that use iodine as their principal purifying agent. The iodine-based tablets are safer, more effective, and retain their potency longer than others.

Pace

Beginning hikers often make a twofold misjudgment: they overestimate the distance they can comfortably travel in a day, and they underestimate the difficulty of the trail. Three or even four miles an hour is an easily attainable pace on level or nearly level trail. However, because of the mountainous terrain, most hikers walk the longer trails in North Georgia at a much slower pace. If you plan to stop to eat and drink, look at wildflowers, enjoy the vistas, and gasp for breath, anticipate an average of only one to two miles an hour on trails with a difficulty rating of strenuous or moderate to strenuous.

Safety Tips

Cold-Weather Hiking and Hypothermia

Many hikers consider winter, with its solitude, snow, and unobstructed views, the best time of the year to hike. For the unprepared and inexperienced, however, winter hiking can be as dangerous as it is beautiful.

Do not underestimate the severity of the weather conditions you will be likely to encounter. Especially at the higher elevations, be prepared for temperatures near or below zero and expect fierce winds on unprotected ridges. Even in mid-March, when temperatures in the 50s are predicted for areas south of the mountains, you may have to contend with freezing temperatures and snow at the higher elevations.

All cold-weather hikers should be aware of hypothermia, its symptoms and its treatment.

What is it? Hypothermia is a lowering of body temperature. A drop of only 5 degrees is very serious. Few people whose body temperature drops more than 10 degrees survive. Hypothermia can occur in air temperatures as high as 41 degrees Fahrenheit (5 degrees Celsius).

How does it happen? Wetness and exhaustion can intensify the effects of exposure to low air temperatures. Many people have died of hypothermia because, thinking they could warm up by keeping in motion, they did not stop to take necessary precautions, such as adding a sweater or putting on rain gear. Wet clothes can lead to heat loss and increase your chances of hypothermia.

New synthetic fibers are better than wool in cold or cold and wet weather. While wool retains its insulating qualities when wet, it remains wet and heavy for a long time. The new fabrics—polypropylene (which retains odors) and its newer derivatives (which do not retain odors) are quick-drying and insulating when wet. Especially when worn in layers, these new fabrics transfer or "wick" the moisture away from your sweaty body. Fleece, which has fibers that do not absorb water, is another good cold-weather fabric.

What are the symptoms? The first symptom is shivering. Continued shivering is serious. Shivering may be followed by slurred speech, impaired judgment, weakness, and loss of coordination. The final symptom is unconsciousness.

What can you do? Get the victim into warm clothes. Make the person rest. Give him or her hot drinks and food. If the condition is very serious, put the victim in a sleeping bag with another person. Make a fire. Put up a tent or make a shelter for the victim. As soon as possible, get the victim to a hospital for further treatment. Do not continue your trip after one of your party has had hypothermia.

Hypothermia information courtesy United States Forest Service.

Fords

If you are not reasonably confident you can make a high-water ford, don't attempt it.

A hiking stick is essential for balance on deep, swift fords.

Walk on the very bottom of the riverbed, on eddy sand or small rocks. If you attempt to step from large, slick underwater rock to large, slick underwater rock, you will probably fall and become much wetter than if you had walked on the bottom.

If you are backpacking and the current is strong enough to carry you downstream if you slip, unfasten the waist buckle of your backpack so you can wriggle out of your pack in a hurry.

With a good backpack cover on it, your backpack will float like a boat. It is much safer to swim your pack across a pool rather than to attempt a dangerous shoals while wearing your pack.

On trails with many fords, such as the Jacks River and Conasauga River Trails in the Cohutta Wilderness, you may want to wear old running shoes that you keep on and keep wet. Boots quickly become heavy and waterlogged, and it is impractical and time consuming to take them off for each of forty-two fords on the Jacks River.

If you are concerned about heavy rain or already rising water, you may want to camp on the same side of the river as the nearest lead-in trail, to give yourself a bailout route.

Poisonous Snakes

The copperhead, the Carolina pigmy rattlesnake, and the timber rattlesnake are indigenous to the North Georgia region. The sluggish, unaggressive copperhead is more common than either of the two more aggressive rattlesnake species.

The eastern cottonmouth (water moccasin) is not found in the Blue Ridge Mountains or in the counties included in the North Georgia region directly south of the Blue Ridge Mountains. There are, however, occasional reports of eastern cottonmouths along the larger streams in the Ridge and Valley and Cumberland Plateau Physiographic Provinces of northwestern Georgia. Most of the large snakes seen in and along the streams of the North Georgia mountains are nonpoisonous northern water snakes, not cottonmouths as is often assumed.

While it is likely that you will see nonpoisonous snakes along the trails of North Georgia, your chances of seeing a poisonous snake are slim. Your chances of being bitten by a poisonous snake are even slimmer—in fact, they are remote. There are records of hikers who have walked the entire Appalachian Trail, from Georgia to Maine, without seeing a single poisonous snake.

More people are killed each year by lightning and by bee and wasp stings than by venomous snakes. There are approximately 8,000 venomous snakebites in the United States per year. Of that number, however, only twelve to fifteen people, mostly the young and elderly, die from snakebite each year. In twenty to thirty percent of snakebite cases, no venom is injected.

Treatment for rattlesnake, copperhead, and cottonmouth bites

Don't:
- Cut incisions and attempt to suck the poison out.
- Use a tourniquet.
- Use ice or cold water on the wound.

Do:
- Use a suction device, such as the Extractor by Sawyer Products. Studies show that an Extractor can remove up to 30 percent of the venom if applied within three minutes. The suction from the Extractor is applied without incision.
- Clean wound with antiseptic soap.
- Apply sterile dressing.
- Remove rings and other constrictive items.
- Keep limb at or below level of heart.
- Keep patient quiet, hydrated, and comfortable. Treat for shock as needed.
- Arrange for a safe and rapid transport to a hospital.
- Remember that activity and anxiety accelerate the absorption of the venom. Walking, however, is acceptable if the victim feels up to it or if there is no other alternative.

Snakebite prevention

Wear long trousers and thick hiking boots. The higher the boots, the more protection you will have against snakebite.

Look before you sit or lie down.

Be careful where you put your hands. Do not reach blindly into holes or crevices. (Do not stick your face close to look, either.)

When a log obstructs your path, step up on it and take a long stride or look on the other side of the log before crossing.

If you are camping, wear shoes and use a flashlight when walking around the campsite after dark.

Where vegetation crowds the trail, slow your pace and use a stick to rustle the vegetation ahead of you.

Be extra observant when walking through or near rocky areas and clear-cuts. These two areas provide prime habitat for poisonous snakes.

Learn the color patterns and other distinctive characteristics of the poisonous snakes.

Hike during the cooler weather of fall, winter, and spring.

Wasps and Hornets

Wasp and hornet numbers increase throughout the spring and summer. Hornets do not usually pose much of a threat unless you inadvertently stand too close to a nest or shake a sapling or branch that supports a nest. The angry hornets from an unseen nest on the end of a horizontal, trail-blocking branch can cause quite a stir after the fifth or sixth person moves the branch.

The most common multiple-sting situation occurs in the fall, when bears and a few other animals dig up yellow jacket nests. Be aware of yellow jacket-sized insects flying in numbers near the ground. Give them a wide berth.

Stings cause two general types of reactions: local and systemic. For some people even one sting can result in an acute systemic reaction causing anaphylactic shock. The treatment for anaphylaxis is the immediate administration of epinephrine. Those who have had life-threatening systemic reactions should always carry a sting kit with them into the woods, even on short hikes.

Ice and antihistamines work well for local reactions. An antihistamine will help alleviate the severity of the reaction, and ice or cold water will lessen the swelling and immediate pain.

Hiking Sticks

When considering safety and survival, most people think of maps and compasses and sharp knives. Although seldom mentioned, a hiking stick contributes more to your safety on an hourly and daily basis than almost anything else you can take along. It is especially important if you are day hiking alone or backpacking. If you haven't fallen in the woods yet, you haven't hiked very much. When you fall while wearing a backpack, you fall fast and hard. A sharp knife may enable you to cut materials to help splint a broken bone, but a walking stick will almost always prevent you from falling and breaking a bone or turning an ankle in the first place.

Wildlife

Seeing a wild animal, even if only for an instant, always adds to the enjoyment and excitement of a hike in the mountains. However, because of its relatively harsh environment, the Blue Ridge Mountain region has the lowest density of wildlife per square mile in Georgia. Spotting wildlife along the trails of North Georgia is a bonus and cannot be guaranteed or expected on any given day or trail. One day you may walk 15 miles and see only an eastern box turtle; the next day you may see two or three deer and several turkey within the first 3 miles. There is only one guarantee: the more miles you hike, the more wildlife you are likely to see.

If you hike many of the trails described in this guide, the chances are good that you will sooner or later see ruffed grouse, gray squirrel, striped skunk, white-tailed deer, turkey, woodchuck, and European wild boar. However, your chances of glimpsing some of northern Georgia's wary omnivores and carnivores—black bear, bobcat, red or gray fox, raccoon, and mink—while walking along a trail are slim. Because these animals are generally most active at night, the best time of day to see them is in the morning shortly after sunrise or in the evening shortly before sunset.

Over the past twenty years, with help from DNR reintroduction, the turkey has made a dramatic comeback in the mountains of North Georgia. In the mid-1970s, catching a glimpse of a turkey while hiking in the mountains was fairly rare. Now, however, a turkey sighting is an occasional occurrence; seeing them on or along Forest Service roads is becoming almost commonplace.

Although the results will not be spectacular, here are a few common-sense suggestions for improving your chances of seeing wildlife along the trail:

Walk alone or in small groups.

Leave your dog at home.

Choose trails that traverse a variety of habitats—ridges, coves, wildlife openings, streams, and so on.

Learn more about the habits and habitats of the animals you are trying to see.

Begin your hike early in the morning (the earlier the better). Although you can see wildlife throughout the day, you will see more wildlife, especially white-tailed deer, in the early morning and near dusk. For day hikers, early morning is the best and most practical time to look for wildlife.

Notes on Hiking in North Georgia

Preservation 2000

To meet the increasing need for more publicly owned wildlands, Governor Zell Miller created the Preservation 2000 program in April 1991. As of 1996, this five-year program has acquired or taken options on 100,367 acres of natural areas, greenways, and other wildlands. The Department of Natural Resources will administer these properties.

Governor Miller appointed an Advisory Council on Land Acquisition to help him establish and accomplish the program's goals. DNR has worked closely with Governor Miller to identify the best lands available for preservation and public use. Acquisition has been distributed across the state to expand recreational opportunity and to protect wetlands, natural areas, and other environmentally important lands and waters. Our new public lands fall into one (and rarely two) of four general categories: wildlife management area, state park, natural area, and greenway. The largest new acquisitions across the North Georgia mountains have already preserved thousands of acres and increased recreational opportunities.

1. Smithgall Woods, Dukes Creek Conservation Area—5,604 acres
2. Rich Mountain Wildlife Management Area—5,067 acres
3. Dawson Forest Wildlife Management Area—4,455 acres
4. Tallulah Gorge State Park—2,730 acres
5. Fort Mountain State Park—1,475 acres
6. Crockford-Pigeon Mountain Wildlife Management Area—976 acres
7. Black Rock Mountain State Park—301 acres

Hurricane Opal

Hurricane Opal caused extensive damage to the North Georgia forests in 1995. Especially hard hit were the mountain areas near Ellijay, Blue Ridge, and Chatsworth. Sustained winds up to 85 miles an hour ripped through the forests in that region when the hardwoods were leafed out. It is difficult to appreciate the power of the storm and the extent of the damage unless you have driven the back roads and hiked through deadfalls.

State Park and Forest Service personnel, as well as all volunteers, deserve a sincere thank-you and a pat on the back for their efforts. Without their months of work neither the roads nor the trails would be cleared for hiking. Thanks once again.

Adopt-a-Trail

The US Forest Service "Adopt-a-Trail" program gives individuals, families, and groups the opportunity to do something worthwhile by becoming Forest Service volunteers. The Forest Service provides all the paint and equipment (saws, shovels, axes, shinguards) you could possibly use or carry. Volunteers provide the time, energy, and enthusiasm needed to blaze and brush out their adopted trail.

Forest Service Roads

Especially during the winter months, Forest Service roads may be closed during and after bad weather. In these days of budget cutting, a road in need of repair may remain closed until more money becomes available. If you are planning to hike a remote trail from late November through late March, especially during cold weather, you may want to call the appropriate ranger district to check road conditions to your destination.

Recreation Areas

Most recreation areas are closed and their approach roads gated during the off-season. The length of the off-season, however, varies from area to area and is subject to change. Most recreation areas open sometime between late March and early May and close between the end of October and the middle of November. Call or write the appropriate ranger district for the exact dates.

Although you will have to walk to their trailheads, you may hike recreation area trails during the off-season. The Forest Service asks two favors from winter hikers: please do not park so that you block access through the gated entrance roads, and please do not leave any trash in recreation area garbage cans.

Wilderness Blazes

Trails within wilderness, including the AT, have a different standard of maintenance from nonwilderness trails. Wilderness trails are blazed less frequently and maintained less rigorously than nonwilderness trails. Even if the Forest Service required equal maintenance, it would be very difficult and more expensive. Chainsaws are not allowed in wilderness.

Campfire Regulations for
Blood Mountain Wilderness

Building, maintaining, attending or using a fire or campfire, or gathering woody material for a fire or campfire is prohibited in the following area: Blood Mountain Shelter and to include 300 feet either side of the Appalachian Trail in the Blood Mountain Wilderness from where the Appalachian Trail crosses Highway 129 at Neels Gap to where the Appalachian Trail crosses Slaughter Creek south of Slaughter Gap.

Special Areas of the Chattahoochee National Forest

Wilderness	Total Acreage	Total Acreage in GA	Year Established
Ellicott Rock	8,274	2,021	1975, 1984 addition
Cohutta	36,977	35,268	1975, 1986 addition
Southern Nantahala	23,714	11,770	1984
Big Frog	8,082	89	1984, 1986 addition
Raven Cliffs	9,115	ALL	1986
Brasstown	12,975	ALL	1986, 1991 addition
Tray Mountain	9,702	ALL	1986
Rich Mountain	9,649	ALL	1986
Blood Mountain	7,800	ALL	1991
Mark Trail	16,400	ALL	1991

National Recreation Area	Total Acreage	Total Acreage In GA	Year Established
Ed Jenkins	23,330	ALL	1991

National Wild & Scenic River	Total Acreage	Total Acreage In GA	Year Established
Chattooga	15,704	7,737	1974

National Scenic Area	Total Acreage	Year Established
Coosa Bald	7,100	1991

Scenic Area	Total Acreage	Year Established
Anna Ruby Falls	1,600	1964
Coleman River	330	1960
Cooper Creek	1,240	1960
DeSoto Falls	650	1963
High Shoals	170	1957
Keown Falls	218	1962
Sosebee Cove	175	1956

Hiking Resources

Map and Pamphlet Information

The following Chattahoochee National Forest maps and pamphlets are available from the supervisor's office in Gainesville or the appropriate Ranger District.

- Cohutta-Big Frog Wilderness map (small fee)
- Ellicott Rock Wilderness map (small fee)
- Southern Nantahala Wilderness map (small fee)
- Chattooga National Wild and Scenic River map (small fee)
- Chattahoochee Admin-Visitor map (small fee)
- Recreation Opportunity Guide: Chattahoochee-Oconee National Forests (no fee at present, but could become a cost item in the future)
- Trail Guide to the Chattahoochee-Oconee National Forests (small fee)
- One-sheet map and description of the Duncan Ridge National Recreational Trail
- One-sheet map and description of the Bartram National Heritage Trail

The Ranger Districts often have additional maps and pamphlets giving short descriptions of trails in their districts.

Topographic Quadrangles (1:24,000) are available from the US Geological Survey Information Service, Box 25286, Denver, CO 80225, (phone number 303-202-4700).

Long Trail Addresses and Map Information

Appalachian National Scenic Trail

Georgia Appalachian Trail Club
P.O. Box 654, Atlanta GA 30301
Voice Mail (404) 634-6495

The Appalachian Trail Conference has excellent maps of the entire trail. The Appalachian Trail Guide to North Carolina-Georgia includes a packet of three maps: the Georgia section, the North Carolina section, and the Great Smoky Mountains National Park section. The Appalachian Trail Conference also sells these maps separately from the book.

Appalachian Trail Conference
P.O. Box 807, Harpers Ferry WV 25425
(304) 535-6331
FAX: (304) 535-2667

The Appalachian Trail maps are also available at many outdoor recreation stores and from Amicalola Falls State Park.

Amicalola Falls State Park
418 Amicalola Falls Lodge Drive, Dawsonville GA 30534
(706) 265-2885

Benton MacKaye Trail
Benton MacKaye Trail Association
P.O. Box 53271, Atlanta GA 30355-1271
(no phone)

Section maps are no longer being produced and there is no comprehensive map as yet. Look for one in the future.

Bartram National Heritage Trail
At present, there is no active Bartram Trail Society in Georgia. Direct questions and comments to:
North Carolina Bartram Trail Society
Route 3, Box 406, Sylva NC 28779

The Forest Service (Tallulah Ranger District) has a one-sheet map of the Bartram Trail.

Tallulah Ranger District
P.O. Box 438
825 Highway 441 South, Clayton GA 30525
(706) 782-3320

Duncan Ridge National Recreation Trail
The Forest Service (Toccoa Ranger District) has a one-sheet map of the trail.
Toccoa Ranger District
990 East Main Street, Suite 1
Blue Ridge GA 30513
(706) 632-3031

National Forest Addresses

USDA Forest Service
Supervisor's Office
1755 Cleveland Highway
Gainesville GA 30501
(770) 536-0541

Armuchee Ranger District
P.O. Box 465
(806 East Villanow Street)
La Fayette GA 30728
(706) 638 1085

Brasstown Ranger District
1881 Highway 515
P.O. Box 9
Blairsville GA 30514
(706) 745-6928

Chattooga Ranger District
P.O. Box 196
Highway 197, North Burton Road
Clarkesville GA 30523
(706) 754-6221

Cohutta Ranger District
401 Old Ellijay Road
Chatsworth GA 30705
(706) 695-6736

Tallulah Ranger District
P.O. Box 438
825 Highway 441 South
Clayton GA 30525
(706) 782-3320

Toccoa Ranger District
990 East Main Street, Suite 1
Blue Ridge GA 30513
(706) 632-3031

State Park Information and Addresses

Camping is allowed in state parks at designated sites only, either in campgrounds or along backcountry trails. A per-night fee is charged for all of these designated sites. State park campsites (backcountry sites included) are administered through a state-wide reservation system. For reservations call: (800) 864-7275. If you live in the metro Atlanta area call: (770) 389-7275.

Please note: Tallulah Gorge State Park handles its own camping reservations. Call (706) 754-7979 for more information.

State parks charge a nominal fee for a permit—the Park Pass—to enter and use the parks (excepting Tallulah Gorge State Park). Wednesdays are free (Smithgall Woods, Dukes Creek Conservation Area is an exception).

Tallulah Gorge State Park does not charge a Park Pass fee. Smithgall Woods, Dukes Creek Conservation Area, which is open Wednesday, Saturday, and Sunday only, does charge a Park Pass fee on Wednesday. The conservation area does not have a campground.

Amicalola Falls State Park
418 Amicalola Falls Lodge Drive
Dawsonville GA 30534
(706) 265-2885

Black Rock Mountain State Park
P.O. Drawer A
Mountain City GA 30562
(706) 746-2141

Cloudland Canyon State Park
Route 2
Rising Fawn GA 30738
(706) 657-4050

Fort Mountain State Park
181 Fort Mountain Park Road
Chatsworth GA 30705
(706) 695-2621

Moccasin Creek State Park
P.O. Box 1634
Clarkesville GA 30523
(706) 947-3194

Smithgall Woods,
Dukes Creek Conservation Area
61 Tsalaki Trail
Helen GA 30545
(706) 878-3087

Tallulah Gorge State Park
P.O. Box 248
Tallulah Falls GA 30573
(706) 754-7970

Unicoi State Park
1788 Highway 356
Helen GA 30545
(706) 878-2201

Vogel State Park
7485 Vogel State Park Road
Blairsville GA 30512
(706) 745-2628

Other Helpful Addresses

Corps of Engineers
Resource Manager's Office
Carters Lake
P.O. Box 96
Oakman GA 30732
(706) 334-2248

Crockford-Pigeon Mountain Wildlife Management Area
Department of Natural Resources
Wildlife Resources–Game Management
2592 Floyd Springs Road
Armuchee GA 30105
(706) 295-6041

Dawson Forest Wildlife Management Area
DNR-WRD
Game Management
2150 Dawsonville Highway
Gainesville GA 30501
(770) 535-5700

Index of Trails

Index of Maps

The Georgia Conservancy

The Georgia Conservancy is an independent, nonprofit organization of citizens, community groups, and businesses dedicated to protecting Georgia's environment and encouraging responsible stewardship of vital natural resources. Our vision for Georgia is a healthy environment, with plentiful, clean water, good air quality, and functioning natural systems.

Since its founding in 1967, The Georgia Conservancy has built a solid reputation for its reasoned, pragmatic approach to environmental problem-solving and its well-practiced ability to build consensus on difficult and complex issues. Through education and advocacy, The Georgia Conservancy plays a key role in developing public policy and enhancing environmental quality. Achievements include the designation of Cumberland Island as a National Seashore, protection of the Cohutta Mountains and Okefenokee Swamp as Wilderness Areas, creation of the Chattahoochee River National Recreational Area, initiation of state growth management policies, development of a national forest management plan, and protection of coastal marshes, sand dunes, and freshwater wetlands.

As Georgia continues its unprecedented growth, the pressures on our environment increase. The Georgia Conservancy is committed to its leadership role as the state's primary resource for environmental information and advocacy.

THE HIKING TRAILS OF NORTH GEORGIA, like The Georgia Conservancy's GUIDE TO THE NORTH GEORGIA MOUNTAINS and A GUIDE TO THE GEORGIA COAST, celebrates our magnificent natural heritage and is a testament to the compelling need to protect it for present and future generations. We thank the many volunteers who assisted with this book.

For information about The Georgia Conservancy, please contact us at:

The Georgia Conservancy
1776 Peachtree Street, NW
Suite 400 South
Atlanta, GA 30309
(404) 876-2900